STEAM POWERED VIDEO'S COMPREHENSIVE RAILROAD ATLAS OF NORTH AMERICA

CALIFORNIA AND NEVADA

MIKE WALKER

Published in England by
Steam Powered Publishing, A Steam Powered Group Company,
Dawes Road, Dunkirk, Nr. Faversham, Kent ME13 9TP

ISBN 1 874745 021

Cover design by SHARP ART, Selling, Kent, United Kingdom.

SYMBOLS & ABBREVIATIONS

Standard gauge line (in service)
Standard gauge electrified line (in service) – see appendix for system
Standard gauge line (abandonded)
Narrow gauge line (in service) – see appendix for gauge
Mixed standard/narrow gauge line (in service)
Narrow gauge line (abandoned) – see appendix for gauge
Mixed standard/narrow gauge line (abandoned)
Principal tunnel
Principal bridge or viaduct
Passenger station – Amtrak/commuter/tourist
Division point, headquarters, etc.
Other operating/timetable locations
Closed station or siding

UP (WP)	Current owner (Previous owner)	See appendix for reporting marks
SP/ATSF	Current owner/Trackage rights	
ATSF–DRGW	Jointly owned & operated track	

National boundary
State or provincial boundary
National Park boundary

◆	Talking detector & designation – reports all trains.
◇	Talking detector & designation – reports on defect only
▲	Summit (elevation in feet a.s.l.)
+	Passenger station – scheduled regular service
ǂ	Passenger station – tourist or museum operation

A	Automatically controlled interlocking
B	General or bulletin office
C	Passenger car yard
D	Draw, lift or swing bridge
E	Engine facility
G	Railroad crossing at grade with gate or gate on line
L	DTC block limits
M	Manually controlled interlocking (may be remotely controlled)
P	Passing siding
R	Register station
S	Railroad crossing at grade with stop sign protection
T	Turning facility (turntable or wye)
U	Railroad crossing unprotected
W	Water tank
X	Crossover on multiple track
Y	Yard

n	Northbound
e	Eastbound
s	Southbound
w	Westbound
m	Mileage
CP	Control point
DTC	Designated traffic control
Bch	Branch
Br	Bridge
Jct	Junction
Stn	Station
Tnl	Tunnel
Twr	Tower
Vdt	Viaduct
Yd	Yard

INTRODUCTION

This second volume of **Steam Powered Video's RAILROAD ATLAS OF NORTH AMERICA** covers the popular train watching states of California and Nevada including such notable locations as the Feather River Canyon, Donner Pass, Tehachapi and Cajon.

The Atlas shows all currently operated common carrier, tourist and major industrial railroads along with abandoned routes. Electric interurban and street railroads are not shown except where they provided common carrier freight service or operate over or adjacent to a common carrier's right of way. Lines shown as narrow or mixed gauge are only shown as such when they are currently so laid or were at abandonment. Lines built as narrow gauge and subsequently rebuilt are shown as standard gauge. It should be noted that some lines shown as "in service" may see very infrequent use whilst some "abandoned" lines may, if the tracks remain in place, be reactivated for a special movement. Some abandoned trackage is simplified or omitted to clarify existing details.

Every effort has been made to show all current operating locations as defined in railroad employee timetables. Letter and symbol codes adjacent to each location give an indication of what facilities may be found there. The approximate location of all "talking defect detectors", along with their identification, together with "Controlled Points" and SP's "Direct Traffic Control" blocks are shown as an aid to locating train movements which may be heard over the radio. Major bridges and tunnels (with a length of over 1000') are also shown.

The Atlas does not show roads as this would be confusing. For detail of road access to lines the DeLorme topographic atlases are recommended whilst the Altamont Press Railfan Timetables provide useful additional operating data. The author and publisher remind readers that the contents of this Atlas are for information only and do not imply any right of public access. Railroads and much of the property surrounding them is private and should be respected as such.

Whilst every care has been taken in the preparation of this volume, cross checking various published sources, company timetables, official guides etc., it is accepted that there may be some minor errors or omissions. In addition, the continuing process of mergers, regional and shortline spinoffs and abandonments within the North American Railroad industry will eventually affect the accuracy of this Atlas. The information herein is compiled to late 1993.

ACKNOWLEDGEMENTS: *Finally, in any work such as this, numerous individuals help to provide information. In particular thanks should be given to the following members of the UK Chapter of the NRHS; John Sears, who spent many hours searching out obscure details, and Richard Cossey and Graham Pike who undertook the mammoth task of compiling the index.*

OPERATIONS

A few words of explanation of the operational aspects of some of the railroads in this Atlas may be useful to avoid confusion.

SOUTHERN PACIFIC has a policy of measuring all mileages from San Francisco (its headquarters) whilst all trains heading in the ultimate direction of San Francisco are regarded as Westbound and those away from San Francisco as Eastbound. This applies throughout the SP system even though the train may be going nowhere near the Bay Area. Many of the company's less heavily used lines are now covered by "Direct Traffic Control" under which they are divided into named blocks which are released as required over the radio. The "West" end of these blocks is always that with the lower mileage, ie nearest San Francisco, while the "East" end has the higher mileage. Throughout the SP system "East" and "West" have little connection with true compass points, probably the worst example of this is in the Soledad Canyon north of Los Angeles (map CA-37) where "East" and "West" ends of DTC blocks are the exact reverse of compass direction and "Westbound" trains are headed due east!

UNION PACIFIC measures mileages from Los Angeles towards Salt Lake City on the old LA&SL and from Oakland to Salt Lake City on the old Western Pacific. It has instigated a system of "Controlled Points" (CP) along its main lines which are defined by a letter and mileage, C for the LA&SL route and F for the WP indicating California/Utah and Feather River Divisions respectively. Separate CP's define each end of a siding thus the lower number is the west end, the higher the east end. Branch line CP's are numbered sequentially in the 900 series to avoid duplication.

Lines where AMTRAK is the controlling operator, including the San Francisco peninsular and Los Angeles "Metrolink" commuter operations, are being designated with named Controlled Points, ie "CP Coast" or "CP Olive", which reflect the location.

SANTA FE has no single milepost numbering. Between Needles and Richmond they run from Belen NM. Separate series run from Barstow to Los Angeles via Pasadena and from San Bernardino to Hobart and San Diego. Santa Fe and UP use Track Warrant Control (TWC) for much of their traffic and these may be issued between any two or more designated points; stations, switches or mileposts for example.

Mike Walker
Marlow, Bucks., Jan. 1994

TABLE OF CONTENTS

MAP GRID

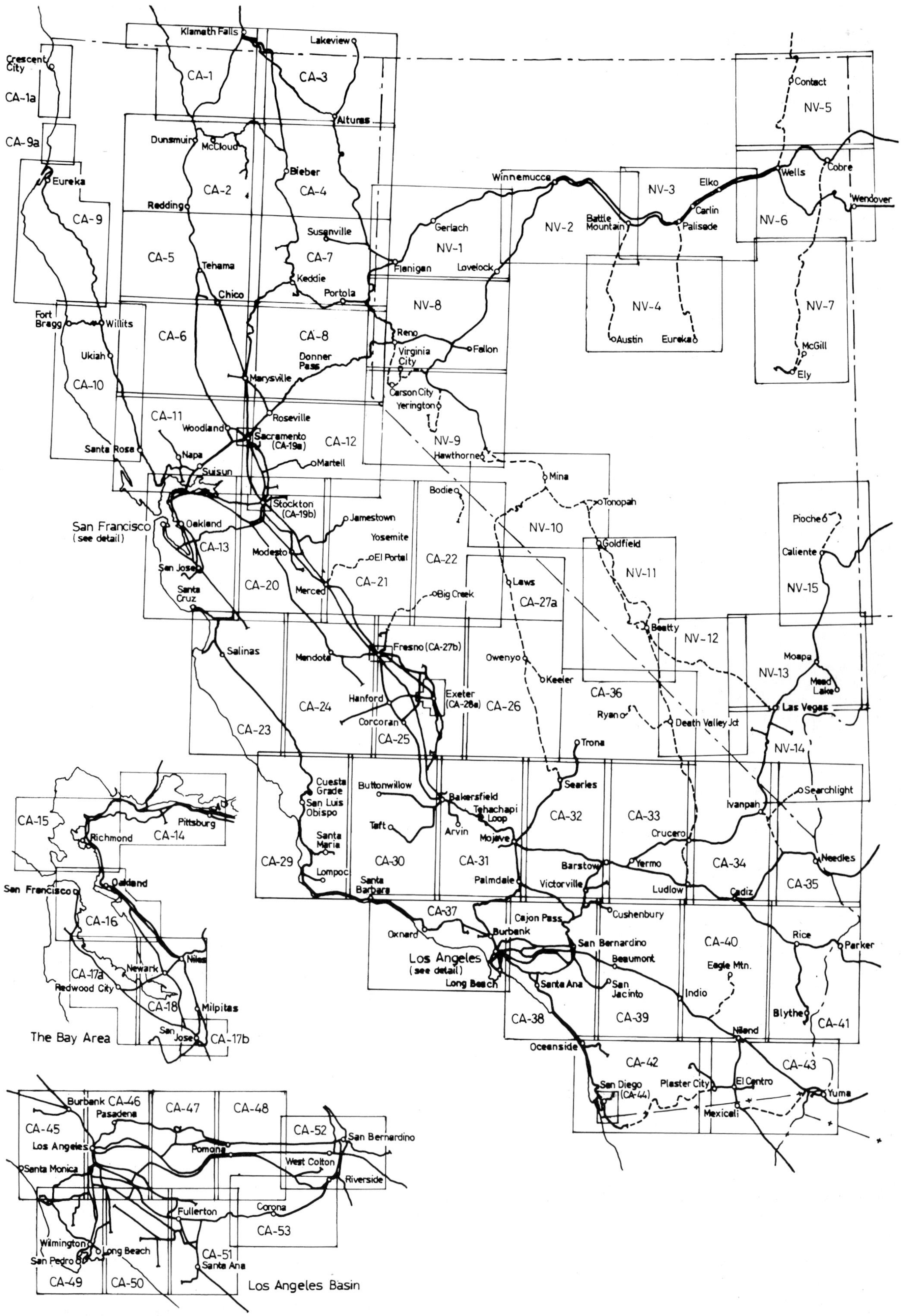

Klamath Falls
Lakeview
Crescent City
CA-1a
CA-1
CA-3
Alturas
CA-9a
Dunsmuir
McCloud
Bieber
Eureka
CA-2
CA-4
Redding
CA-9
Susanville
CA-5
Tehama
CA-7
Keddie
Portola
Chico
Fort Bragg
Willits
CA-6
CA-8
Ukiah
Donner Pass
CA-10
Marysville
CA-11
Roseville
Woodland
Sacramento (CA-19a)
CA-12
Santa Rosa
Napa
Suisun
Martell
Stockton (CA-19b)
San Francisco (see detail)
Oakland
Jamestown
CA-13
Yosemite
Modesto
El Portal
San Jose
CA-20
CA-21
CA-22
Merced
Big Creek
Santa Cruz
Salinas
Fresno (CA-27b)
Mendota
Hanford
Exeter (CA-28a)
CA-24
CA-26
CA-23
Corcoran
CA-25
Bodie
Laws
CA-27a
Owenyo
Keeler
Cuesta Grade
San Luis Obispo
Buttonwillow
Bakersfield
Tehachapi Loop
Taft
Arvin
Mojave
Santa Maria
CA-29
CA-30
CA-31
Lompoc
Santa Barbara
Palmdale
CA-37
Oxnard
Burbank
Los Angeles (see detail)
Long Beach
Cajon Pass
Contact
NV-5
Wells
Cobre
Wendover
Winnemucca
Elko
NV-3
Carlin
Battle Mountain
Palisade
NV-6
Gerlach
NV-2
NV-1
Flanigan
Lovelock
NV-4
NV-7
NV-8
Reno
Austin
Eureka
McGill
Ely
Virginia City
Fallon
Carson City
Yerington
NV-9
Hawthorne
Mina
Tonopah
NV-10
Goldfield
Pioche
Caliente
NV-11
NV-15
Beatty
NV-12
Moapa
NV-13
Mead Lake
CA-36
Las Vegas
Ryan
Death Valley Jct
Trona
NV-14
Searles
Searchlight
Ivanpah
CA-32
CA-33
Crucero
Needles
Barstow
Yermo
CA-34
Victorville
Ludlow
Cadiz
CA-35
Cushenbury
San Bernardino
CA-40
Rice
Parker
Beaumont
Eagle Mtn.
Santa Ana
San Jacinto
Indio
CA-38
CA-39
Blythe
CA-41
Niland
Oceanside
CA-42
CA-43
San Diego (CA-44)
Plaster City
El Centro
Yuma
Mexicali

CA-15
Pittsburg
Richmond
CA-14
San Francisco
Oakland
CA-16
Niles
CA-17a
Newark
Redwood City
CA-18
Milpitas
San Jose
CA-17b
The Bay Area

Burbank
CA-46
CA-47
CA-48
Pasadena
CA-45
CA-52
San Bernardino
Los Angeles
Pomona
West Colton
Santa Monica
Riverside
Fullerton
Corona
CA-53
Wilmington
Long Beach
CA-51
San Pedro
Santa Ana
CA-49
CA-50
Los Angeles Basin

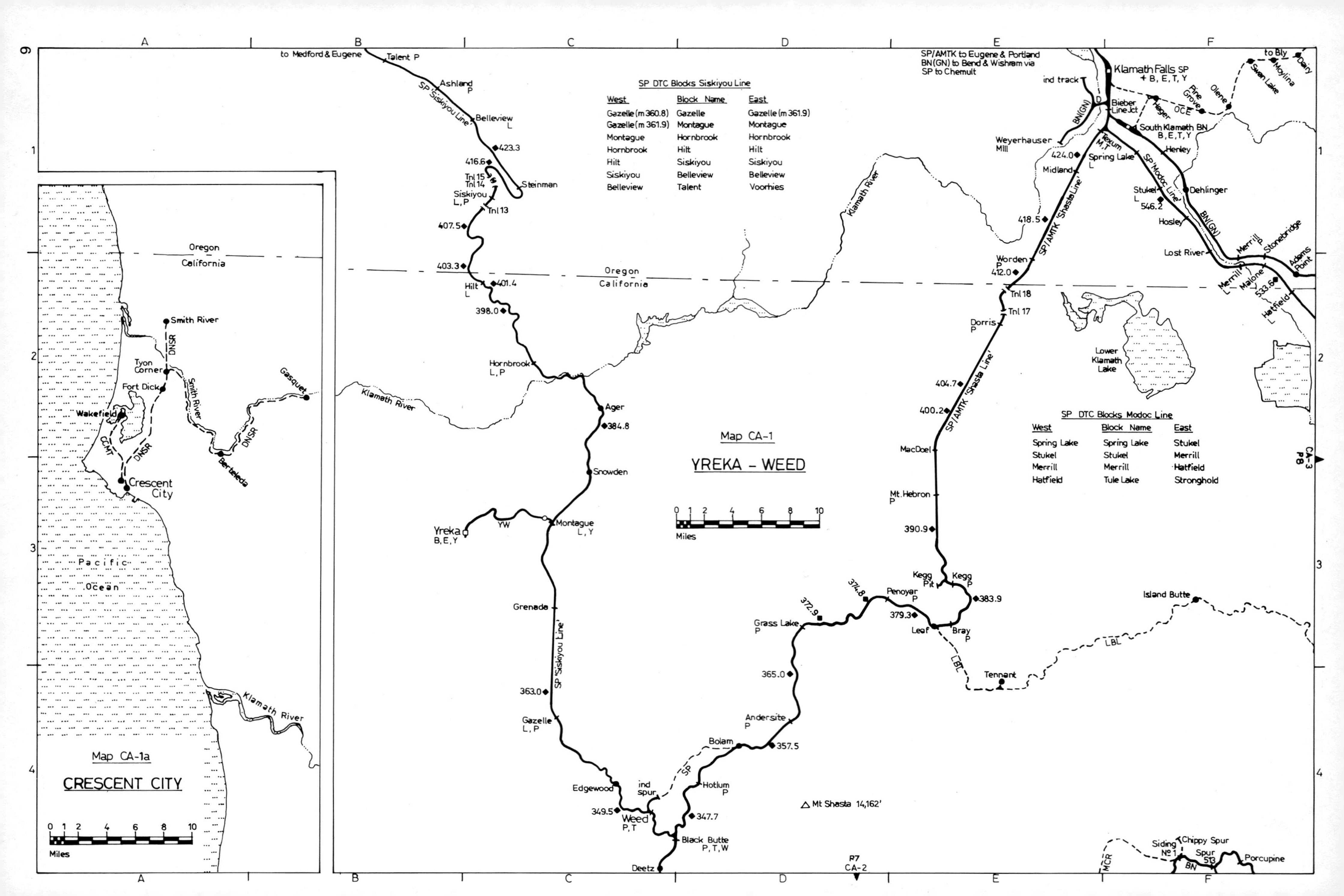
Map CA-1
YREKA - WEED
0 1 2 4 6 8 10
Miles
SP DTC Blocks Siskiyou Line
West | Block Name | East
Gazelle (m 360.8) | Gazelle | Gazelle (m 361.9)
Gazelle (m 361.9) | Montague | Montague
Montague | Hornbrook | Hornbrook
Hornbrook | Hilt | Hilt
Hilt | Siskiyou | Siskiyou
Siskiyou | Belleview | Belleview
Belleview | Talent | Voorhies
SP DTC Blocks Modoc Line
West | Block Name | East
Spring Lake | Spring Lake | Stukel
Stukel | Stukel | Merrill
Merrill | Merrill | Hatfield
Hatfield | Tule Lake | Stronghold
SP/AMTK to Eugene & Portland
BN(GN) to Bend & Wishram via
SP to Chemult
to Medford & Eugene
Talent P
Ashland P
SP 'Siskiyou Line'
Belleview L
423.3
416.6
Tnl 15
Tnl 14
Steinman
Siskiyou L, P
Tnl 13
407.5
403.3
Oregon
California
Hilt L
401.4
398.0
Hornbrook L, P
Klamath River
Ager
384.8
Snowden
Yreka B, E, Y
YW
Montague L, Y
Grenada
363.0
Gazelle L, P
Edgewood
349.5
Weed P, T
ind spur
SP
Deetz
Black Butte P, T, W
347.7
Hotlum P
Bolam
357.5
Andersite P
365.0
Grass Lake P
372.9
374.8
Penoyar P
379.3
Leaf
Bray P
Kegg Pit
Kegg P
383.9
LBL
Tennant
Island Butte
Mt Shasta 14,162'
P7
CA-2
390.9
Mt. Hebron P
MacDoel
400.2
404.7
SP/AMTK 'Shasta Line'
Dorris P
Tnl 17
Tnl 18
Worden P
412.0
418.5
Midland
424.0
Weyerhauser Mill
ind track
BN(GN)
Klamath Falls SP + B, E, T, Y
Bieber Line Jct
Texum M, T
Spring Lake L
Hager
OCE
Pine Grove
Olene
Swan Lake
Moylina
Dairy
to Bly
South Klamath BN B, E, T, Y
Henley
Dehlinger
SP 'Modoc Line'
Stukel L
546.2
Hosley
Lost River
Merrill P
Stonebridge
Adams Point
Merrill L
Malone
533.6
Hatfield L
Lower Klamath Lake
CA-3
P8
Siding No 1
Chippy Spur
Spur 513
Porcupine
MCR
Map CA-1a
CRESCENT CITY
0 1 2 4 6 8 10
Miles
Smith River
DNSR
Tyon Corner
Fort Dick
Wakefield
CCMT
Smith River
Gasquet
Berteleda
Crescent City
Pacific Ocean
Klamath River

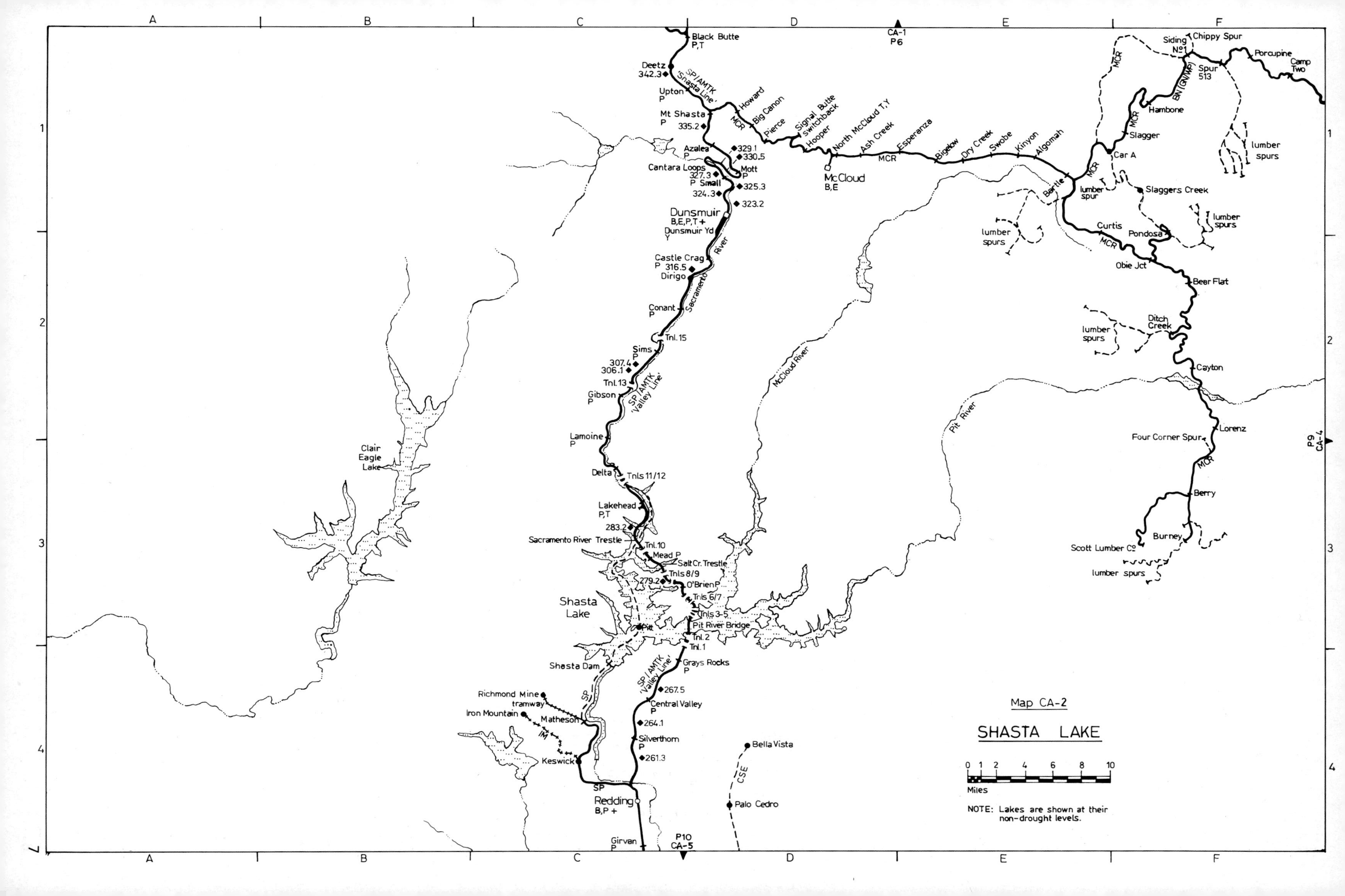

Map CA-2
SHASTA LAKE
0 1 2 4 6 8 10
Miles
NOTE: Lakes are shown at their non-drought levels.
Black Butte P,T
Deetz 342.3
SP/AMTK 'Shasta Line'
Upton P
Mt Shasta P
335.2
Howard
Big Canon
MCR
Pierce
Signal Butte
Switchback
Hooper
North McCloud T,Y
Ash Creek
Esperanza
Bigelow
Dry Creek
Swobe
Kinyon
Algomah
Bartle
McCloud B,E
CA-1 P6
Azalea P
329.1
330.5
Mott P
Cantara Loops
327.3
P Small
325.3
324.3
323.2
Dunsmuir B,E,P,T +
Dunsmuir Yd Y
Castle Crag P
316.5
Dirigo
Sacramento River
Conant P
Tnl.15
Sims P
307.4
306.1
Tnl.13
SP/AMTK 'Valley Line'
Gibson P
Lamoine P
Delta
Tnls 11/12
Lakehead P,T
283.2
Sacramento River Trestle
Tnl.10
Mead P
Salt Cr. Trestle
Tnls 8/9
279.2
O'Brien P
Tnls 6/7
Tnls 3-5
Pit River Bridge
Pit
Tnl.2
Tnl.1
Shasta Lake
Shasta Dam
Grays Rocks P
267.5
Central Valley P
264.1
Silverthorn P
261.3
Richmond Mine
tramway
Iron Mountain
Matheson
IM
SP
Keswick
Redding B,P +
Girvan P
P10 CA-5
Bella Vista
CSE
Palo Cedro
Clair Eagle Lake
McCloud River
Pit River
Siding No 1
Chippy Spur
Porcupine
Camp Two
Spur 513
BN (GN/WP)
Hambone
Slagger
Car A
lumber spurs
lumber spur
Slaggers Creek
Curtis
Pondosa
Obie Jct
Beer Flat
Ditch Creek
Cayton
Lorenz
Four Corner Spur
Berry
Burney
Scott Lumber Co
P9 CA-4
A
B
C
D
E
F
1
2
3
4

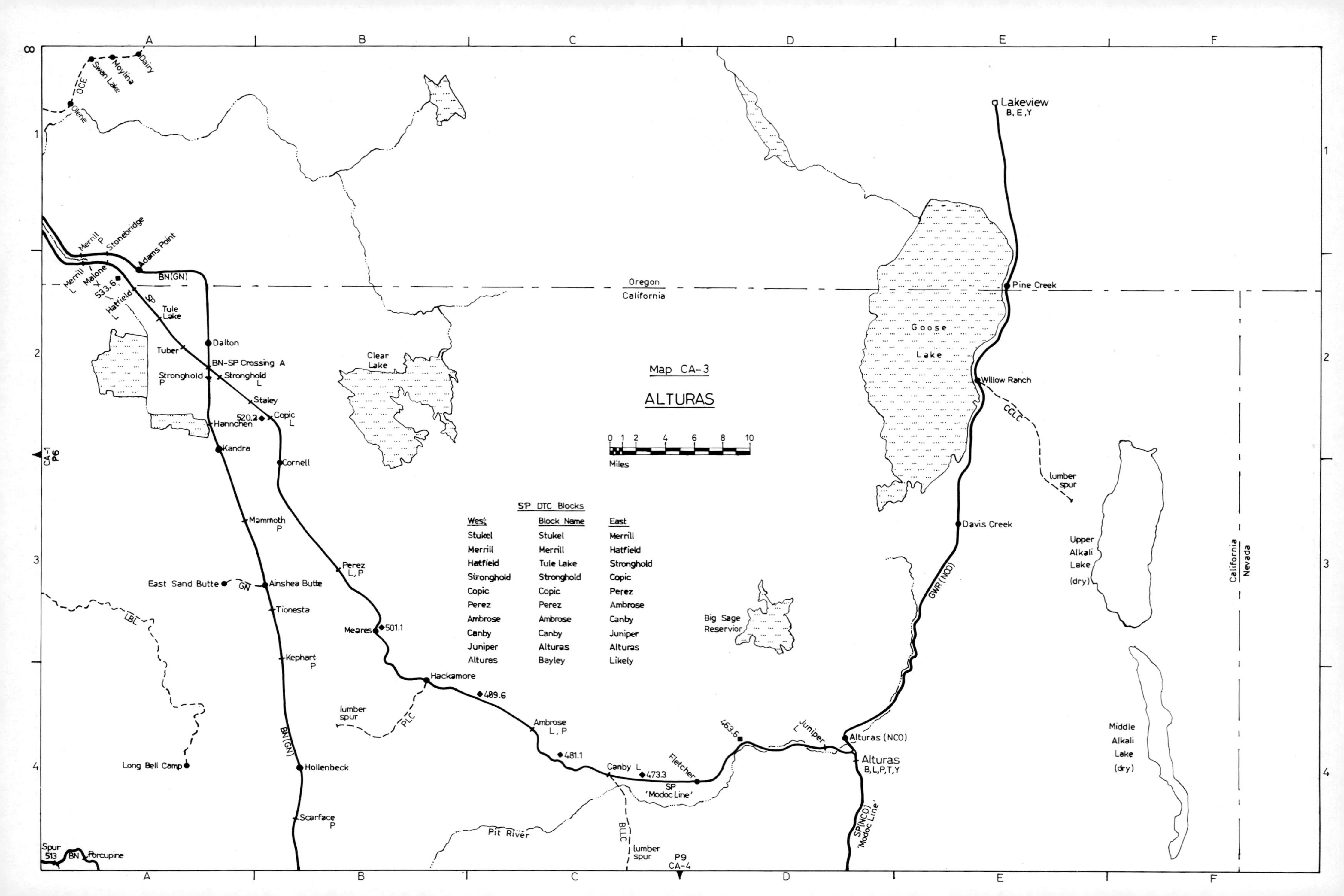
Map CA-3
ALTURAS
0 1 2 4 6 8 10
Miles
SP DTC Blocks
West
Stukel
Merrill
Hatfield
Stronghold
Copic
Perez
Ambrose
Canby
Juniper
Alturas
Block Name
Stukel
Merrill
Tule Lake
Stronghold
Copic
Perez
Ambrose
Canby
Alturas
Bayley
East
Merrill
Hatfield
Stronghold
Copic
Perez
Ambrose
Canby
Juniper
Alturas
Likely
Oregon
California
Nevada
Goose Lake
Clear Lake
Big Sage Reservior
Upper Alkali Lake (dry)
Middle Alkali Lake (dry)
Pit River
Lakeview B, E, Y
Pine Creek
Willow Ranch
CCLC
lumber spur
Davis Creek
GWR (NCO)
Alturas (NCO)
Alturas B, L, P, T, Y
SP(NCO) 'Modoc Line'
Juniper L
463.6
Fletcher
SP 'Modoc Line'
Canby L
473.3
BLLC
lumber spur
P9 CA-4
481.1
Ambrose L, P
489.6
Hackamore
PLC
lumber spur
Meares
501.1
Perez L, P
Cornell
Copic L
520.2
Staley
Stronghold L
BN-SP Crossing A
Stronghold P
Hannchen
Kandra
Dalton
Tuber
Tule Lake
SP
Hatfield L
533.6
Malone
Merrill L
Merrill P
Stonebridge
Adams Point
BN(GN)
Mammoth P
East Sand Butte
GN
Ainshea Butte
Tionesta
Kephart P
Hollenbeck
BN(GN)
Scarface P
LBL
Long Bell Camp
Spur 513
BN
Porcupine
CA-1 P6
Dairy
Moylina
Swan Lake
OCE
Olene
A
B
C
D
E
F
1
2
3
4

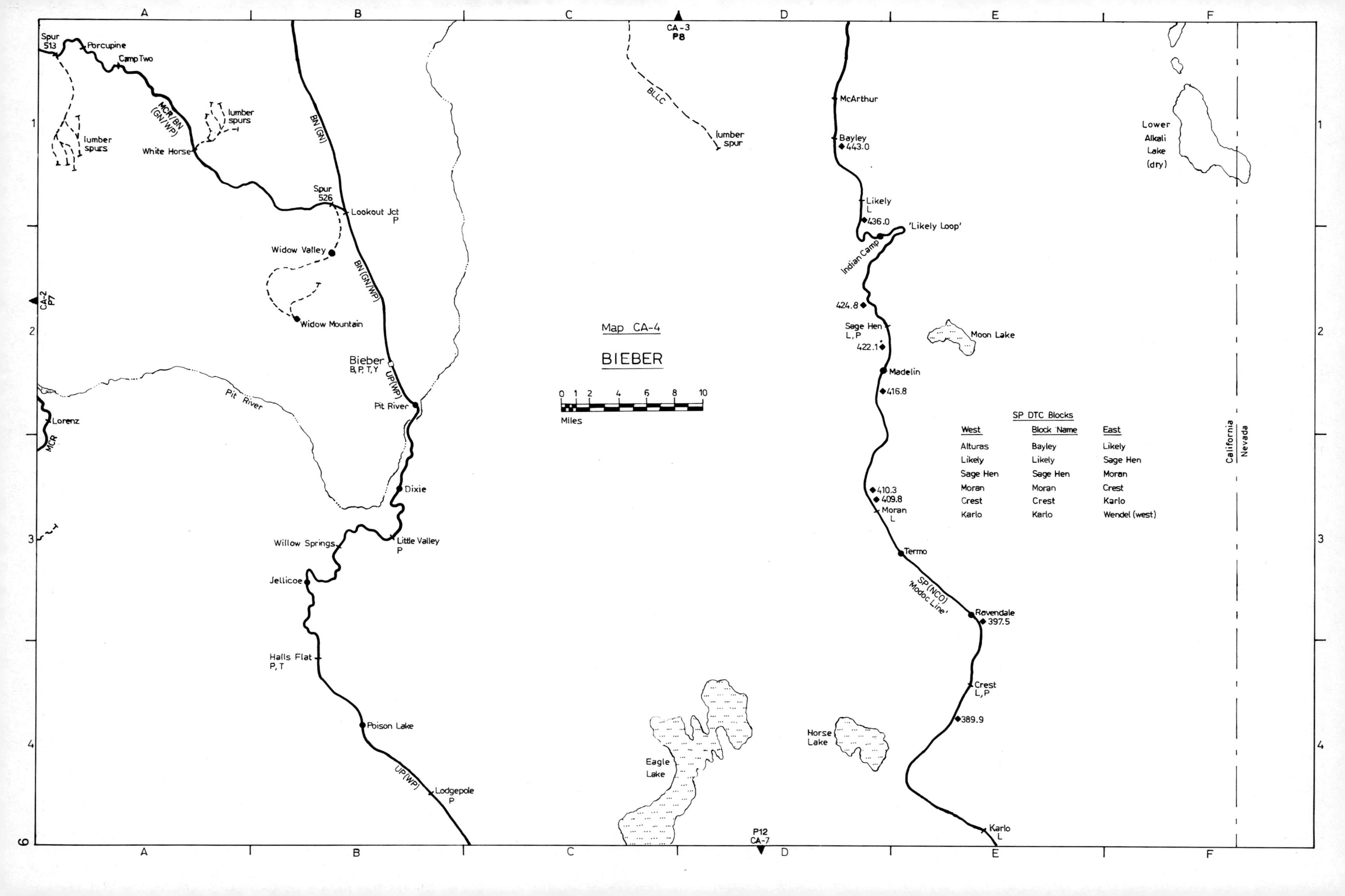
Map CA-4
BIEBER
0 1 2 4 6 8 10
Miles
SP DTC Blocks
West
Block Name
East
Alturas
Bayley
Likely
Likely
Likely
Sage Hen
Sage Hen
Sage Hen
Moran
Moran
Moran
Crest
Crest
Crest
Karlo
Karlo
Karlo
Wendel (west)
CA-3
P8
CA-2
P7
P12
CA-7
Spur 513
Porcupine
Camp Two
MCR/BN (GN/WP)
lumber spurs
White Horse
Spur 526
Lookout Jct P
BN (GN)
BN (GN/WP)
Widow Valley
Widow Mountain
Bieber B, P, T, Y
UP (WP)
Pit River
Lorenz
MCR
Dixie
Little Valley P
Willow Springs
Jellicoe
Halls Flat P, T
Poison Lake
Lodgepole P
BLLC
lumber spur
McArthur
Bayley
443.0
Likely L
436.0
'Likely Loop'
Indian Camp
424.8
Sage Hen L, P
422.1
Madelin
416.8
410.3
409.8
Moran L
Termo
SP (NCO) 'Modoc Line'
Rovendale
397.5
Crest L, P
389.9
Karlo L
Moon Lake
Horse Lake
Eagle Lake
Lower Alkali Lake (dry)
California
Nevada

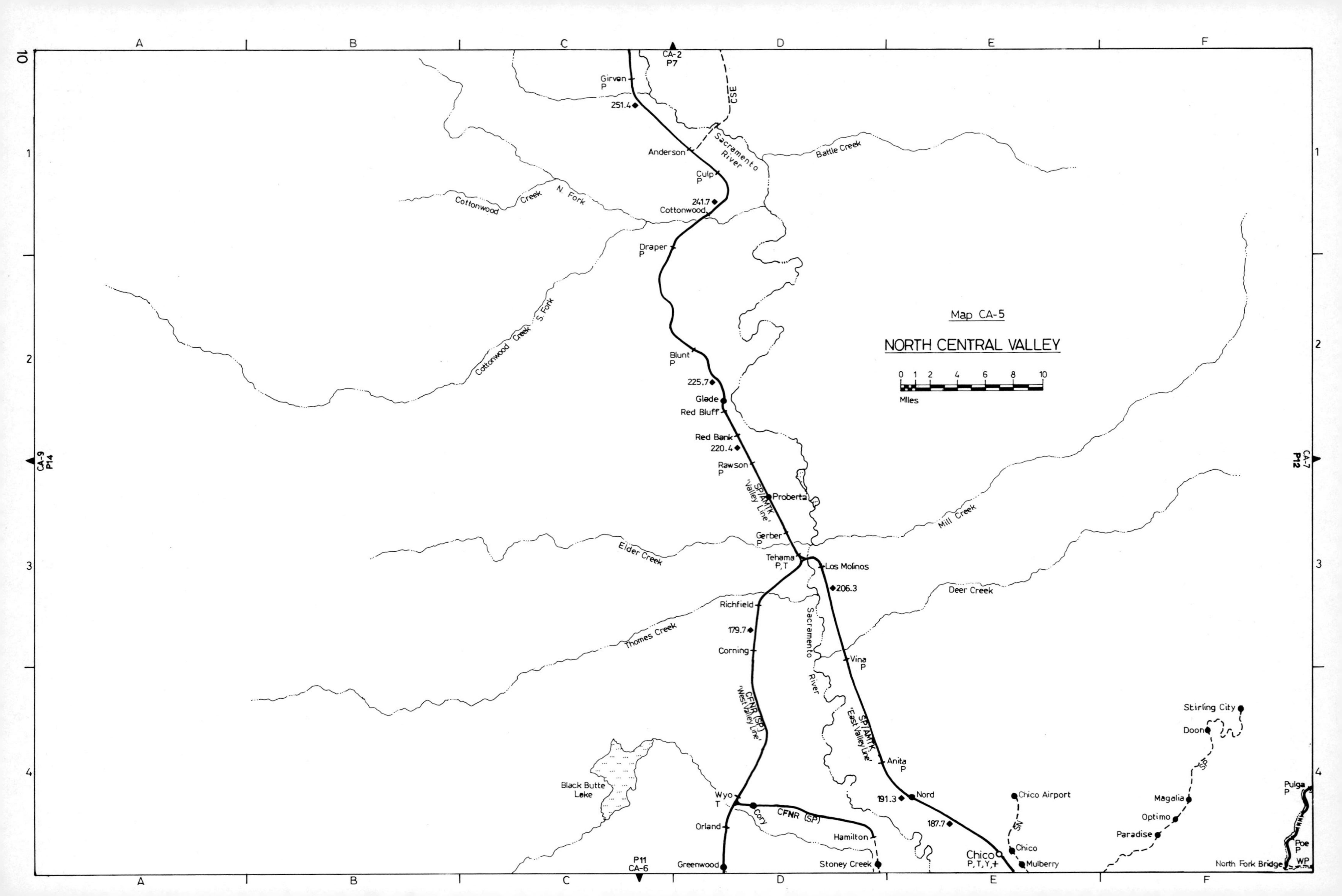

Map CA-5
NORTH CENTRAL VALLEY
0 1 2 4 6 8 10
Miles
CA-2
P7
CA-9
P14
CA-7
P12
P11
CA-6
CSE
Girvan P
251.4
Sacramento River
Battle Creek
Anderson
Culp P
241.7
Cottonwood
Cottonwood Creek N. Fork
Draper P
Cottonwood Creek S. Fork
Blunt P
225.7
Glade
Red Bluff
Red Bank
220.4
Rawson P
SP/AMTK 'Valley Line'
Proberta
Mill Creek
Gerber P
Elder Creek
Tehama P, T
Los Molinos
206.3
Deer Creek
Richfield
179.7
Thomes Creek
Corning
Sacramento River
Vina P
CFNR (SP) 'West Valley Line'
SP/AMTK 'East Valley Line'
Stirling City
Doon
SP
Anita P
Black Butte Lake
Wyo T
Nord
191.3
Chico Airport
Magalia
Optimo
Paradise
Cory
CFNR (SP)
Orland
Hamilton
187.7
NS
Chico
Chico P, T, Y, +
Mulberry
Greenwood
Stoney Creek
Pulga P
Poe P
North Fork Bridge
WP

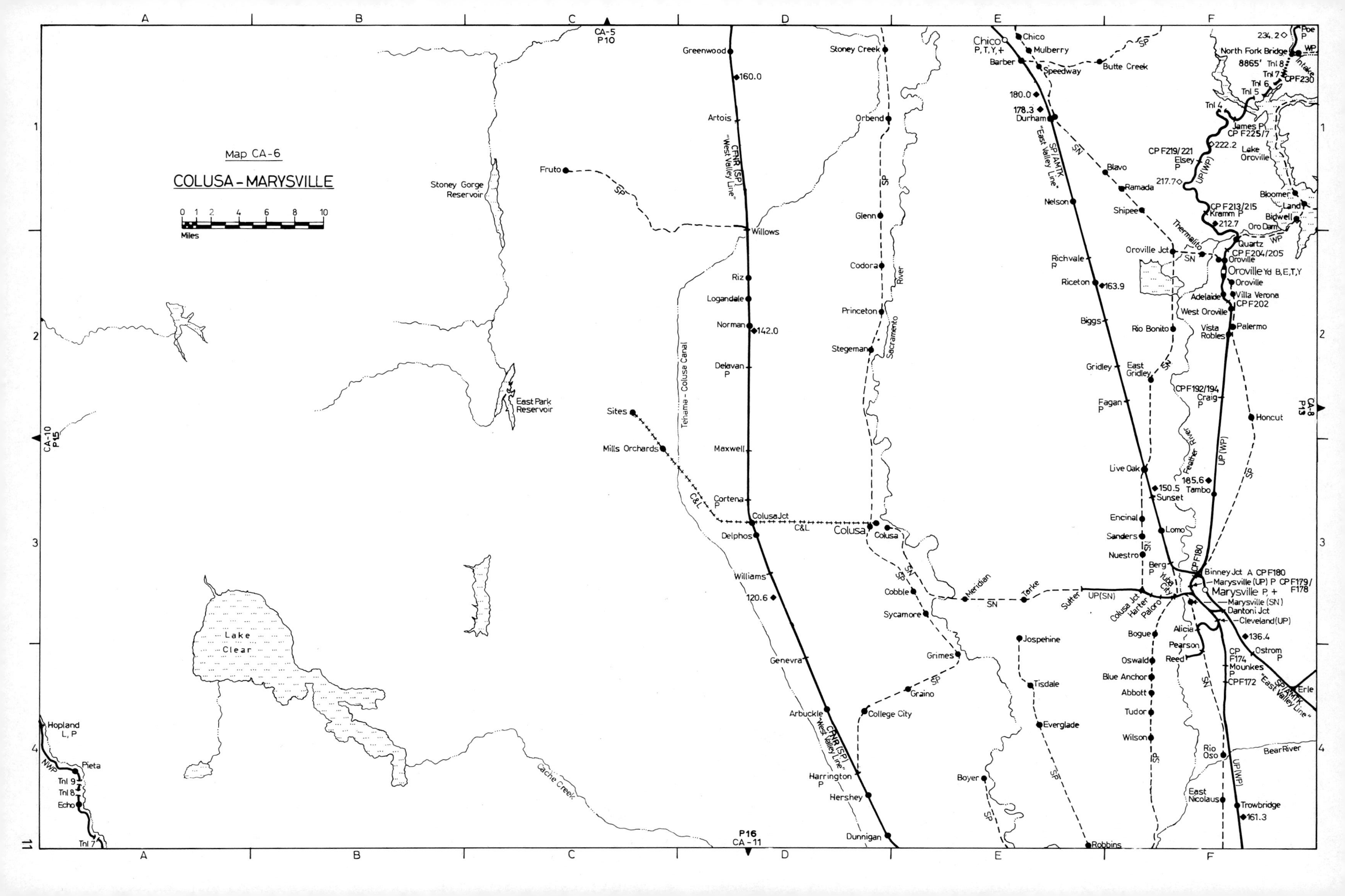
Map CA-6
COLUSA - MARYSVILLE
0 1 2 4 6 8 10
Miles
CA-5
P10
CA-8
P13
CA-10
P15
P16
CA-11
Chico
P, T, Y, +
Chico
Mulberry
Barber
Speedway
Butte Creek
180.0
178.3
Durham
SP/AMTK
"East Valley Line"
Blavo
Ramada
Nelson
Shipee
Richvale
P
Riceton
163.9
Biggs
Gridley
Fagan
P
Live Oak
150.5
Sunset
Encinal
Sanders
Nuestro
Lomo
Berg
P
Yuba City
Oroville Jct
Thermalito
Rio Bonito
East
Gridley
Quartz
CP F204/205
Oroville
Oroville Yd B,E,T,Y
Oroville
Adelaide
Villa Verona
CP F202
West Oroville
Vista
Robles
Palermo
CP F192/194
Craig
P
Honcut
Feather River
185.6
Tambo
UP (WP)
SP
SN
CP F219/221
Elsey
P
222.2
217.7
Lake
Oroville
CP F213/215
Kramm P
212.7
Oro Dam
Bloomer
Land
Bidwell
WP
James P
CP F225/7
Tnl 4
Tnl 5
Tnl 6
Tnl 7
Tnl 8
8865'
North Fork Bridge
CP F230
Intake
234.2
Poe
P
CP F180
Binney Jct A CP F180
Marysville (UP) P CP F179/F178
Marysville P, +
Marysville (SN)
Dantoni Jct
Cleveland (UP)
136.4
CP
F174
Mounkes
P
CP F172
Ostrom
P
Erle
Colusa Jct
Harter
Paloro
Alicia
Pearson
Reed
Bogue
Oswald
Blue Anchor
Abbott
Tudor
Wilson
Rio
Oso
Bear River
East
Nicolaus
Trowbridge
161.3
Robbins
Sutter
UP (SN)
Tarke
Meridian
Josephine
Tisdale
Everglade
Boyer
Stoney Creek
Orbend
Glenn
Codora
Princeton
Stegeman
Sacramento River
Colusa
Colusa
Cobble
Sycamore
Grimes
Graino
College City
Greenwood
160.0
Artois
CFNR (SP)
"West Valley Line"
Willows
Riz
Logandale
Norman
142.0
Delevan
P
Maxwell
Cortena
P
Colusa Jct
C&L
Delphos
Williams
120.6
Genevra
Arbuckle
Harrington
P
Hershey
Dunnigan
Tehama - Colusa Canal
Sites
Mills Orchards
Fruto
Stoney Gorge
Reservoir
East Park
Reservoir
Lake
Clear
Cache Creek
Hopland
L, P
Pieta
NWP
Tnl 9
Tnl 8
Echo
Tnl 7
A
B
C
D
E
F
1
2
3
4

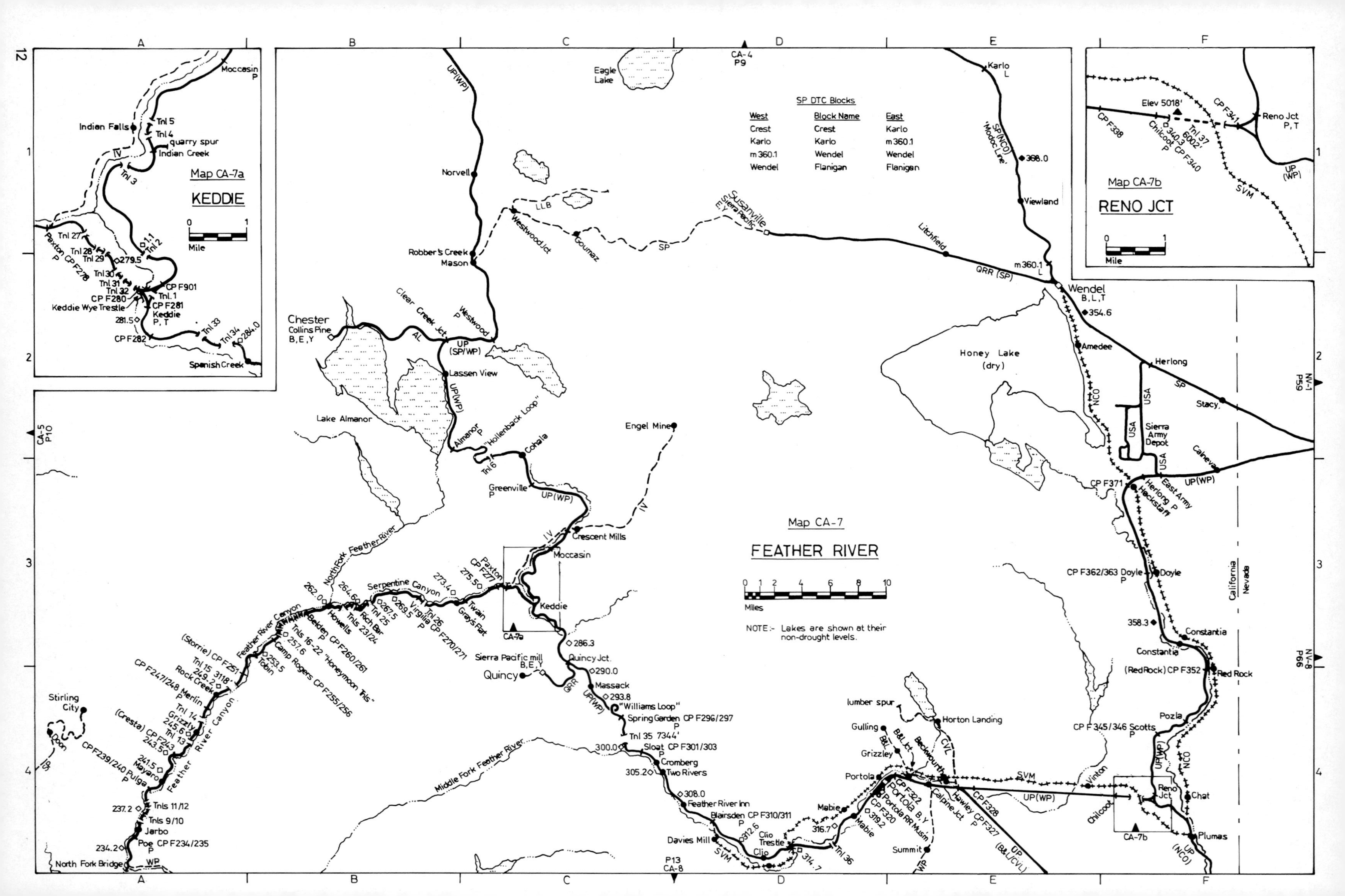

SP DTC Blocks

West	Block Name	East
Crest	Crest	Karlo
Karlo	Karlo	m 360.1
m 360.1	Wendel	Wendel
Wendel	Flanigan	Flanigan

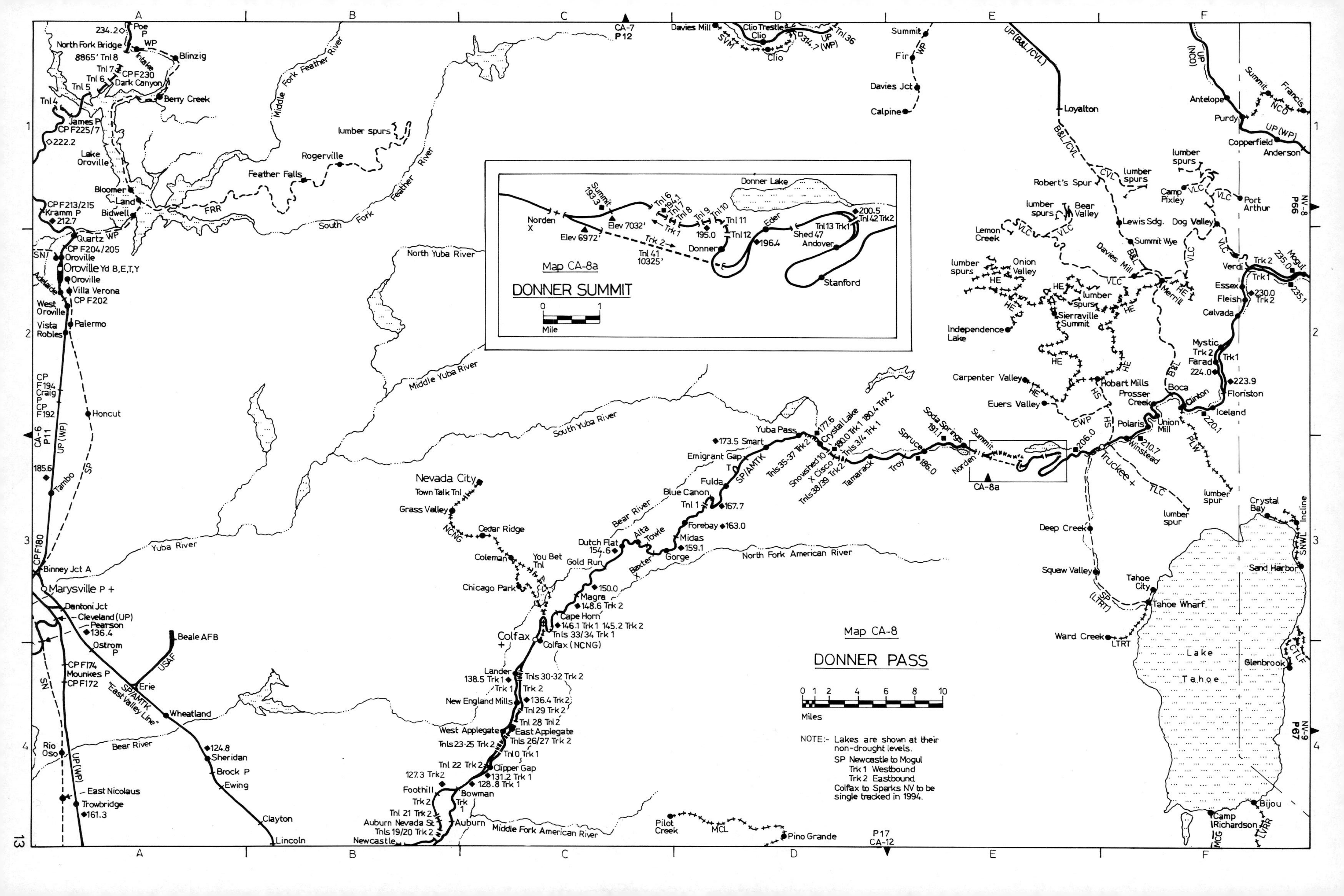

Map CA-8
DONNER PASS
0 1 2 4 6 8 10
Miles
NOTE:- Lakes are shown at their non-drought levels.
SP Newcastle to Mogul
Trk 1 Westbound
Trk 2 Eastbound
Colfax to Sparks NV to be single tracked in 1994.
Map CA-8a
DONNER SUMMIT
0 1
Mile
Norden X
Summit 193.3
Elev 6972'
Elev 7032'
Tnl 6
194.1
Tnl 7
Tnl 8
Trk 1
Trk 2
Tnl 41 10325'
Tnl 9
Tnl 10
195.0
Tnl 11
Tnl 12
Donner
Eder
196.4
Shed 47
Andover
Tnl 13 Trk1
200.5
Tnl 42 Trk2
Stanford
Donner Lake
CA-7 P12
CA-6 P11
P17 CA-12
NV-8 P66
NV-9 P67
CA-8a
234.2
Poe P
WP
North Fork Bridge
8865' Tnl 8
Intake
Blinzig
Tnl 7
CP F230
Tnl 6
Dark Canyon
Tnl 5
Berry Creek
Tnl 4
James P
CP F225/7
222.2
Lake Oroville
Bloomer
Land
Bidwell
CP F213/215
Kramm P
212.7
Quartz WP
SNT
CP F204/205
Oroville
Oroville Yd B,E,T,Y
Adelaide
Oroville
Villa Verona
West Oroville
CP F202
Vista Robles
Palermo
CP F194
Craig P
CP F192
Honcut
UP (WP)
SP
185.6
Tambo
CP F180
Binney Jct A
Marysville P +
Dantoni Jct
Cleveland (UP)
Pearson
136.4
Ostrom P
Beale AFB
USAF
CP F174
Mounkes P
CP F172
SN
Erie
SP/AMTK
"East Valley Line"
Wheatland
Rio Oso
Bear River
124.8
Sheridan
Brock P
Ewing
East Nicolaus
Trowbridge
161.3
Clayton
Lincoln
Middle Fork Feather River
lumber spurs
Rogerville
Feather Falls
FRR
South Fork Feather River
North Yuba River
Middle Yuba River
South Yuba River
Yuba River
Nevada City
Town Talk Tnl
Grass Valley
NCNG
Cedar Ridge
Coleman
You Bet Tnl
Chicago Park
Gold Run
Dutch Flat 154.6
Alta
Towle
Baxter
Bear River
Midas
159.1
Gorge
Forebay
163.0
Blue Canon
Tnl 1
167.7
Fulda
Emigrant Gap
SP/AMTK
173.5 Smart
Yuba Pass
177.6
Crystal Lake
Tnls 35-37 Trk 2
Snowshed 10
X Cisco
180.0 Trk 1
180.4 Trk 2
Tnls 3/4 Trk 1
Tnls 38/39 Trk 2
Tamarack
Troy
Spruce
186.0
Soda Springs 191.1
Summit
Norden
North Fork American River
150.0
Magra
148.6 Trk 2
Cape Horn
146.1 Trk 1
145.2 Trk 2
Tnls 33/34 Trk 1
Colfax
Colfax (NCNG)
Lander
138.5 Trk 1
Tnls 30-32 Trk 2
Trk 1
Trk 2
New England Mills
136.4 Trk 2
Tnl 29 Trk 2
Tnl 28 Trk 2
West Applegate
East Applegate
Tnls 23-25 Trk 2
Tnls 26/27 Trk 2
Tnl 0 Trk 1
Tnl 22 Trk 2
Clipper Gap
131.2 Trk 1
127.3 Trk 2
128.8 Trk 1
Foothill
Bowman
Trk 2
Trk 1
Tnl 21 Trk 2
Auburn Nevada St
Tnls 19/20 Trk 2
Auburn
Newcastle
Middle Fork American River
Pilot Creek
MCL
Pino Grande
Davies Mill
SVM
Clio Trestle
Clio
314.7
UP (WP)
Tnl 36
Summit
Fir
WP
Davies Jct
Calpine
UP (B&L/CVL)
Loyalton
B&L/CVL
Robert's Spur
CVL
lumber spurs
Bear Valley
Lemon Creek
VLC
Lewis Sdg.
Summit Wye
Davies Mill
B&L
Onion Valley
HE
Sierraville Summit
Independence Lake
Carpenter Valley
Euers Valley
Hobart Mills
HS
CWP
Prosser Creek
Camp Pixley
Dog Valley
Port Arthur
Merrill
Boca
Clinton
Polaris
Union Mill
210.7
Winstead
PLW
206.0
Truckee +
TLC
lumber spur
Verdi
Trk 2
Trk 1
235.0
Mogul
235.1
Essex
Fleish
230.0 Trk 2
Calvada
Mystic
Trk 2
Farad
224.0
223.9
Floriston
Iceland
220.1
UP (NCO)
Antelope
Summit
Francis
NCO
Purdy
UP (WP)
Copperfield
Anderson
Crystal Bay
Incline
SNWL
Sand Harbor
Deep Creek
Squaw Valley
Tahoe City
Tahoe Wharf
SP (LTRT)
Ward Creek
LTRT
Lake Tahoe
Glenbrook
CTLF
Camp Richardson
MCG
Bijou
LVRR
A
B
C
D
E
F
1
2
3
4

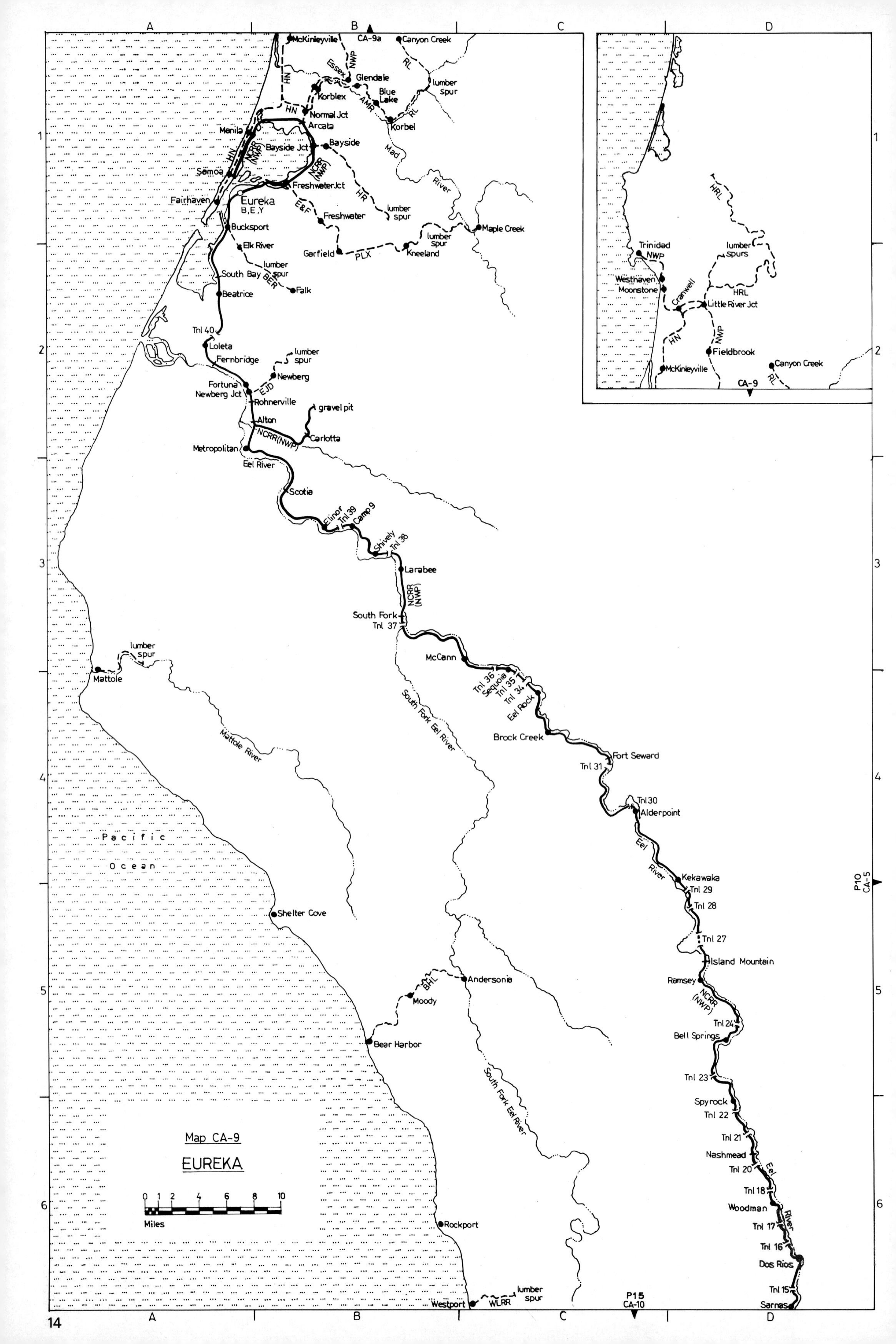
Map CA-9
EUREKA
0 1 2 4 6 8 10
Miles
Pacific Ocean
McKinleyville
CA-9a
Canyon Creek
NWP
Essex
RL
HN
Glendale
lumber spur
Korblex
Blue Lake
AMR
Normal Jct
Arcata
Korbel
Manila
Bayside Jct
Bayside
Mad River
NCRR (NWP)
Samoa
Freshwater Jct
Fairhaven
Eureka
B,E,Y
E&F
HR
Freshwater
Maple Creek
Bucksport
Elk River
Garfield
PLX
Kneeland
South Bay
BER
Falk
Beatrice
Tnl 40
Loleta
Fernbridge
Newberg
Fortuna
Newberg Jct
EJD
Rohnerville
gravel pit
Alton
Carlotta
NCRR(NWP)
Metropolitan
Eel River
Scotia
Elinor
Tnl 39
Camp 9
Shively
Tnl 38
Larabee
South Fork
Tnl 37
McCann
Tnl 36
Sequoia
Tnl 35
Tnl 34
Eel Rock
South Fork Eel River
Mattole
Mattole River
Brock Creek
Fort Seward
Tnl 31
Tnl 30
Alderpoint
Eel River
Kekawaka
Tnl 29
Tnl 28
Tnl 27
Island Mountain
Ramsey
Shelter Cove
Andersonia
BHL
Moody
Bear Harbor
Tnl 24
Bell Springs
Tnl 23
Spyrock
Tnl 22
Tnl 21
Nashmead
Tnl 20
Tnl 18
Woodman
Tnl 17
Tnl 16
Dos Rios
Tnl 15
Sarnas
Rockport
Westport
WLRR
P15
CA-10
P10
CA-5
Trinidad
HRL
lumber spurs
Westhaven
Moonstone
Cramwell
Little River Jct
Fieldbrook
CA-9

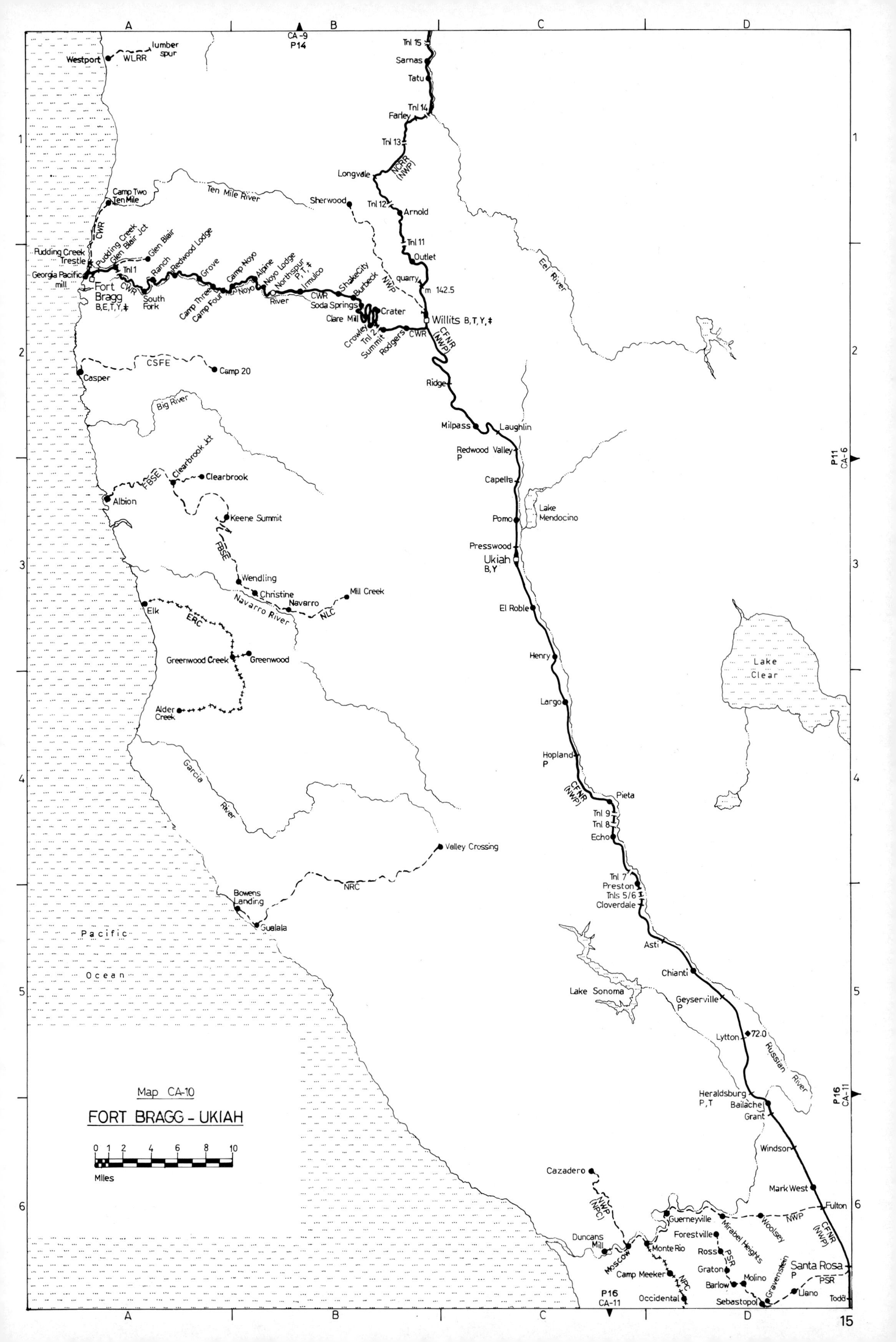

Map CA-10
FORT BRAGG - UKIAH
0 1 2 4 6 8 10
Miles
A
B
C
D
1
2
3
4
5
6
CA-9
P14
P11
CA-6
P16
CA-11
P16
CA-11
Westport
WLRR
lumber spur
Tnl 15
Sarnas
Tatu
Tnl 14
Farley
Tnl 13
Longvale
NCRR (NWP)
Sherwood
Tnl 12
Arnold
Tnl 11
Outlet
quarry
m 142.5
Camp Two
Ten Mile
Ten Mile River
CWR
Pudding Creek
Trestle
Pudding Creek
Glen Blair Jct
Glen Blair
Georgia Pacific mill
Tnl 1
Ranch
Redwood Lodge
Grove
Camp Noyo
Alpine
Noyo Lodge
Northspur
P, T, ‡
Irmulco
ShakeCity
Burbeck
NWP
Fort Bragg
B, E, T, Y, ‡
CWR
South Fork
Camp Three
Camp Four
Noyo
Noyo River
CWR
Soda Springs
Crater
Willits B, T, Y, ‡
Clare Mill
Crowley
Tnl 2
Summit
Rodgers
CWR
CFNR (NWP)
Eel River
CSFE
Casper
Camp 20
Ridge
Big River
Milpass
Laughlin
Redwood Valley
P
FBSE
Clearbrook Jct
Clearbrook
Capella
Albion
Lake Mendocino
Keene Summit
Pomo
FBSE
Presswood
Ukiah
B, Y
Wendling
Christine
Mill Creek
Navarro
Navarro River
NLC
Elk
ERC
El Roble
Greenwood Creek
Greenwood
Henry
Lake Clear
Largo
Alder Creek
Garcia River
Hopland
P
CFNR (NWP)
Pieta
Tnl 9
Tnl 8
Echo
Valley Crossing
NRC
Tnl 7
Preston
Tnls 5/6
Cloverdale
Bowens Landing
Gualala
Pacific
Ocean
Asti
Chianti
Lake Sonoma
Geyserville
P
Lytton
72.0
Russian River
Heraldsburg
P, T
Bailache
Grant
Windsor
Cazadero
Mark West
NWP (NPC)
Fulton
Guerneyville
Woolsey
NWP
Forestville
Mirabel Heights
CFNR (NWP)
Duncans Mill
Moscow
Monte Rio
Ross
PSR
Santa Rosa
P
Camp Meeker
NPC
Graton
Molino
Barlow
Gravenstein
PSR
Llano
Occidental
Sebastopol
Todd

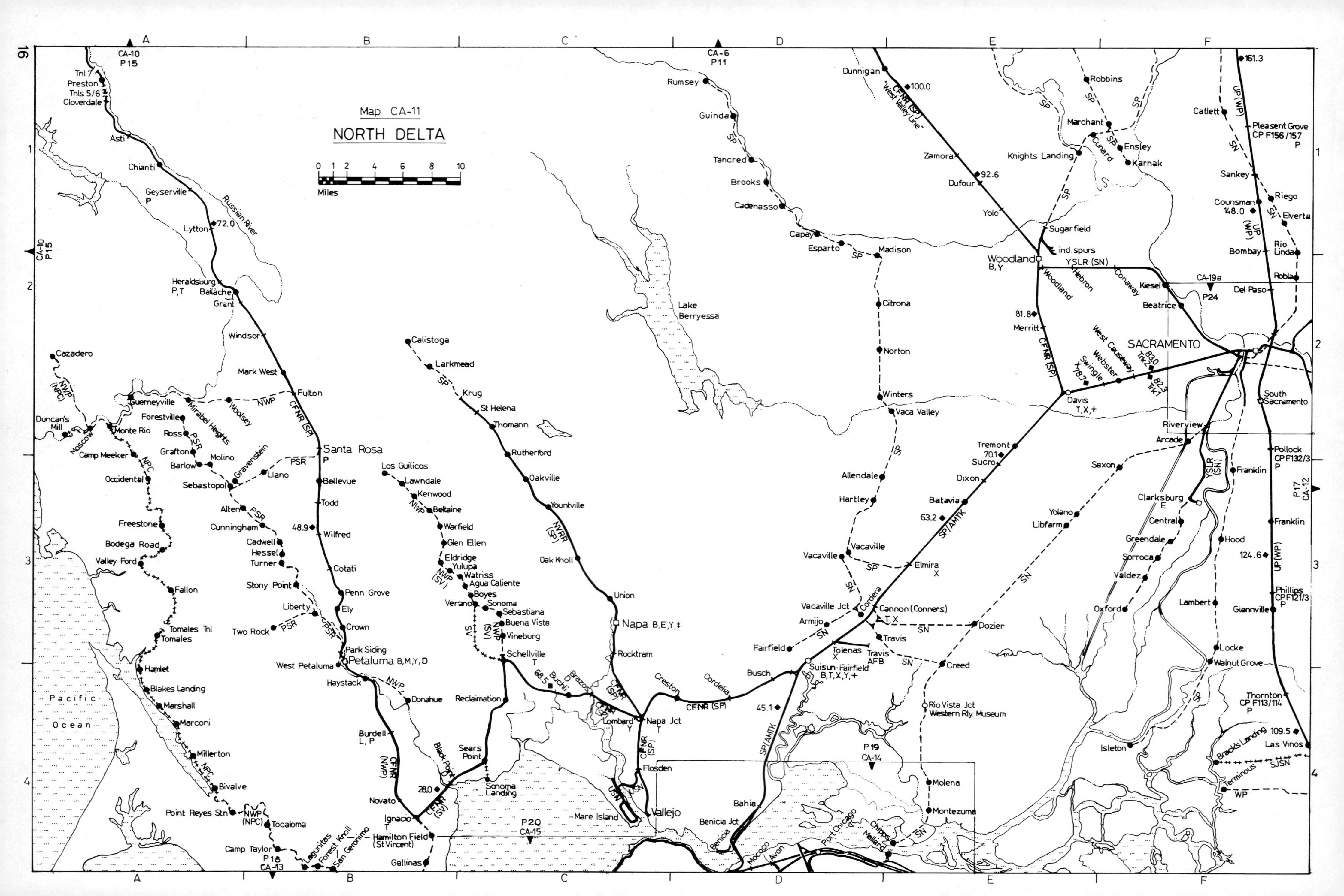

Map CA-11
NORTH DELTA
0 1 2 4 6 8 10
Miles
SACRAMENTO
Woodland B,Y
Davis T,X,+
Napa B,E,Y,‡
Petaluma B,M,Y,D
Santa Rosa P
Vallejo
Suisun-Fairfield B,T,X,Y,+
Lake Berryessa
Russian River
Pacific Ocean
Mare Island
Rio Vista Jct Western Rly. Museum
Travis AFB
CFNR (SP) "West Valley Line"
CFNR (SP)
CFNR (NWP)
SP/AMTK
UP (WP)
NVRR (SP)
YSLR (SN)
NWP (SV)
NWP (NPC)
CA-10 P15
CA-6 P11
CA-19a P24
P17 CA-12
P19 CA-14
P2Q CA-15
P18 CA-13
Tnl 7
Preston
Tnls 5/6
Cloverdale
Asti
Chianti
Geyserville P
Lytton
72.0
Heraldsburg P,T
Bailache
Grant
Windsor
Mark West
Fulton
Santa Rosa P
Bellevue
Todd
48.9
Wilfred
Cotati
Penn Grove
Ely
Crown
Park Siding
West Petaluma
Haystack
Donahue
Burdell L,P
Novato
Ignacio T
Hamilton Field (St Vincent)
Gallinas
Black Point
28.0
Sears Point
Sonoma Landing
Reclamation
Schellville T
68.5
Buchli
Brazos D
Lombard Y
Napa Jct T
Flosden
Creston
Cordelia
Busch
45.1
Fairfield
Armijo
Vacaville Jct
Cordera
Cannon (Conners) T,X
Travis
Tolenas X
Dozier
Creed
Vacaville
Elmira X
Batavia
63.2
Dixon
Sucro
70.1
Tremont
Swingle X
78.7
Webster
West Causeway
830 Trk2
82.3 Trk1
Calistoga
Larkmead
Krug
St Helena
Thomann
Rutherford
Oakville
Yountville
Oak Knoll
Union
Rocktram
Los Guilicos
Lawndale
Kenwood
Beltaine
Warfield
Glen Ellen
Eldridge
Yulupa
Watriss
Agua Caliente
Boyes
Verano
Sonoma
Sebastiana
Buena Vista
Vineburg
Cazadero
Duncan's Mill
Moscow
Monte Rio
Guerneyville
Forestville
Mirabel Heights
Woolsey
Ross
Grafton
Barlow
Molino
Gravenstein
Llano
Sebastopol
Camp Meeker
Occidental
Alten
Cunningham
Cadwell
Hessel
Turner
Stony Point
Liberty
Two Rock
Freestone
Bodega Road
Valley Ford
Fallon
Tomales Tnl
Tomales
Hamlet
Blakes Landing
Marshall
Marconi
Millerton
Bivalve
Point Reyes Stn
Tocaloma
Camp Taylor
Lagunitas
Forest Knoll
San Geronimo
Rumsey
Guinda
Tancred
Brooks
Cadenasso
Capay
Esparto
Madison
Citrona
Norton
Winters
Vaca Valley
Allendale
Hartley
Dunnigan
100.0
Zamora
92.6
Dufour
Yolo
Robbins
Marchant
Cunard
Ensley
Karnak
Knights Landing
Sugarfield
ind. spurs
Hebron
Conaway
Kiesel
Beatrice
81.8
Merritt
161.3
Catlett
Pleasent Grove CP F156/157 P
Sankey
Riego
Counsman
148.0
Elverta
Bombay
Rio Linda
Robla
Del Paso
South Sacramento
Riverview
Arcade
Pollock CP F132/3 P
Franklin
Saxon
Clarksburg E
Central
Greendale
Sorroca
Valdez
Oxford
Yolano
Libfarm
Hood
124.6
Lambert
Gianville
Phillips CP F121/3 P
Locke
Walnut Grove
Thornton CP F113/114 P
Isleton
Bracks Landing
109.5
Las Vinos
Terminous
WP
SJSN
Molena
Montezuma
Chipps
Mallard
Port Chicago
Avon
Mococo
Benicia
Benicia Jct
Bahia

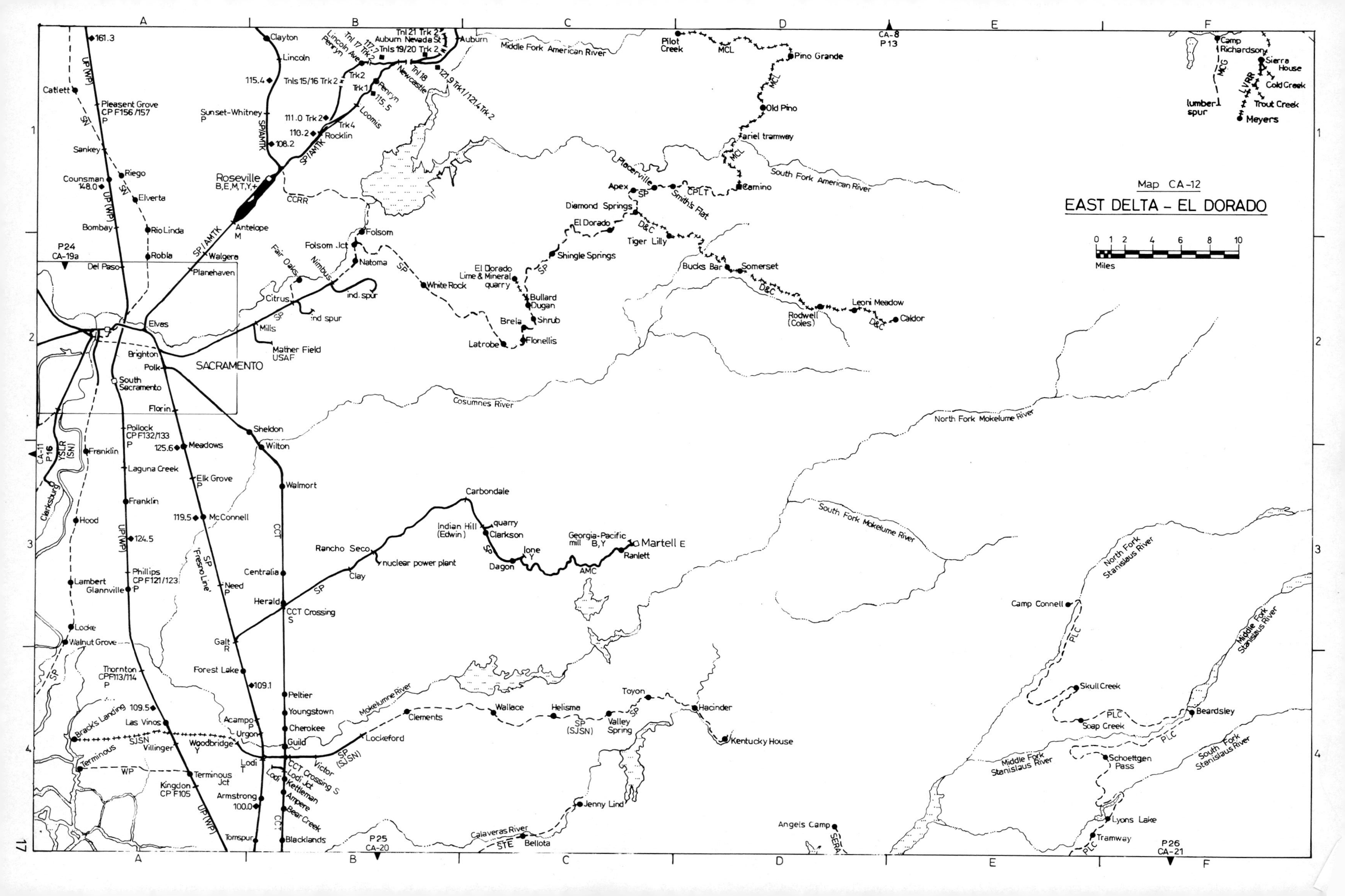
Map CA-12
EAST DELTA - EL DORADO
0 1 2 4 6 8 10
Miles
SACRAMENTO
Roseville
B,E,M,T,Y,+
Antelope
M
Walgera
Planehaven
Folsom
Folsom Jct
Natoma
Nimbus
Fair Oaks
Citrus
Mills
Mather Field
USAF
ind. spur
ind spur
White Rock
Latrobe
Brela
Shrub
Flonellis
Bullard
Dugan
El Dorado
Lime & Mineral
quarry
Shingle Springs
El Dorado
Diamond Springs
Placerville
Apex
Smith's Flat
Camino
ariel tramway
Tiger Lilly
Bucks Bar
Somerset
Rodwell
(Coles)
Leoni Meadow
Caldor
Old Pino
Pino Grande
Pilot
Creek
Camp
Richardson
Sierra
House
Cold Creek
Trout Creek
Meyers
lumber1
spur
Auburn
Auburn Nevada St
Tnls 19/20 Trk 2
Tnl 21 Trk 2
Tnl 17 Trk 2
Tnl 18
Newcastle
121.9 Trk1/121.4 Trk 2
Lincoln Ave
Penryn
115.5
Trk2
Trk1
Trk4
Loomis
Rocklin
110.2
111.0 Trk 2
108.2
Tnls 15/16 Trk 2
115.4
Lincoln
Clayton
Sunset-Whitney
P
161.3
Catlett
Pleasent Grove
CP F156/157
P
Sankey
Riego
Counsman
148.0
Elverta
Bombay
Rio Linda
Robla
Del Paso
P24
CA-19a
Elves
Brighton
Polk
South
Sacramento
Florin
Pollock
CP F132/133
P
125.6
Meadows
Laguna Creek
Elk Grove
P
Franklin
Franklin
119.5
McConnell
124.5
Hood
Sheldon
Wilton
Walmort
Phillips
CP F121/123
Glannville
P
Lambert
Need
P
SP
'Fresno Line'
Centralia
Herald
CCT Crossing
S
Galt
R
Forest Lake
109.1
Clay
Rancho Seco
nuclear power plant
Carbondale
Indian Hill
(Edwin)
quarry
Clarkson
Dagon
Ione
Y
Georgia-Pacific
mill
B, Y
Ranlett
Martell E
AMC
Locke
Walnut Grove
Thornton
CPF113/114
P
109.5
Las Vinos
Bracks Landing
SJSN
Villinger
Terminous
WP
Woodbridge
Y
Acampo
P
Urgon
Lodi
T
Terminous
Jct
Kingdon
CP F105
Armstrong
100.0
Tomspur
Peltier
Youngstown
Cherokee
Guild
Victor
CCT Crossing S
Lodi Jct
Kettleman
Ampere
Bear Creek
Blacklands
Lockeford
SP
(SJSN)
Clements
Wallace
Helisma
Valley
Spring
Toyon
Hacinder
Kentucky House
Jenny Lind
Bellota
STE
Calaveras River
P25
CA-20
Angels Camp
SERA
Camp Connell
Skull Creek
Soap Creek
Beardsley
Schoettgen
Pass
Lyons Lake
Tramway
P26
CA-21
Cosumnes River
North Fork Mokelume River
South Fork Mokelume River
Mokelumne River
Middle Fork American River
South Fork American River
North Fork
Stanislaus River
Middle Fork
Stanislaus River
South Fork
Stanislaus River
UP (WP)
SP/AMTK
CCT
CCRR
CPLT
PLC
MCL
MCG
LVRR
D&C
SN
CA-8
P13
CA-11
P16
YSLR
(SN)
Clarksburg

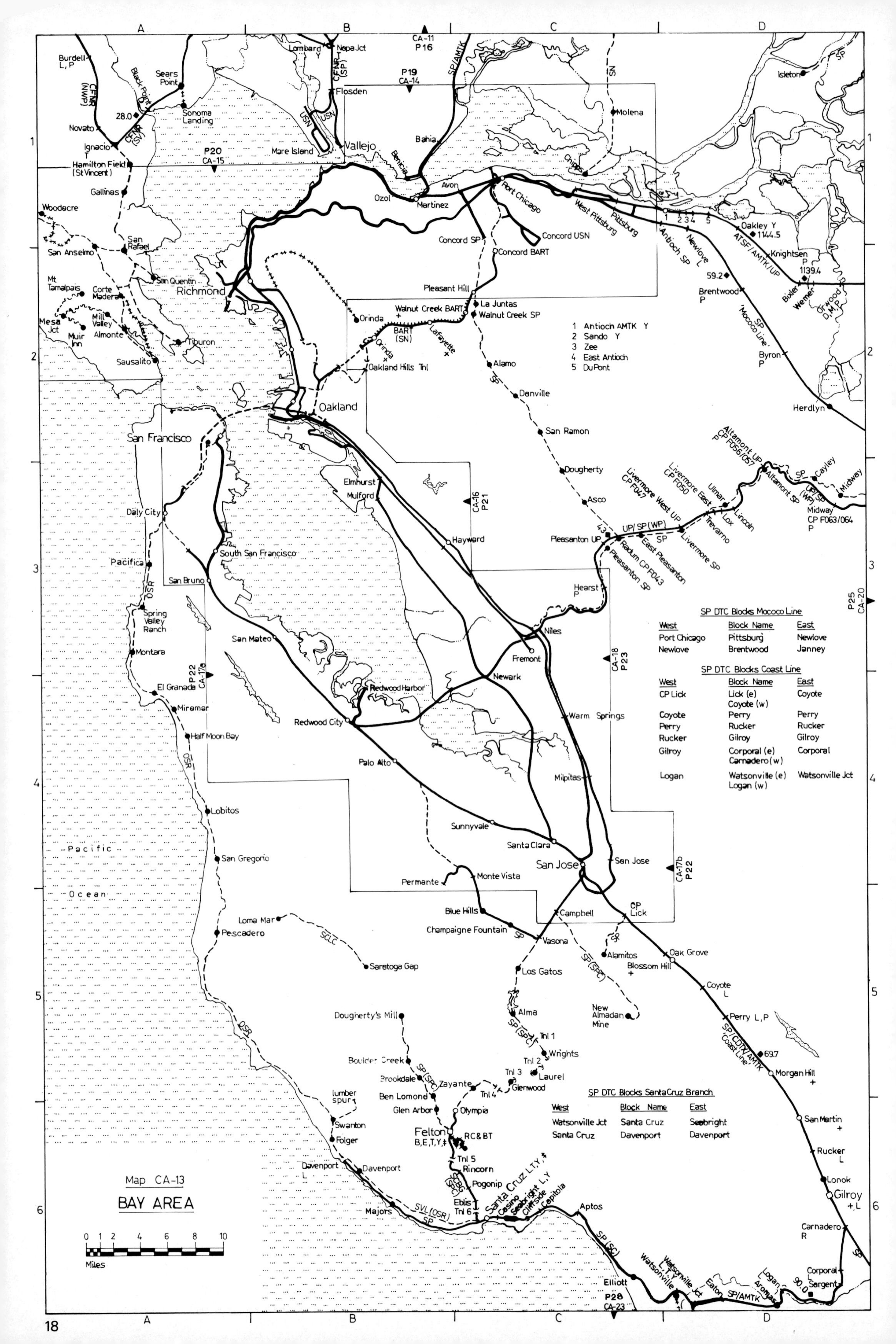

Map CA-13
BAY AREA
Miles
0 1 2 4 6 8 10
Pacific
Ocean
San Francisco
Oakland
Richmond
San Jose
Burdell L, P
Black Point
Sears Point
Sonoma Landing
Novato
28.0
Ignacio T
Hamilton Field (St Vincent)
Lombard Y
Napa Jct
Flosden
Mare Island
Vallejo
Benicia
Bahia
Molena
Chipps
Isleton
Gallinas
Woodacre
San Anselmo
San Rafael
San Quentin
Mt Tamalpais
Corte Madera
Mill Valley
Almonte
Mesa Jct
Muir Inn
Tiburon
Sausalito
Ozol
Martinez
Avon
Port Chicago
West Pittsburg
Pittsburg
Concord SP
Concord USN
Concord BART
Antioch SP
Newlove L
Oakley Y 1144.5
Knightsen P 1139.4
ATSF/AMTK/UP
59.2
Brentwood P
Bixler
Werner
Orwood D, M, P
SP 'Mococo Line'
Byron P
Herdlyn
Pleasant Hill
La Juntas
Walnut Creek SP
Walnut Creek BART
Orinda
BART (SN)
Lafayette
Oakland Hills Tnl
Alamo
Danville
San Ramon
Dougherty
Asco
1 Antioch AMTK Y
2 Sando Y
3 Zee
4 East Antioch
5 DuPont
Altamont UP P CP F056/057
Altamont SP
Cayley
Midway
Midway CP F063/064 P
Livermore East CP F050
Livermore West UP CP F047
Ulmar
Lox
Lincoln
Trevarno
Livermore SP
UP/SP (WP)
Pleasanton UP
East Pleasanton
Radum CP F043
Pleasanton SP
Hearst P
Elmhurst
Mulford
Hayward
Daly City
South San Francisco
Pacifica
San Bruno
Spring Valley Ranch
Montara
San Mateo
El Granada
Miramar
Half Moon Bay
OSR
Niles
Fremont
Newark
Redwood Harbor
Redwood City
Warm Springs
Palo Alto
Milpitas
Lobitos
Sunnyvale
Santa Clara
San Gregorio
San Jose
Permante
Monte Vista
Blue Hills
Champaigne Fountain
Campbell
CP Lick
Vasona
Loma Mar
Pescadero
SCLC
Saratoga Gap
Los Gatos
SP (SPC)
Alamitos
Blossom Hill
Oak Grove
Coyote L
New Almadan Mine
Alma
Perry L, P
Dougherty's Mill
Tnl 1
Wrights
SP/CDTX/AMTK 'Coast Line'
69.7
Boulder Creek
Tnl 2
Laurel
Morgan Hill
Brookdale
Zayante
Tnl 3
Glenwood
Tnl 4
Ben Lomond
lumber spur
Glen Arbor
Olympia
Swanton
Felton B, E, T, Y, ‡
RC&BT
Folger
Tnl 5
Rincorn
Davenport L
Davenport
Pogonip
Santa Cruz L, T, Y, ‡
Casino
Seabright L, Y
Cliffside
Capitola
Aptos
Eblis
Tnl 6
Majors
SVL (OSR)
SP (SC)
San Martin
Rucker L
Lonok
Gilroy + L
Carnadero R
Corporal
Sargent
90.0
Elliott
Watsonville L, T, Y
Watsonville Jct
Eaton
SP/AMTK
Logan
Aromas
P16 CA-11
P19 CA-14
P20 CA-15
CA-16 P21
P22 CA-17a
CA-18 P23
CA-17b P22
P25 CA-20
P28 CA-23
SP DTC Blocks Mococo Line
West | Block Name | East
Port Chicago | Pittsburg | Newlove
Newlove | Brentwood | Janney
SP DTC Blocks Coast Line
West | Block Name | East
CP Lick | Lick (e) Coyote (w) | Coyote
Coyote | Perry | Perry
Perry | Rucker | Rucker
Rucker | Gilroy | Gilroy
Gilroy | Corporal (e) Carnadero (w) | Corporal
Logan | Watsonville (e) Logan (w) | Watsonville Jct
SP DTC Blocks Santa Cruz Branch
West | Block Name | East
Watsonville Jct | Santa Cruz | Seabright
Santa Cruz | Davenport | Davenport

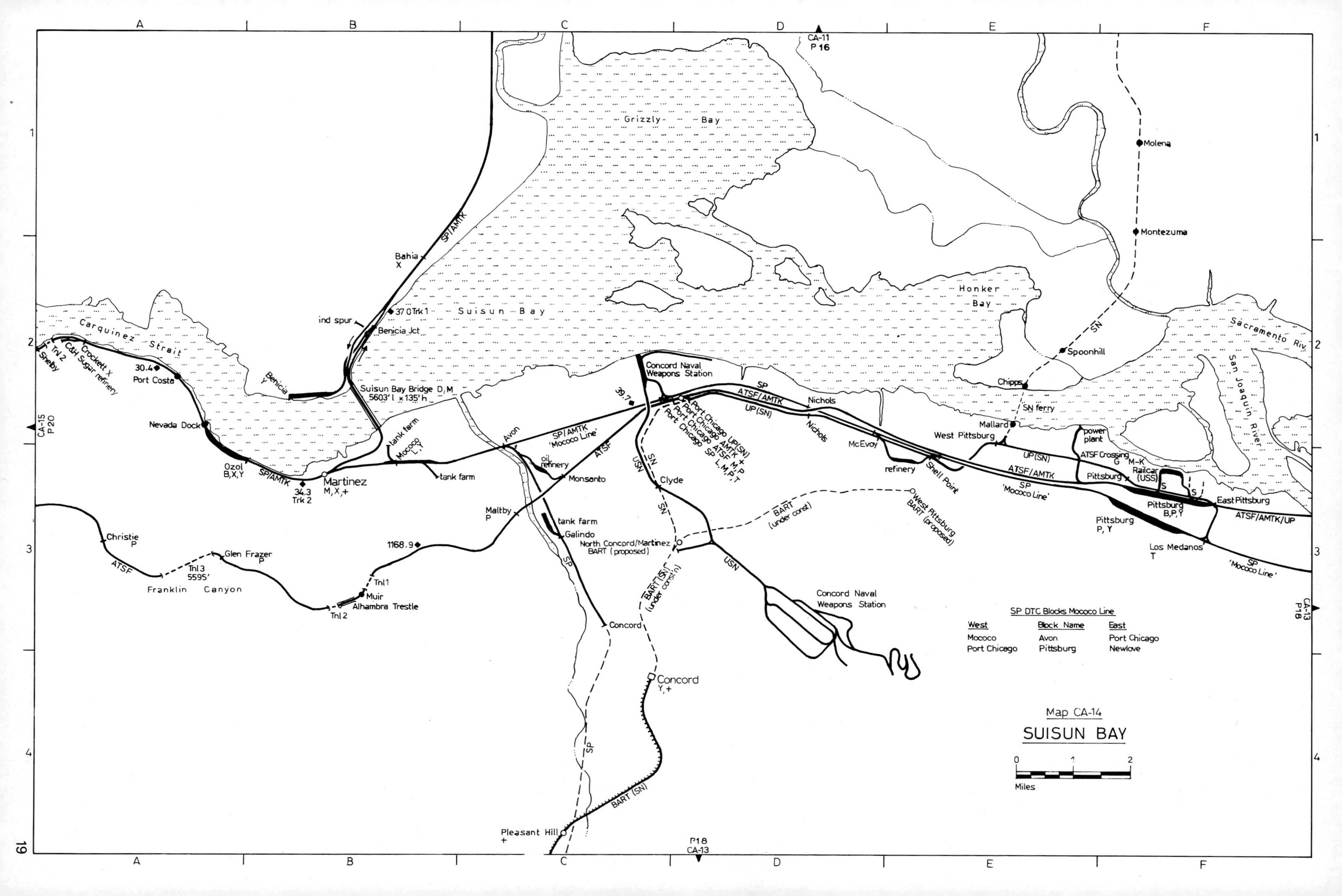
Map CA-14
SUISUN BAY
0
1
2
Miles
SP DTC Blocks Mococo Line
West
Block Name
East
Mococo
Avon
Port Chicago
Port Chicago
Pittsburg
Newlove
Sacramento Riv.
San Joaquin River
Honker Bay
Grizzly Bay
Suisun Bay
Carquinez Strait
Molena
Montezuma
Spoonhill
Chipps
SN ferry
SN
Mallard
West Pittsburg
Shell Point
refinery
McEvoy
Nichols
Nichols
SP
ATSF/AMTK
UP(SN)
UP(SN)
ATSF/AMTK
SP 'Mococo Line'
power plant
ATSF Crossing
G
M-K
Pittsburg
Railcar (USS)
S
S
Pittsburg B,P,Y
Pittsburg P,Y
Los Medanos T
East Pittsburg
ATSF/AMTK/UP
SP 'Mococo Line'
CA-13 P18
CA-11 P16
CA-15 P20
P18 CA-13
West Pittsburg BART (proposed)
BART (under const)
Concord Naval Weapons Station
Concord Naval Weapons Station
USN
Port Chicago UP(SN)
Port Chicago AMTK +
Port Chicago ATSF M,P
Port Chicago SP L,M,P,T
Clyde
39.7
SN
SN
USN
North Concord/Martinez BART (proposed)
BART (SN) (under constr.)
Concord Y,+
Concord
BART (SN)
SP
SP
Pleasant Hill +
SP/AMTK 'Mococo Line'
ATSF
Monsanto
oil refinery
tank farm
Galindo
Avon
Maltby P
tank farm
tank farm
Mococo L,Y
1168.9
Tnl 1
Muir
Alhambra Trestle
Tnl 2
Martinez M,X,+
34.3 Trk 2
Suisun Bay Bridge D,M 5603' l x 135' h
Benicia Jct
37.0 Trk 1
Bahia X
SP/AMTK
ind spur
Benicia Y
SP/AMTK
Ozol B,X,Y
Nevada Dock
Glen Frazer P
Tnl 3 5595'
Franklin Canyon
Christie P
ATSF
Port Costa
30.4
Crockett X
C&H Sugar refinery
Tnl 2
Shelby
A
B
C
D
E
F
1
2
3
4

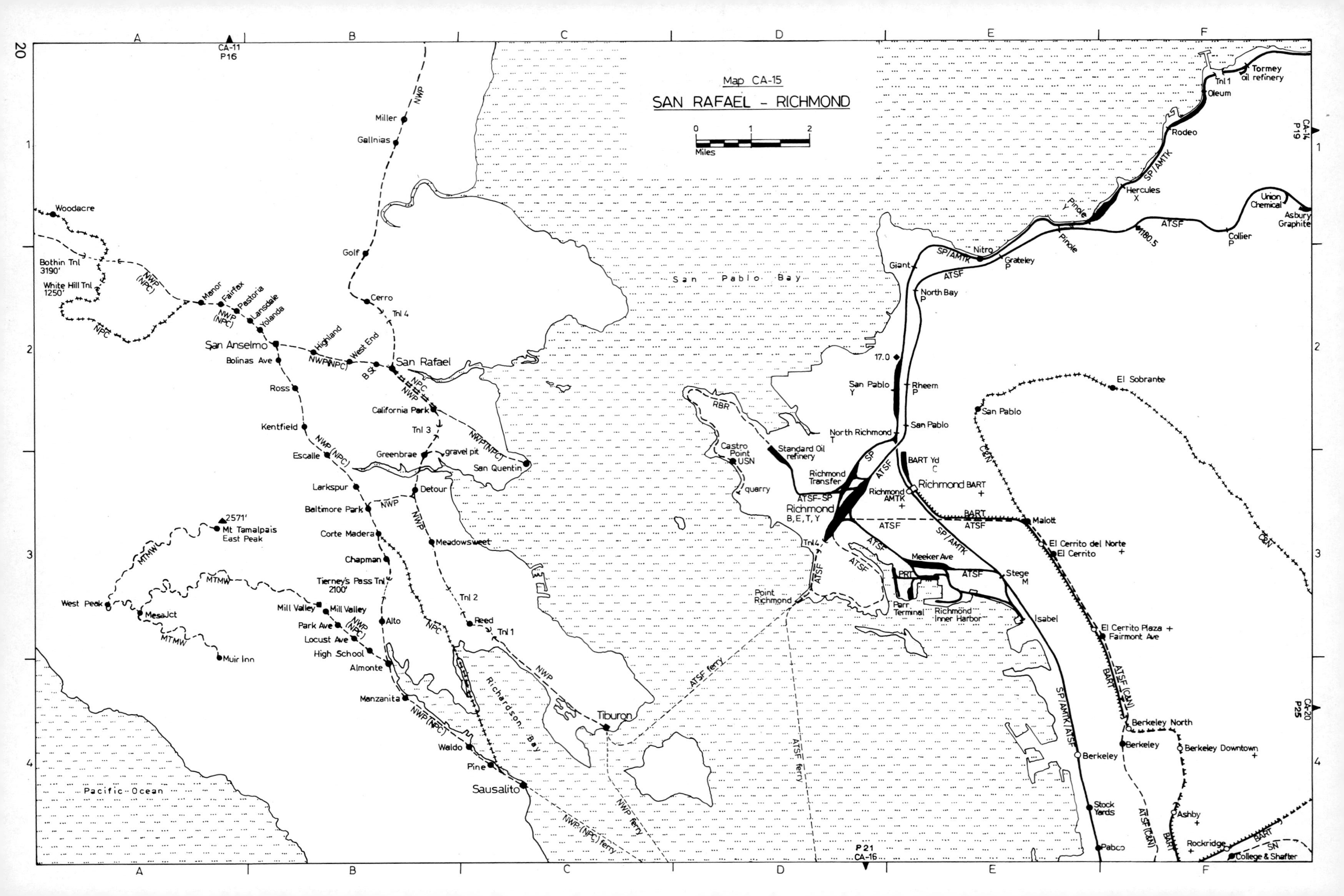

Map CA-15
SAN RAFAEL - RICHMOND
0
1
2
Miles
CA-11
P16
CA-14
P19
CA-20
P25
P 21
CA-16
Miller
Gallnias
NWP
Golf
Cerro
Tnl 4
Woodacre
Bothin Tnl
3190'
White Hill Tnl
1250'
NWP (NPC)
NPC
Manor
Fairfax
Pastoria
Lansdale
Yolanda
NWP (NPC)
San Anselmo
Bolinas Ave
Highland
West End
NWP (NPC)
B St
San Rafael
NPC
NWP
Ross
Kentfield
California Park
Tnl 3
NWP (NPC)
Escalle
NWP (NPC)
Greenbrae
gravel pit
San Quentin
Larkspur
Detour
Baltimore Park
NWP
2571'
Mt Tamalpais
East Peak
MTMW
Corte Madera
Meadowsweet
Chapman
Tierney's Pass Tnl
2100'
Tnl 2
West Peak
Mesa Jct
MTMW
Mill Valley
Mill Valley
Park Ave
NWP (NPC)
Locust Ave
Alto
NPC
Reed
Tnl 1
MTMW
Muir Inn
High School
Almonte
Richardson Bay
NWP
Manzanita
NWP (NPC)
Tiburon
ATSF ferry
Waldo
Pine
Sausalito
Pacific Ocean
NWP ferry
NWP (NPC) ferry
ATSF ferry
San Pablo Bay
Tnl 1
Tormey
oil refinery
Oleum
Rodeo
SP/AMTK
Hercules
X
Union Chemical
Asbury Graphite
Pinole
Y
Pinole
ATSF
180.5
Collier
P
Nitro
SP/AMTK
Grateley
P
Giant
ATSF
North Bay
P
17.0
San Pablo
Y
Rheem
P
El Sobrante
San Pablo
RBR
North Richmond
T
San Pablo
C&N
Castro Point
USN
Standard Oil refinery
SP
ATSF
BART Yd
C
Richmond Transfer
Richmond AMTK
Richmond BART
quarry
ATSF-SP
Richmond
B, E, T, Y
BART
ATSF
Malott
ATSF
SP/AMTK
El Cerrito del Norte
El Cerrito
Tnl 4
ATSF
Meeker Ave
ATSF
ATSF
Stege
M
PRT
ATSF
Point Richmond
Parr Terminal
Richmond Inner Harbor
Isabel
El Cerrito Plaza
Fairmont Ave
SP/AMTK/ATSF
BART
ATSF (C&N)
Berkeley North
Berkeley
Berkeley Downtown
Berkeley
Stock Yards
ATSF (C&N)
BART
Ashby
Pabco
Rockridge
BART
SN
College & Shafter
A
B
C
D
E
F
1
2
3
4

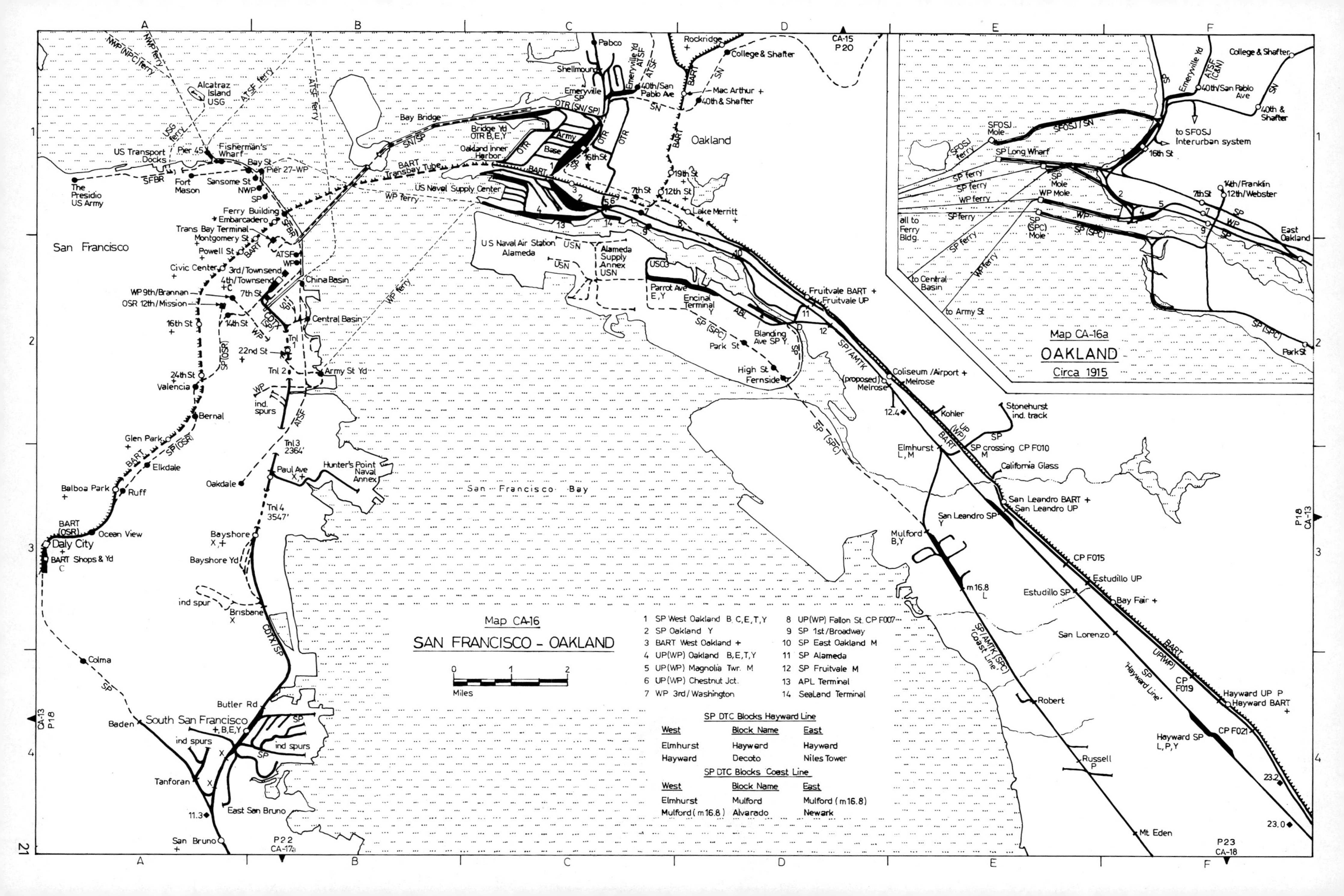
Map CA-16
SAN FRANCISCO - OAKLAND
0 1 2
Miles
1 SP West Oakland B,C,E,T,Y
2 SP Oakland Y
3 BART West Oakland +
4 UP(WP) Oakland B,E,T,Y
5 UP(WP) Magnolia Twr. M
6 UP(WP) Chestnut Jct.
7 WP 3rd/Washington
8 UP(WP) Fallon St. CP F007
9 SP 1st/Broadway
10 SP East Oakland M
11 SP Alameda
12 SP Fruitvale M
13 APL Terminal
14 SeaLand Terminal
SP DTC Blocks Hayward Line
West Block Name East
Elmhurst Hayward Hayward
Hayward Decoto Niles Tower
SP DTC Blocks Coast Line
West Block Name East
Elmhurst Mulford Mulford (m16.8)
Mulford (m16.8) Alvarado Newark
Map CA-16a
OAKLAND
Circa 1915
San Francisco
Oakland
San Francisco Bay
CA-15
P20
CA-13
P18
P22
CA-17a
P23
CA-18
The Presidio US Army
US Transport Docks
Pier 45
Fisherman's Wharf
Alcatraz Island USG
Fort Mason
Sansome St
Bay St
Pier 27-WP
NWP
Ferry Building
Embarcadero
Trans Bay Terminal
Montgomery St
Powell St
Civic Center
3rd/Townsend
4th/Townsend
7th St
WP 9th/Brannan
OSR 12th/Mission
16th St
14th St
22nd St
24th St
Valencia
Bernal
Glen Park
Elkdale
Balboa Park
Ruff
Ocean View
Daly City
BART Shops & Yd
China Basin
Central Basin
Army St Yd
Tnl 1
Tnl 2
Tnl 3 2364'
Tnl 4 3547'
ind. spurs
Oakdale
Paul Ave
Hunter's Point Naval Annex
Bayshore
Bayshore Yd
ind spur
Brisbane
Butler Rd
South San Francisco
ind spurs
East San Bruno
Tanforan
San Bruno
Baden
Colma
Bay Bridge
Transbay Tube
US Naval Supply Center
Bridge Yd OTR B,E,Y
Oakland Inner Harbor
Army Base
Pabco
Shellmound
Emeryville SP
Emeryville Yd
40th/San Pablo Ave
Rockridge
College & Shafter
Mac Arthur
40th & Shafter
19th St
12th St
Lake Merritt
US Naval Air Station Alameda
Alameda Supply Annex USN
Parrot Ave E,Y
Encinal Terminal Y
Blanding Ave SP Y
Park St
High St
Fernside
Fruitvale BART
Fruitvale UP
Coliseum /Airport
Melrose
(proposed) Melrose
Kohler
Stonehurst ind. track
SP crossing CP F010
Elmhurst L, M
California Glass
San Leandro BART
San Leandro UP
San Leandro SP Y
Mulford B,Y
m 16.8 L
CP F015
Estudillo UP
Estudillo SP
Bay Fair
San Lorenzo
SP 'Hayward Line'
SP/AMTK (SPC) 'Coast Line'
Robert
Russell P
Mt Eden
CP F019
Hayward UP P
Hayward BART
CP F021
Hayward SP L,P,Y
SFOSJ Mole
SFOSJ ferry
SP Long Wharf
SP Mole
WP Mole
SP (SPC) Mole
SP ferry
WP ferry
all to Ferry Bldg.
to Central Basin
to Army St
to SFOSJ Interurban system
7th St
14th/Franklin
12th/Webster
East Oakland
Park St

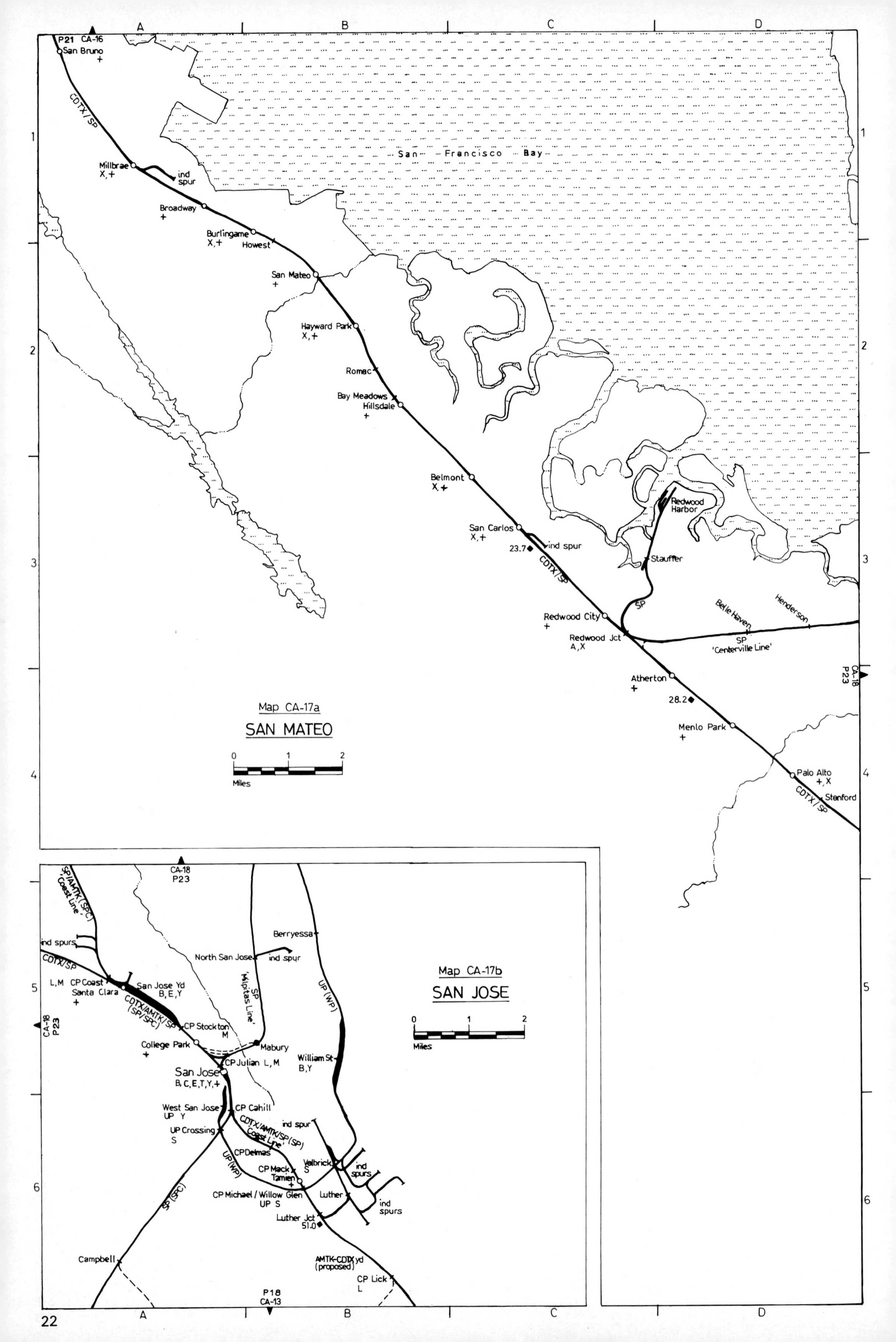
Map CA-17a
SAN MATEO
Miles
San Francisco Bay
P21 CA-16
San Bruno
CDTX / SP
Millbrae X, +
ind spur
Broadway
Burlingame X, +
Howest
San Mateo
Hayward Park X, +
Romac
Bay Meadows
Hillsdale
Belmont X, +
San Carlos X, +
23.7
ind spur
Redwood Harbor
Stauffer
SP
Redwood City
Redwood Jct A, X
Belle Haven
Henderson
SP 'Centerville Line'
Atherton
28.2
Menlo Park
Palo Alto +, X
Stanford
CA-18 P23
Map CA-17b
SAN JOSE
SP/AMTK (SPC) 'Coast Line'
ind spurs
CDTX/SP
L, M CP Coast
Santa Clara
San Jose Yd B, E, Y
CDTX/AMTK/SP (SP/SPC)
CP Stockton M
College Park
San Jose B, C, E, T, Y, +
CP Julian L, M
Mabury
North San Jose
ind spur
Berryessa
SP 'Milpitas Line'
UP (WP)
William St B, Y
West San Jose UP Y
CP Cahill
UP Crossing S
CDTX/AMTK/SP (SP) 'Coast Line'
CP Delmas
CP Mack
Tamien
Valbrick S
ind spurs
CP Michael / Willow Glen UP S
Luther
Luther Jct
51.0
SP (SPC)
Campbell
AMTK-CDTX yd (proposed)
CP Lick L
P18 CA-13

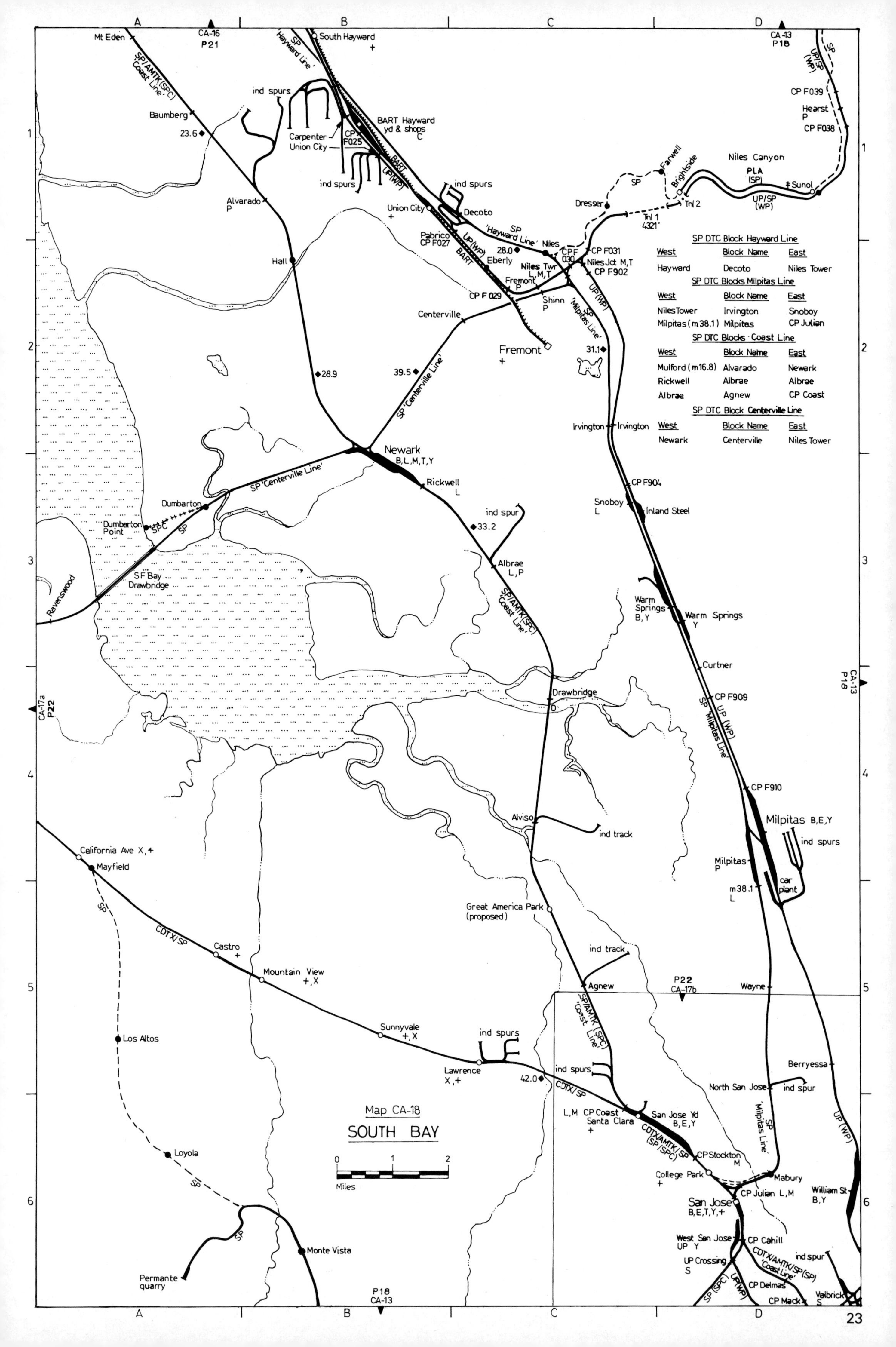

Map CA-18
SOUTH BAY
Miles
0
1
2
SP DTC Block Hayward Line
West
Block Name
East
Hayward
Decoto
Niles Tower
SP DTC Blocks Milpitas Line
West
Block Name
East
Niles Tower
Irvington
Snoboy
Milpitas (m 38.1)
Milpitas
CP Julian
SP DTC Blocks Coast Line
West
Block Name
East
Mulford (m 16.8)
Alvarado
Newark
Rickwell
Albrae
Albrae
Albrae
Agnew
CP Coast
SP DTC Block Centerville Line
West
Block Name
East
Newark
Centerville
Niles Tower
Mt Eden
CA-16
P21
South Hayward
SP 'Hayward Line'
SP/AMTK (SPC) 'Coast Line'
ind spurs
Baumberg
23.6
BART Hayward yd & shops
C
Carpenter
Union City
CP F025
BART
UP (WP)
Alvarado
P
Union City
Decoto
Pabrico
CP F027
28.0
Eberly
Hall
Niles
CP F031
Niles Jct M, T
CP F902
Niles Twr
L, M, T
Fremont
P
CP F029
Shinn
P
Centerville
Fremont
SP 'Milpitas Line'
31.1
28.9
39.5
SP 'Centerville Line'
Irvington
Irvington
Newark
B, L, M, T, Y
Rickwell
L
CP F904
Snoboy
L
Inland Steel
Dumbarton
Dumbarton Point
SPC
SP
ind spur
33.2
Albrae
L, P
SF Bay Drawbridge
Ravenswood
Warm Springs
B, Y
Warm Springs
Y
Curtner
CP F909
SP 'Milpitas Line'
UP (WP)
Drawbridge
CA-17a
P22
CA-13
P18
CP F910
Milpitas B, E, Y
ind spurs
Milpitas
P
car plant
m 38.1
L
Alviso
ind track
California Ave X, +
Mayfield
SP
CDTX/SP
Castro
Mountain View
+, X
Great America Park (proposed)
ind track
Agnew
P22
CA-17b
Wayne
SP/AMTK (SPC) 'Coast Line'
Los Altos
Sunnyvale
+, X
ind spurs
Lawrence
X, +
42.0
ind spurs
CDTX/SP
Berryessa
North San Jose
ind spur
L, M
CP Coast
Santa Clara
San Jose Yd
B, E, Y
CDTX/AMTK/SP (SP/SPC)
CP Stockton
M
College Park
Mabury
Loyola
SP
San Jose
B, E, T, Y, +
CP Julian L, M
William St
B, Y
Monte Vista
West San Jose
UP Y
CP Cahill
UP Crossing
S
CDTX/AMTK/SP (SP) 'Coast Line'
ind spur
Permanente quarry
P18
CA-13
SP (SPC)
UP (WP)
CP Delmas
CP Mack
Valbrick
S
Niles Canyon
PLA (SP)
Sunol
UP/SP (WP)
Farwell
Brightside
SP
Dresser
Tnl 2
Tnl 1
4321'
CA-13
P18
SP
UP/SP (WP)
CP F039
Hearst
P
CP F038
A
B
C
D
1
2
3
4
5
6

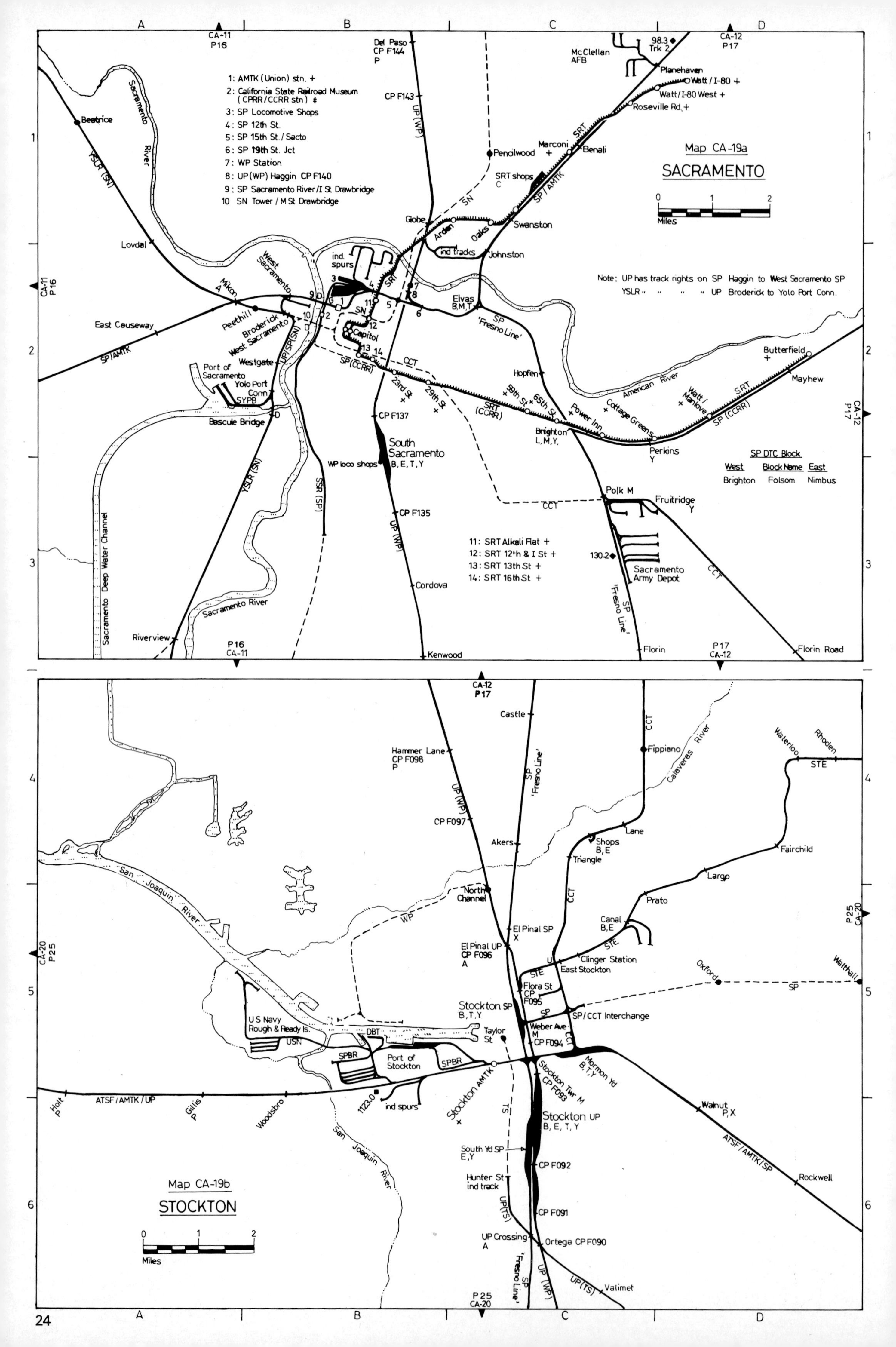
Map CA-19a
SACRAMENTO
Miles
1: AMTK (Union) stn. +
2: California State Railroad Museum (CPRR/CCRR stn) ‡
3: SP Locomotive Shops
4: SP 12th St.
5: SP 15th St./Sacto
6: SP 19th St. Jct
7: WP Station
8: UP (WP) Haggin CP F140
9: SP Sacramento River/I St Drawbridge
10 SN Tower/M St. Drawbridge
Note: UP has track rights on SP Haggin to West Sacramento SP
YSLR " " " " UP Broderick to Yolo Port Conn.
11: SRT Alkali Flat +
12: SRT 12th & I St +
13: SRT 13th St +
14: SRT 16th St +
SP DTC Block
West Block Name East
Brighton Folsom Nimbus
Beatrice
Sacramento River
YSLR (SN)
Lovdal
Mikon A
Peethill
East Causeway
SP/AMTK
Del Paso CP F144 P
CP F143
UP (WP)
McClellan AFB
98.3 Trk 2
Planehaven
Watt/I-80 +
Watt/I-80 West +
Roseville Rd. +
Pencilwood
Marconi +
Benali
SRT shops C
SRT
SP/AMTK
SN
Globe
Arden
Oaks
Swanston
ind tracks
Johnston
ind. spurs
West Sacramento
Elvas B,M,T
SP 'Fresno Line'
Broderick
West Sacramento
UP/SP (SN)
Capitol
SP (CCRR)
CCT
Westgate
Port of Sacramento
Yolo Port Conn
SYPB
Bascule Bridge
23rd St
29th St
59th St
65th St
SRT (CCRR)
Hopfen
American River
Butterfield
Mayhew
Power Inn
Cottage Greens
Watt/Manlove
SRT
SP (CCRR)
Brighton L,M,Y,
Perkins Y
CP F137
South Sacramento B,E,T,Y
WP loco shops
SSR (SP)
CP F135
UP (WP)
Polk M
Fruitridge Y
130.2
Sacramento Army Depot
CCT
SP 'Fresno Line'
Cordova
Sacramento Deep Water Channel
Sacramento River
Riverview
Kenwood
Florin
Florin Road
P16 CA-11
P17 CA-12
Map CA-19b
STOCKTON
Miles
Castle
Hammer Lane CP F098 P
UP (WP)
CP F097
SP 'Fresno Line'
CCT
Fippiano
Calaveras River
Waterloo
Rhoden
STE
Lane
Shops B,E
Triangle
Akers
Fairchild
Largo
Prato
North Channel
WP
Canal B,E
STE
El Pinal SP X
El Pinal UP CP F096 A
Clinger Station
East Stockton
Oxford
Walthall
SP
San Joaquin River
Flora St CP F095
Stockton SP B,T,Y
SP/CCT Interchange
U S Navy Rough & Ready Is.
USN
DBT
Taylor St
Weber Ave M
CP F094
SPBR
Port of Stockton
Mormon Yd B,T,Y
Stockton AMTK
Stockton Twr M
CP F093
Holt P
ATSF/AMTK/UP
Gillis P
Woodsbro
1123.0
ind spurs
Walnut P,X
Stockton UP B,E,T,Y
SL
ATSF/AMTK/SP
South Yd SP E,Y
CP F092
Hunter St ind track
Rockwell
San Joaquin River
UP (TS)
CP F091
UP Crossing A
Ortega CP F090
SP 'Fresno Line'
UP (WP)
UP (TS)
Valimet
CA-20 P25
P25 CA-20
CA-12 P17

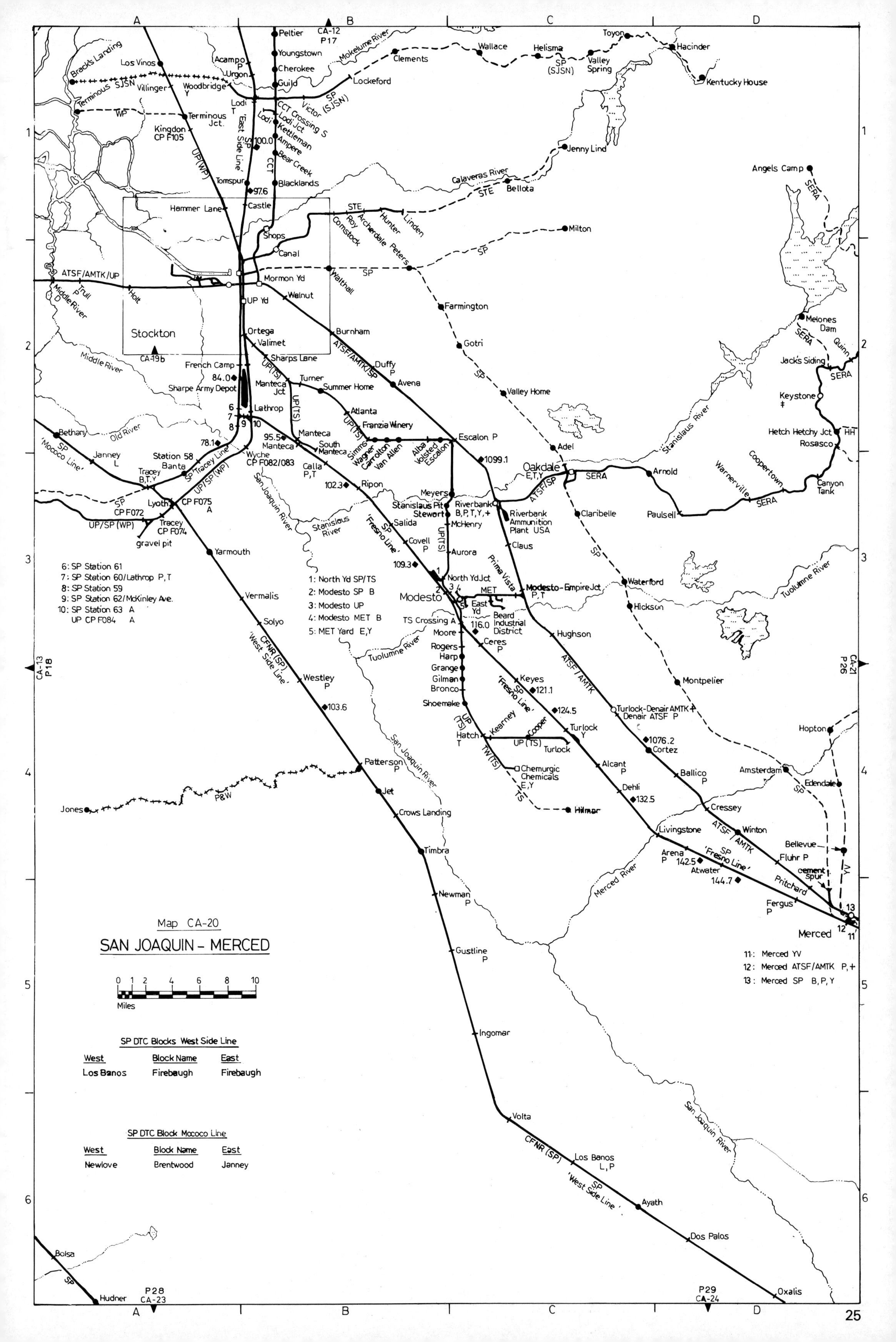

Map CA-20
SAN JOAQUIN - MERCED
0 1 2 4 6 8 10
Miles
SP DTC Blocks West Side Line
West | Block Name | East
Los Banos | Firebaugh | Firebaugh
SP DTC Block Mococo Line
West | Block Name | East
Newlove | Brentwood | Janney
6: SP Station 61
7: SP Station 60/Lathrop P, T
8: SP Station 59
9: SP Station 62/McKinley Ave.
10: SP Station 63 A
UP CP F084 A
1: North Yd SP/TS
2: Modesto SP B
3: Modesto UP
4: Modesto MET B
5: MET Yard E, Y
11: Merced YV
12: Merced ATSF/AMTK P, +
13: Merced SP B, P, Y
CA-12 P17
CA-13 P18
CA-21 P26
P28 CA-23
P29 CA-24
Stockton
CA-19b
Modesto
Merced
Oakdale E, T, Y
Peltier
Youngstown
Cherokee
Guild
Acampo P
Urgon
Los Vinos
Brack's Landing
Terminous SJSN
Villinger
Woodbridge Y
Lodi T
Terminous Jct.
Kingdon CP F105
Clements
Lockeford
Wallace
Helisma
Toyon
Hacinder
Kentucky House
Valley Spring
SP (SJSN)
Mokelumne River
Victor
CCT Crossing S
Lodi Jct
Kettleman
Ampere
Bear Creek
Blacklands
100.0
97.6
Tomspur
'East Side Line'
UP (WP)
CCT
Jenny Lind
Calaveras River
Bellota
STE
Angels Camp
SERA
Hammer Lane
Castle
Shops
Canal
Linden
Hunter
Archerdale
Peters
Roy
Comstock
Milton
ATSF/AMTK/UP
Trull
Holt
Middle River D
Mormon Yd
UP Yd
Walthall
Walnut
Farmington
Burnham
Ortega
Valimet
Sharps Lane
French Camp
84.0
Sharpe Army Depot
Duffy P
Avena
Turner
Summer Home
Manteca Jct
Atlanta
Franzia Winery
Gotri
Valley Home
Melones Dam
Quinn
Jacks Siding
Keystone
Hetch Hetchy Jct HH
Rosasco
Canyon Tank
Lathrop
Bethany
Old River
Janney L
'Mococo Line'
Station 58
Banta
Tracey B, T, Y
78.1
95.5
Manteca
South Manteca
Simms
Wagner
Carrolton
Van Allen
Alba
Volsted
Escalon
Escalon P
1099.1
Adel
Wyche CP F082/083
Calla P, T
Ripon
102.3
Lyoth
CP F072
CP F075 A
Tracey CP F074
UP/SP (WP)
SP Tracey Line
gravel pit
Meyers
Stanislaus Pit
Stewart
Riverbank B, P, T, Y, +
Riverbank Ammunition Plant USA
McHenry
Claribelle
Arnold
Paulsell
Warnerville
Coopertown
Salida
Covell P
'Fresno Line'
Stanislaus River
San Joaquin River
Yarmouth
Aurora
Claus
Prima Vista
109.3
North Yd Jct
MET
Modesto-Empire Jct P, T
Waterford
Hickson
Tuolumne River
East Yd
Beard Industrial District
Vermalis
Solyo
TS Crossing A
Moore
116.0
Ceres P
Rogers
Harp
Grange
Gilman
Bronco
Shoemake
Hughson
Keyes
121.1
124.5
Montpelier
Westley P
CFNR (SP)
'West Side Line'
103.6
Hatch T
Kearney
Cooper
UP (TS)
Turlock
Turlock Y
Turlock-Denair AMTK +
Denair ATSF P
1076.2
Cortez
Hopton
TW (TS)
Chemurgic Chemicals E, Y
Patterson P
Jet
Alcant P
Dehli
132.5
Hilmar
Ballico P
Amsterdam
Edendale
Jones
P&W
Crows Landing
Cressey
Livingstone
Winton
Timbra
Arena P
142.5
Atwater
144.7
Fluhr P
Bellevue
cement spur
Pritchard
Fergus P
Merced River
Newman P
Gustline P
Ingomar
Volta
Los Banos L, P
Ayath
Dos Palos
Oxalis
Bolsa
Hudner

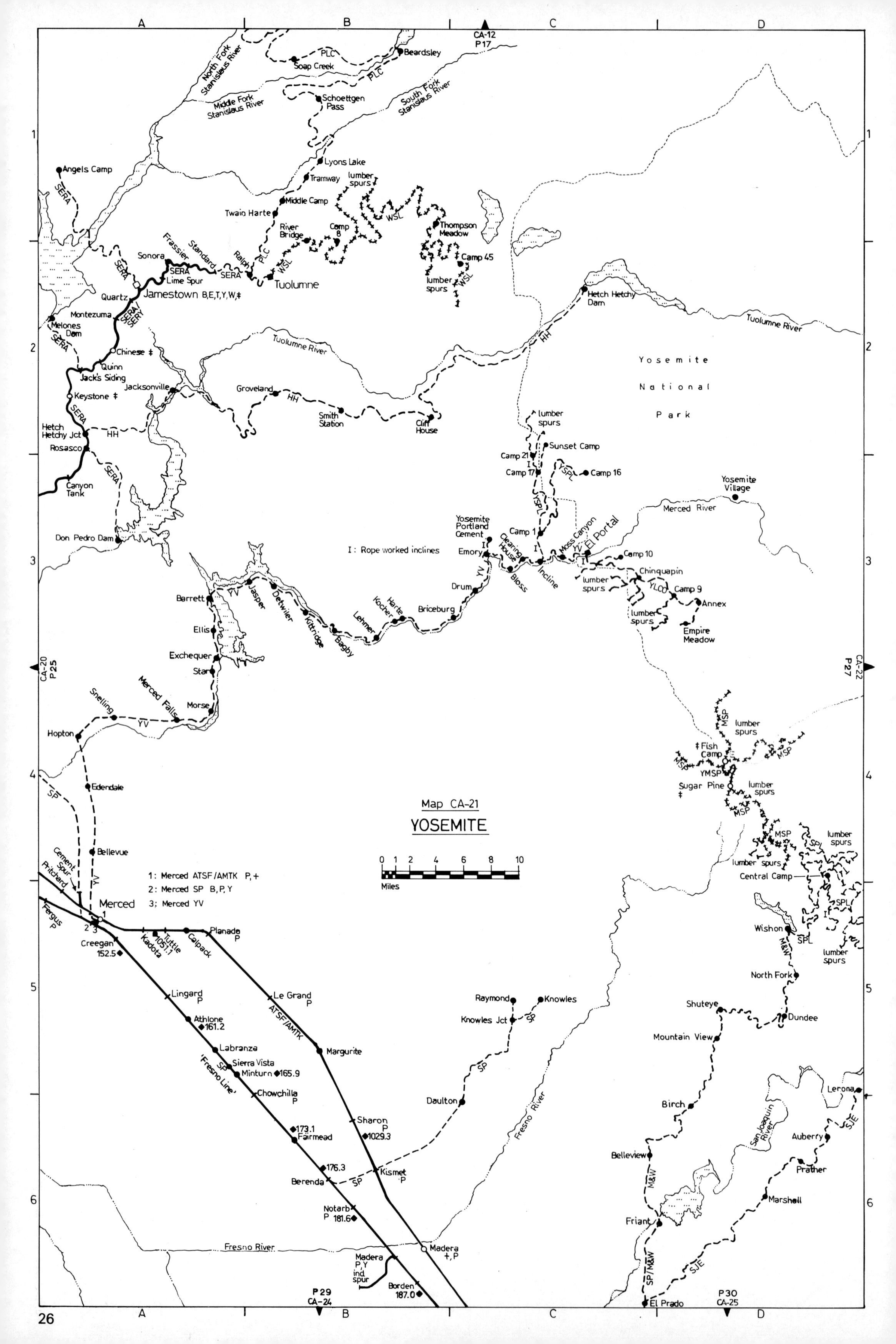

Map CA-21
YOSEMITE
Yosemite National Park
I : Rope worked inclines
1: Merced ATSF/AMTK P, +
2: Merced SP B, P, Y
3; Merced YV
Miles
0 1 2 4 6 8 10
CA-12 P17
CA-20 P25
CA-22 P27
P29 CA-24
P30 CA-25
Angels Camp
Beardsley
Soap Creek
Schoettgen Pass
Lyons Lake
Tramway
Middle Camp
Twain Harte
River Bridge
Camp 8
Thompson Meadow
Camp 45
lumber spurs
Sonora
Lime Spur
Jamestown B,E,T,Y,W,‡
Tuolumne
Quartz
Montezuma
Melones Dam
Chinese ‡
Quinn
Jack's Siding
Keystone ‡
Jacksonville
Groveland
Smith Station
Cliff House
Hetch Hetchy Jct
Rosasco
Canyon Tank
Don Pedro Dam
Hetch Hetchy Dam
Tuolumne River
North Fork Stanislaus River
Middle Fork Stanislaus River
South Fork Stanislaus River
Merced River
Fresno River
San Joaquin River
Sunset Camp
Camp 21
Camp 17
Camp 16
Camp 1
Yosemite Portland Cement
Emory
Clearing House
Bloss
Incline
Moss Canyon
El Portal
Yosemite Village
Camp 10
Chinquapin
Camp 9
Annex
Empire Meadow
Barrett
Jasper
Detwiler
Kittridge
Bagby
Lehmer
Kocher
Harte
Briceburg
Drum
Ellis
Exchequer
Star
Morse
Merced Falls
Snelling
Hopton
Edendale
Bellevue
Cement Spur
Pritchard
Merced
Fergus P
Creegan 152.5
Kadota
Tuttle 1051.1
Calpack
Planada P
Lingard P
Athlone 161.2
Le Grand P
Labranza
Sierra Vista
Minturn 165.9
'Fresno Line'
Chowchilla P
Margurite
173.1
Fairmead
Sharon P
1029.3
176.3
Berenda
Kismet P
Notarb P 181.6
Madera +, P
Madera P, Y ind spur
Borden 187.0
Raymond
Knowles
Knowles Jct
Daulton
Fish Camp ‡
YMSP
Sugar Pine ‡
Central Camp
Wishon
North Fork
Shuteye
Dundee
Mountain View
Birch
Belleview
Friant
El Prado
Lerona
Auberry
Prather
Marshall
SERA
PLC
WSL
HH
YV
YSPL
YLCO
MSP
SPL
SP
M&W
SP/M&W
SJE
ATSF/AMTK
Frassier
Standard
Ralph

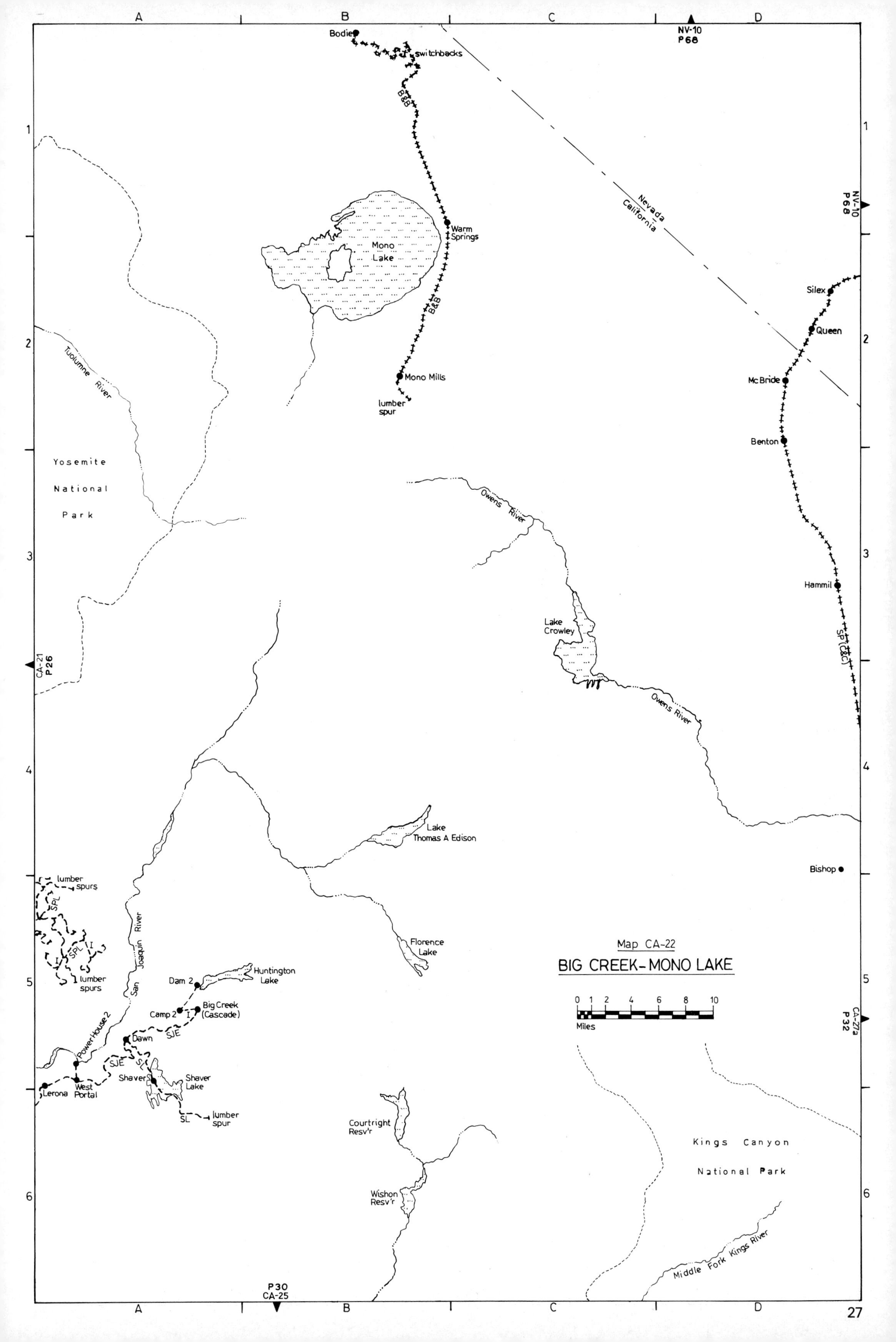
Map CA-22
BIG CREEK-MONO LAKE
0 1 2 4 6 8 10
Miles
NV-10
P68
CA-21
P26
CA-27a
P32
P30
CA-25
Bodie
switchbacks
B&B
Warm Springs
Mono Lake
Mono Mills
lumber spur
Nevada
California
Silex
Queen
McBride
Benton
Hammil
SP (C&C)
Tuolumne River
Yosemite National Park
Owens River
Lake Crowley
Lake Thomas A Edison
Bishop
Florence Lake
San Joaquin River
lumber spurs
SPL
I
Huntington Lake
Dam 2
Camp 2
Big Creek (Cascade)
SJE
Dawn
Power House 2
SL
Shaver
Shaver Lake
West Portal
Lerona
lumber spur
Courtright Resv'r
Wishon Resv'r
Kings Canyon National Park
Middle Fork Kings River

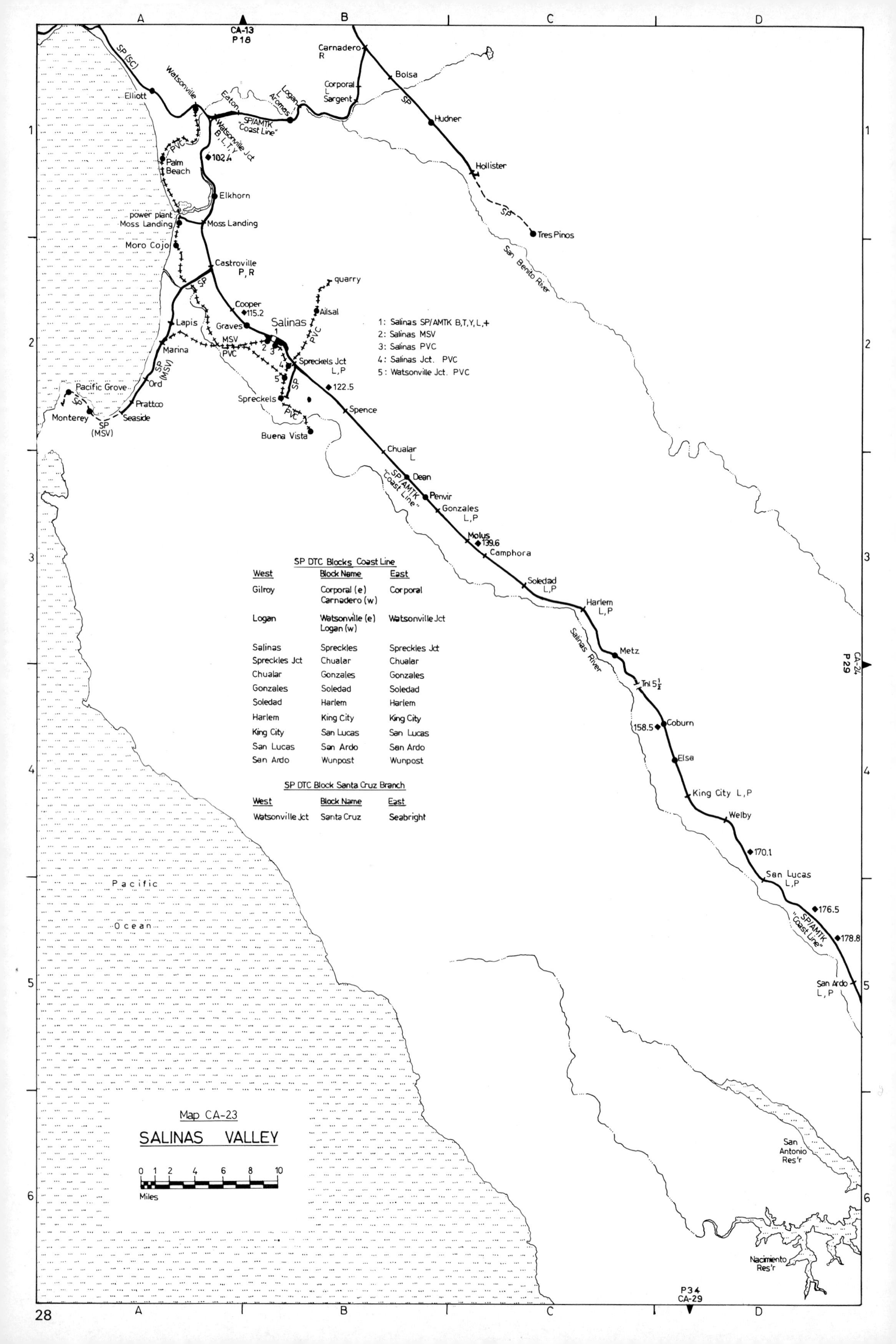

SP DTC Blocks Coast Line

West	Block Name	East
Gilroy	Corporal (e) Carnadero (w)	Corporal
Logan	Watsonville (e) Logan (w)	Watsonville Jct
Salinas	Spreckles	Spreckles Jct
Spreckles Jct	Chualar	Chualar
Chualar	Gonzales	Gonzales
Gonzales	Soledad	Soledad
Soledad	Harlem	Harlem
Harlem	King City	King City
King City	San Lucas	San Lucas
San Lucas	San Ardo	San Ardo
San Ardo	Wunpost	Wunpost

SP DTC Block Santa Cruz Branch

West	Block Name	East
Watsonville Jct	Santa Cruz	Seabright

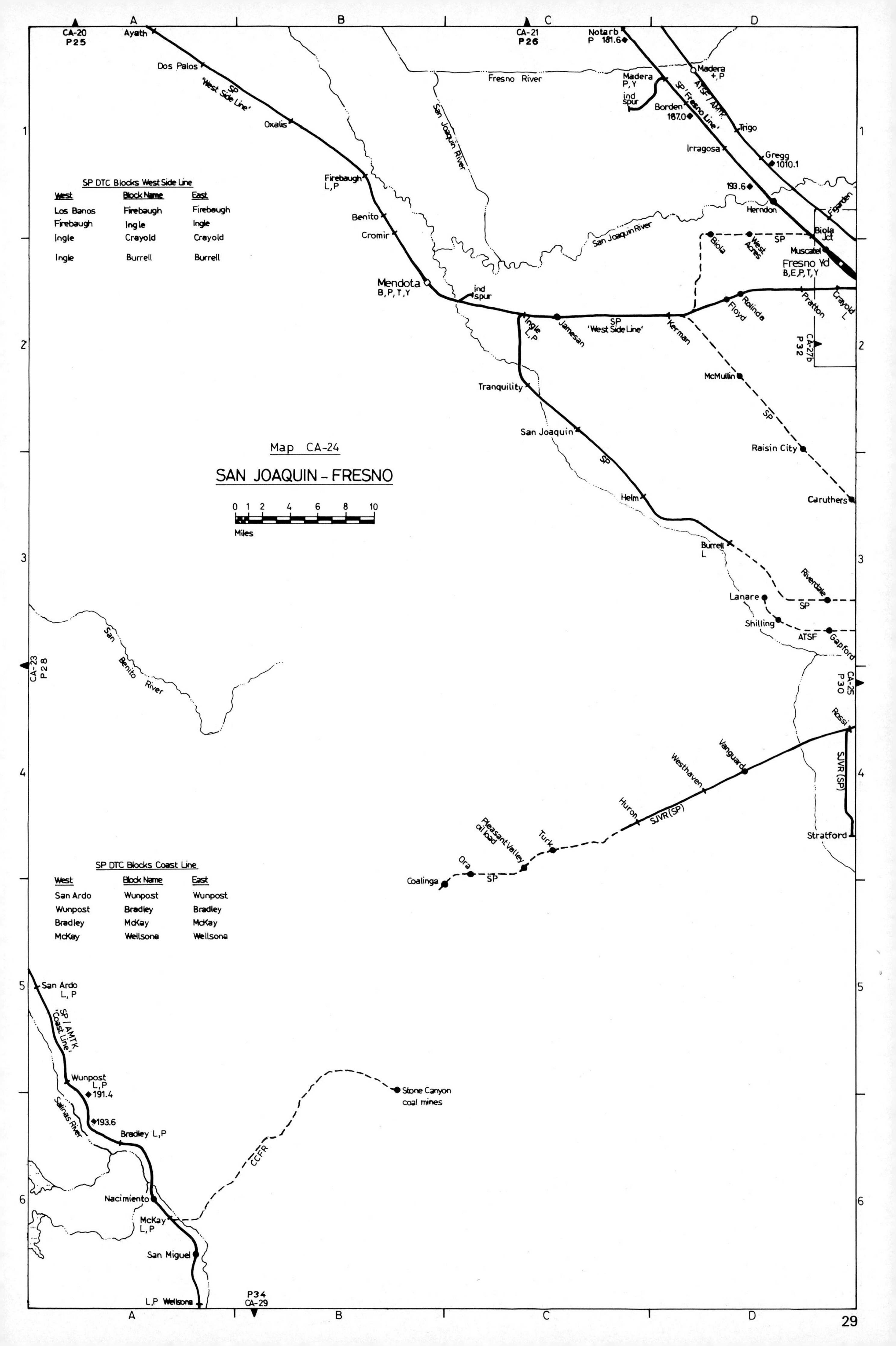

Map CA-24
SAN JOAQUIN - FRESNO
0 1 2 4 6 8 10
Miles
SP DTC Blocks West Side Line
West | Block Name | East
Los Banos | Firebaugh | Firebaugh
Firebaugh | Ingle | Ingle
Ingle | Crayold | Crayold
Ingle | Burrell | Burrell
SP DTC Blocks Coast Line
West | Block Name | East
San Ardo | Wunpost | Wunpost
Wunpost | Bradley | Bradley
Bradley | McKay | McKay
McKay | Wellsona | Wellsona
CA-20 P25
Ayath
Dos Palos
SP 'West Side Line'
Oxalis
Firebaugh L, P
Benito
Cromir
Mendota B, P, T, Y
ind spur
Ingle L, P
Jamesan
SP 'West Side Line'
Kerman
Tranquility
San Joaquin
SP
Helm
Burrell L
Riverdale
Lanare
SP
Shilling
ATSF
Gapford
CA-21 P26
Notarb P 181.6
Madera P, Y
ind spur
Madera +, P
Borden 187.0
SP 'Fresno Line'
ATSF / AMTK
Trigo
Irragosa
Gregg 1010.1
193.6
Herndon
Figarden
Biola Jct
Biola
West Acres
SP
Muscatel
Fresno Yd B, E, P, T, Y
Floyd
Rolinda
Pratton
Crayold L
CA-27b P32
McMullin
SP
Raisin City
Caruthers
Fresno River
San Joaquin River
San Joaquin River
San Benito River
CA-23 P28
CA-25 P30
Rossi
SJVR (SP)
Vanguard
Westhaven
Huron
SJVR (SP)
Turk
Pleasant Valley oil load
Ora
SP
Coalinga
Stratford
San Ardo L, P
SP / AMTK 'Coast Line'
Wunpost L, P
191.4
193.6
Salinas River
Bradley L, P
CCFR
Stone Canyon coal mines
Nacimiento
McKay L, P
San Miguel
L, P Wellsona
P34 CA-29
A
B
C
D
1
2
3
4
5
6

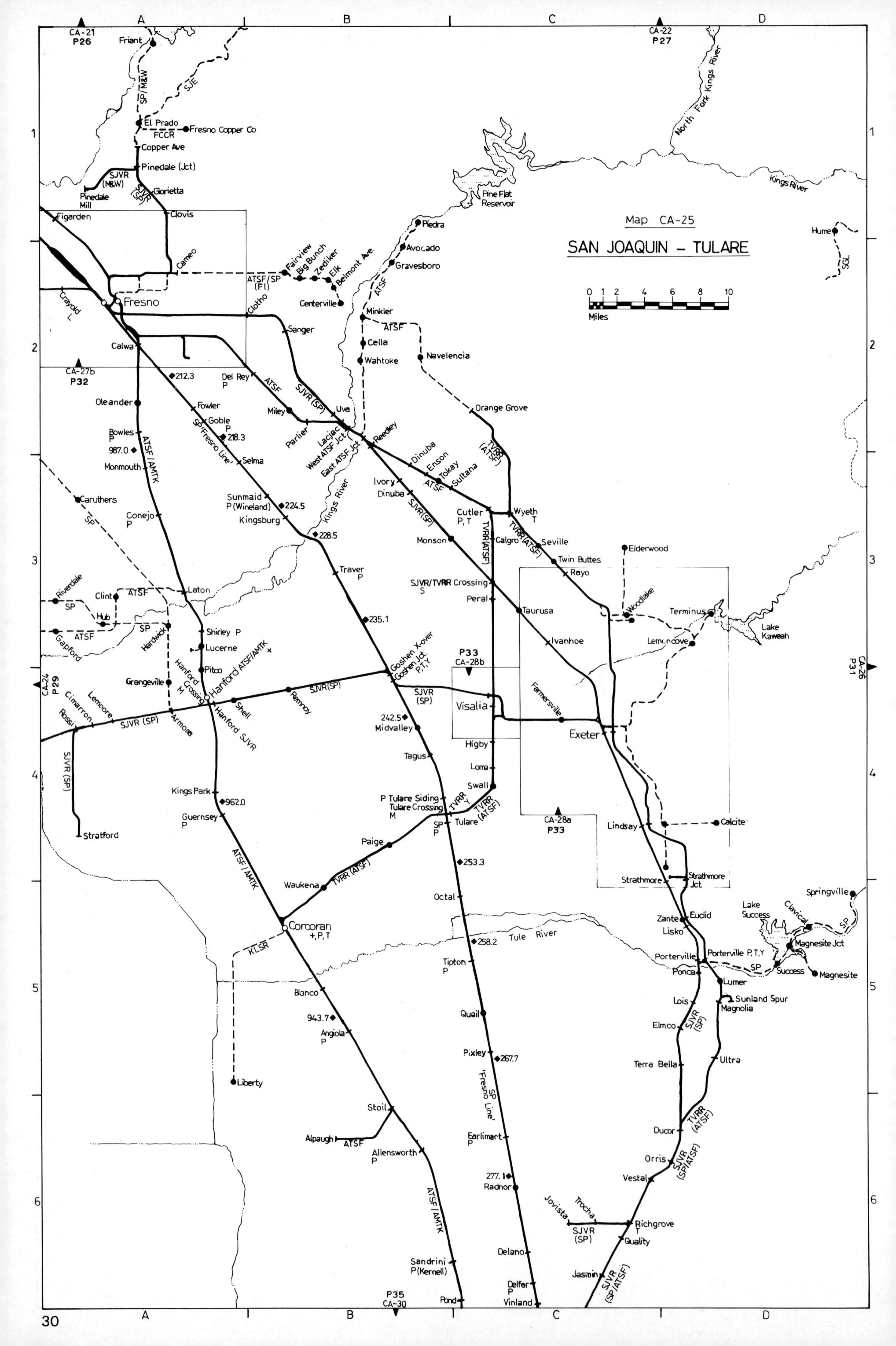

Map CA-25
SAN JOAQUIN - TULARE
Miles
Fresno
Clovis
Visalia
Exeter
Hanford
Corcoran
Tulare
Porterville
Reedley
Dinuba
Selma
Fowler
Kingsburg
Sanger
Lindsay
Delano
Kings River
Tule River
North Fork Kings River
Pine Flat Reservoir
Lake Kaweah
Lake Success

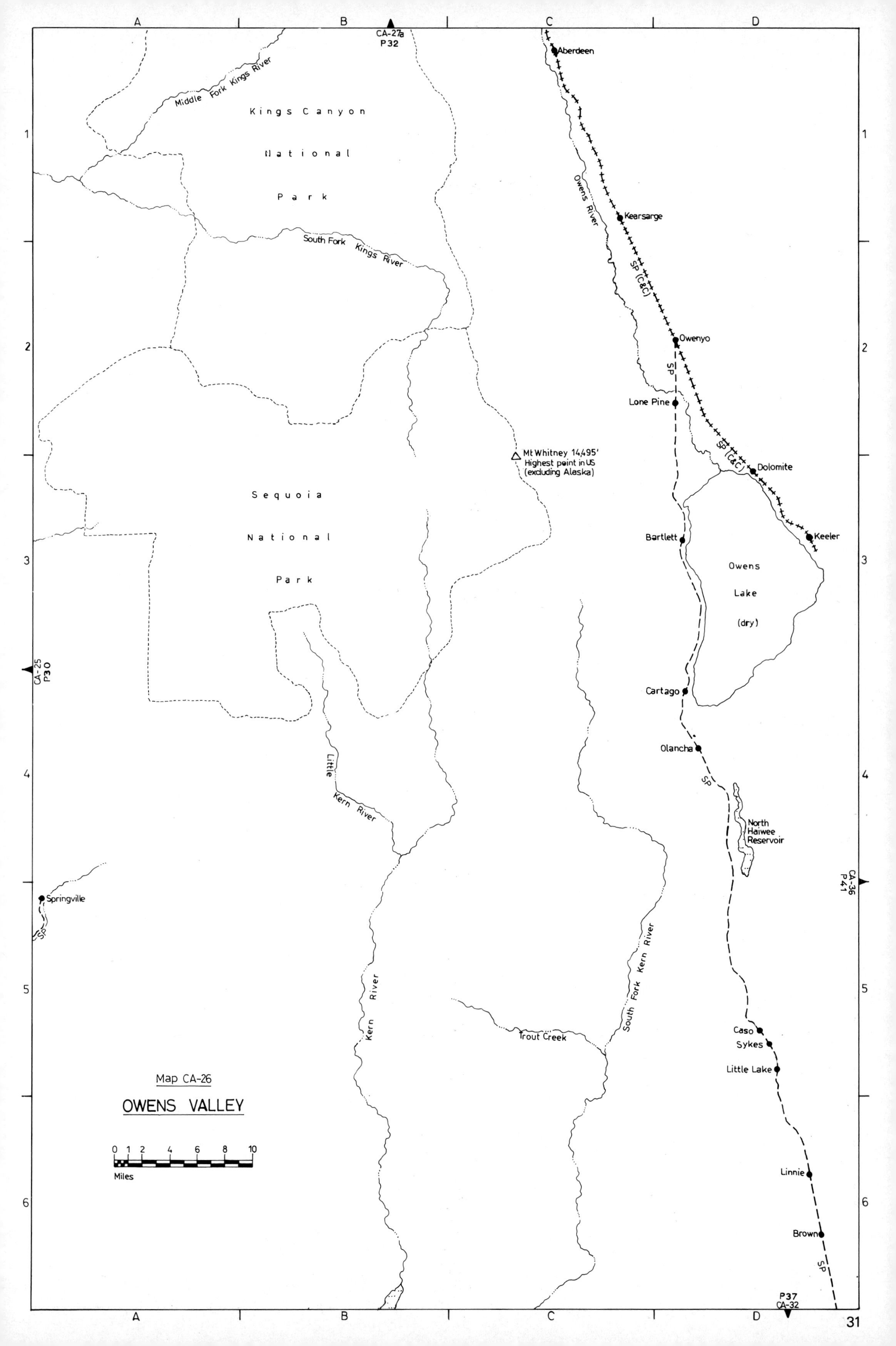
A
B
C
D
CA-27a
P32
Aberdeen
Middle Fork Kings River
Kings Canyon
National
Park
Owens River
Kearsarge
South Fork Kings River
SP (C&C)
Owenyo
SP
Lone Pine
Mt Whitney 14,495'
Highest point in US
(excluding Alaska)
Dolomite
Sequoia
National
Park
Bartlett
Keeler
Owens
Lake
(dry)
CA-25
P30
Cartago
Olancha
SP
Little
Kern River
North
Haiwee
Reservoir
CA-36
P41
Springville
SP
Kern River
South Fork Kern River
Trout Creek
Caso
Sykes
Little Lake
Map CA-26
OWENS VALLEY
0 1 2 4 6 8 10
Miles
Linnie
Brown
SP
P37
CA-32
1
2
3
4
5
6

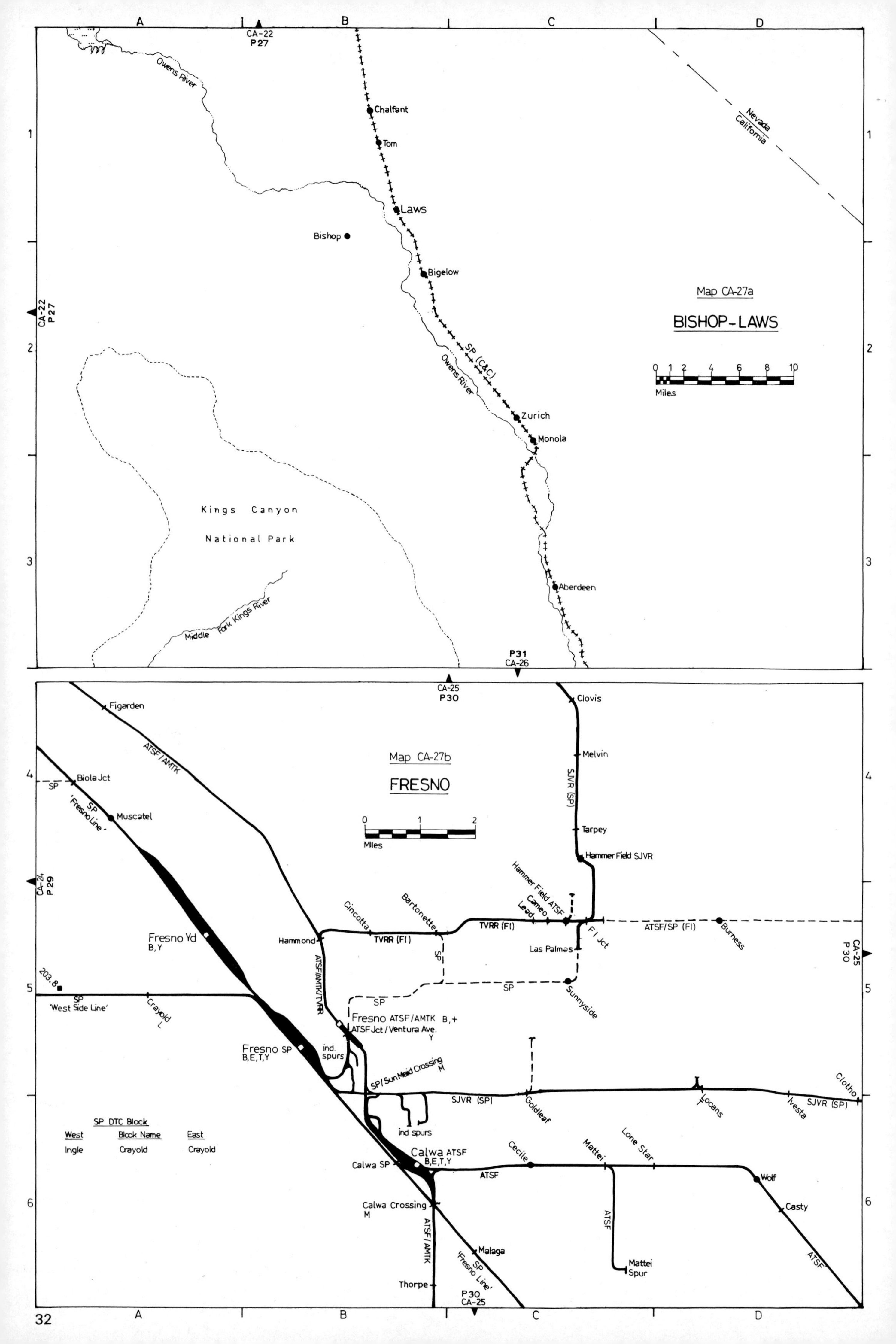
Map CA-27a
BISHOP-LAWS
0 1 2 4 6 8 10
Miles
Owens River
Chalfant
Tom
Laws
Bishop
Bigelow
SP (C&C)
Zurich
Monola
Aberdeen
Nevada
California
Kings Canyon
National Park
Middle Fork Kings River
CA-22
P27
P31
CA-26
CA-25
P30
Map CA-27b
FRESNO
0 1 2
Miles
Figarden
ATSF/AMTK
Biola Jct
SP
'Fresno Line'
Muscatel
Clovis
Melvin
SJVR (SP)
Tarpey
Hammer Field SJVR
Hammer Field ATSF
Cameo
Lead
TVRR (FI)
FI Jct
ATSF/SP (FI)
Burness
Las Palmas
Sunnyside
Cincotta
Bartonette
Hammond
ATSF/AMTK/TVRR
Fresno Yd
B, Y
203.8
'West Side Line'
Crayold
L
Fresno ATSF/AMTK B,+
ATSF Jct/Ventura Ave.
Y
Fresno SP
B,E,T,Y
ind. spurs
SP/Sun Maid Crossing
M
SJVR (SP)
Goldleaf
Locans
T
Ivesta
Clotho
ind spurs
SP DTC Block
West Block Name East
Ingle Crayold Crayold
Calwa ATSF
B,E,T,Y
Calwa SP
ATSF
Cecile
Mattei
Lone Star
Wolf
Casty
Calwa Crossing
M
ATSF/AMTK
Malaga
Mattei Spur
Thorpe
CA-24
P29

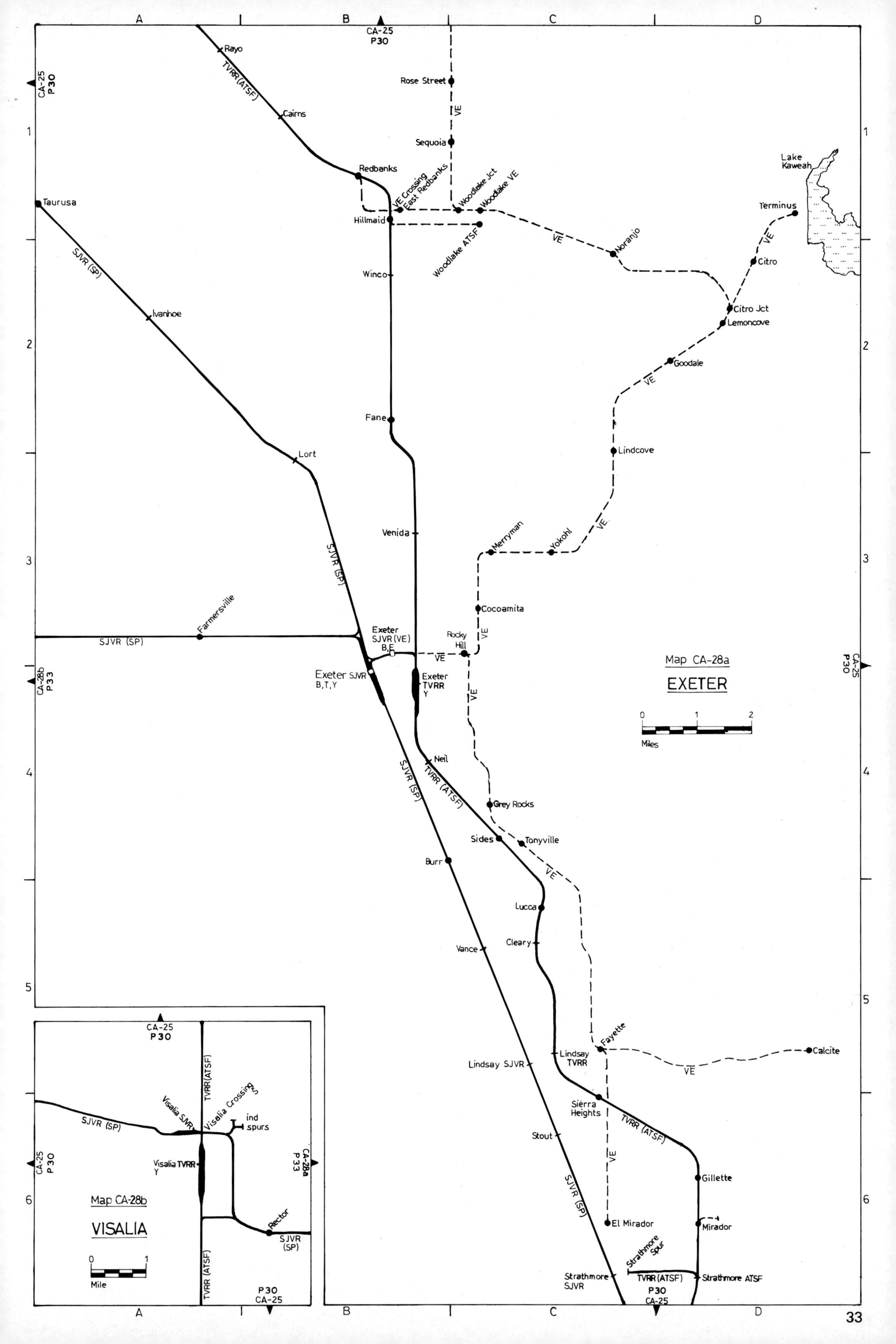
Map CA-28a
EXETER
0 1 2
Miles
Rayo
TVRR (ATSF)
Cairns
Redbanks
VE Crossing
East Redbanks
Rose Street
Sequoia
VE
Woodlake Jct
Woodlake VE
Woodlake ATSF
Hillmaid
Taurusa
Winco
Noranjo
Lake Kaweah
Terminus
Citro
Citro Jct
Lemoncove
Goodale
SJVR (SP)
Ivanhoe
Fane
Lindcove
Lort
Venida
Merryman
Yokohl
Cocoamita
Farmersville
Exeter SJVR (VE) B,F
Rocky Hill
Exeter SJVR B,T,Y
Exeter TVRR Y
Neil
Grey Rocks
Sides
Tonyville
Burr
Lucca
Cleary
Vance
Lindsay TVRR
Fayette
Calcite
Lindsay SJVR
Sierra Heights
Stout
Gillette
El Mirador
Mirador
Strathmore Spur
Strathmore SJVR
TVRR (ATSF)
Strathmore ATSF
CA-25 P30
CA-28b P33
Map CA-28b
VISALIA
0 1
Mile
Visalia SJVR
Visalia Crossing
ind spurs
Visalia TVRR Y
Rector
CA-28a P33
A B C D
1 2 3 4 5 6

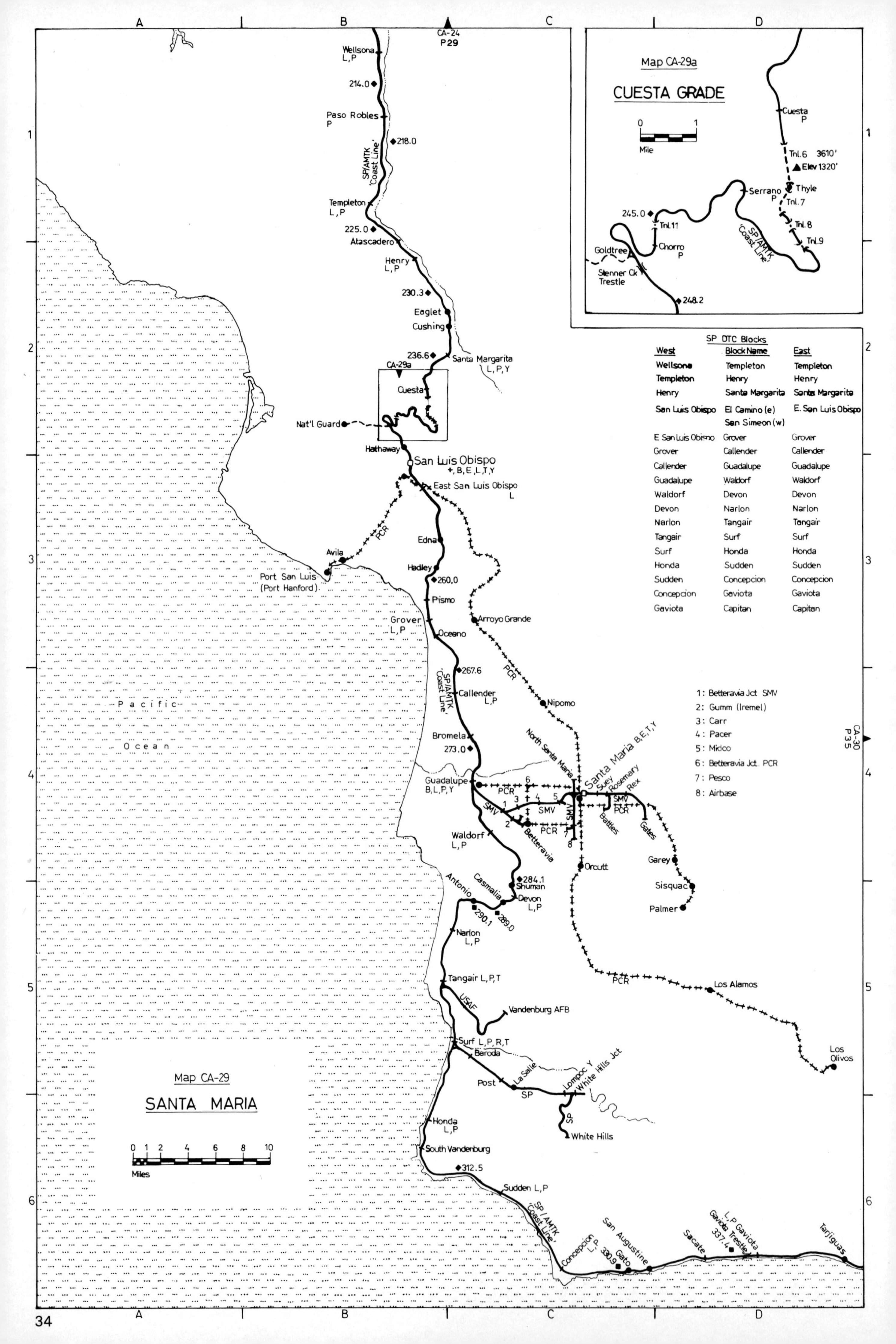

SP DTC Blocks

West	Block Name	East
Wellsona	Templeton	Templeton
Templeton	Henry	Henry
Henry	Santa Margarita	Santa Margarita
San Luis Obispo	El Camino (e) San Simeon (w)	E. San Luis Obispo
E San Luis Obispo	Grover	Grover
Grover	Callender	Callender
Callender	Guadalupe	Guadalupe
Guadalupe	Waldorf	Waldorf
Waldorf	Devon	Devon
Devon	Narlon	Narlon
Narlon	Tangair	Tangair
Tangair	Surf	Surf
Surf	Honda	Honda
Honda	Sudden	Sudden
Sudden	Concepcion	Concepcion
Concepcion	Gaviota	Gaviota
Gaviota	Capitan	Capitan

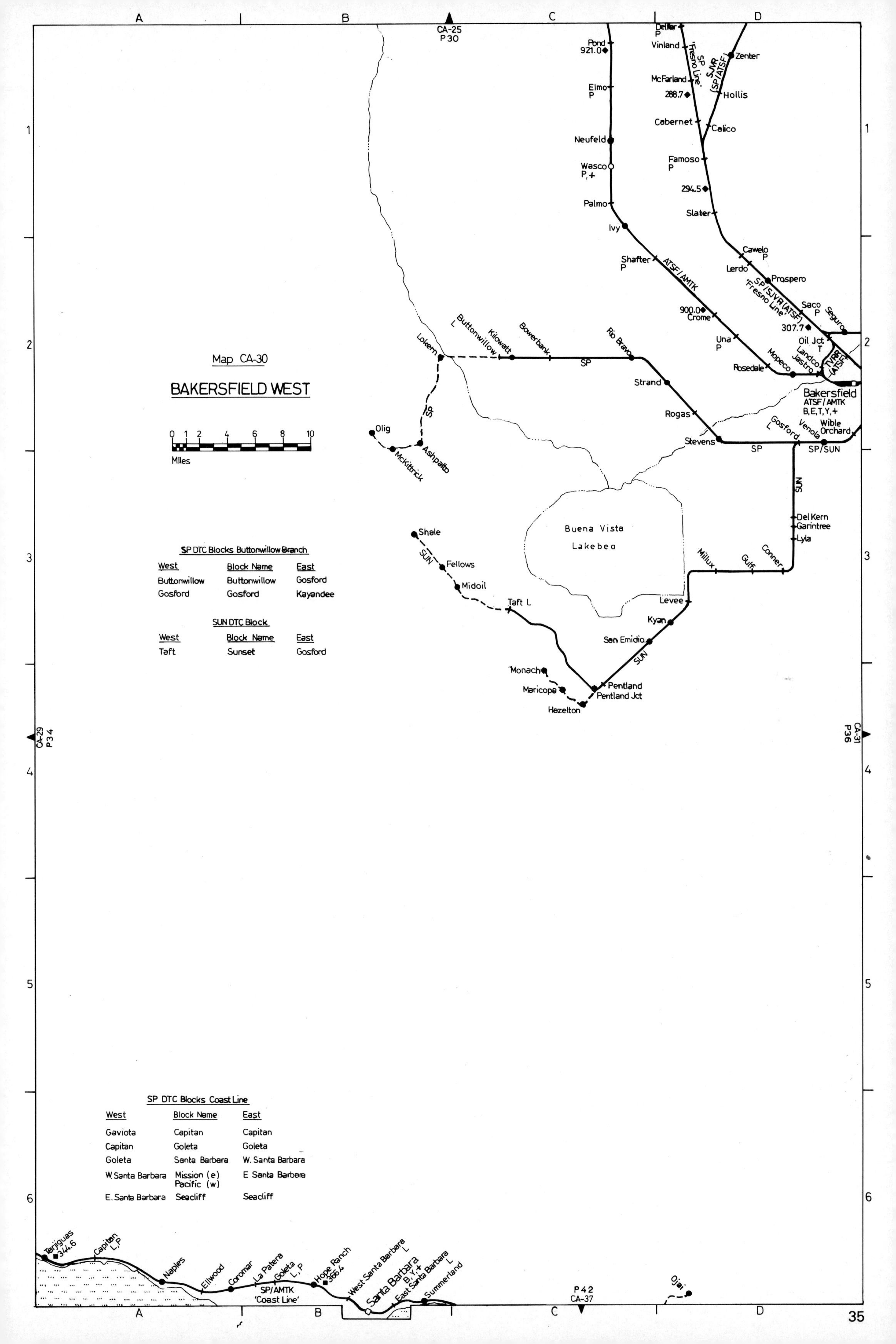

SP DTC Blocks Buttonwillow Branch

West	Block Name	East
Buttonwillow	Buttonwillow	Gosford
Gosford	Gosford	Kayandee

SUN DTC Block

West	Block Name	East
Taft	Sunset	Gosford

SP DTC Blocks Coast Line

West	Block Name	East
Gaviota	Capitan	Capitan
Capitan	Goleta	Goleta
Goleta	Santa Barbara	W. Santa Barbara
W. Santa Barbara	Mission (e) Pacific (w)	E. Santa Barbara
E. Santa Barbara	Seacliff	Seacliff

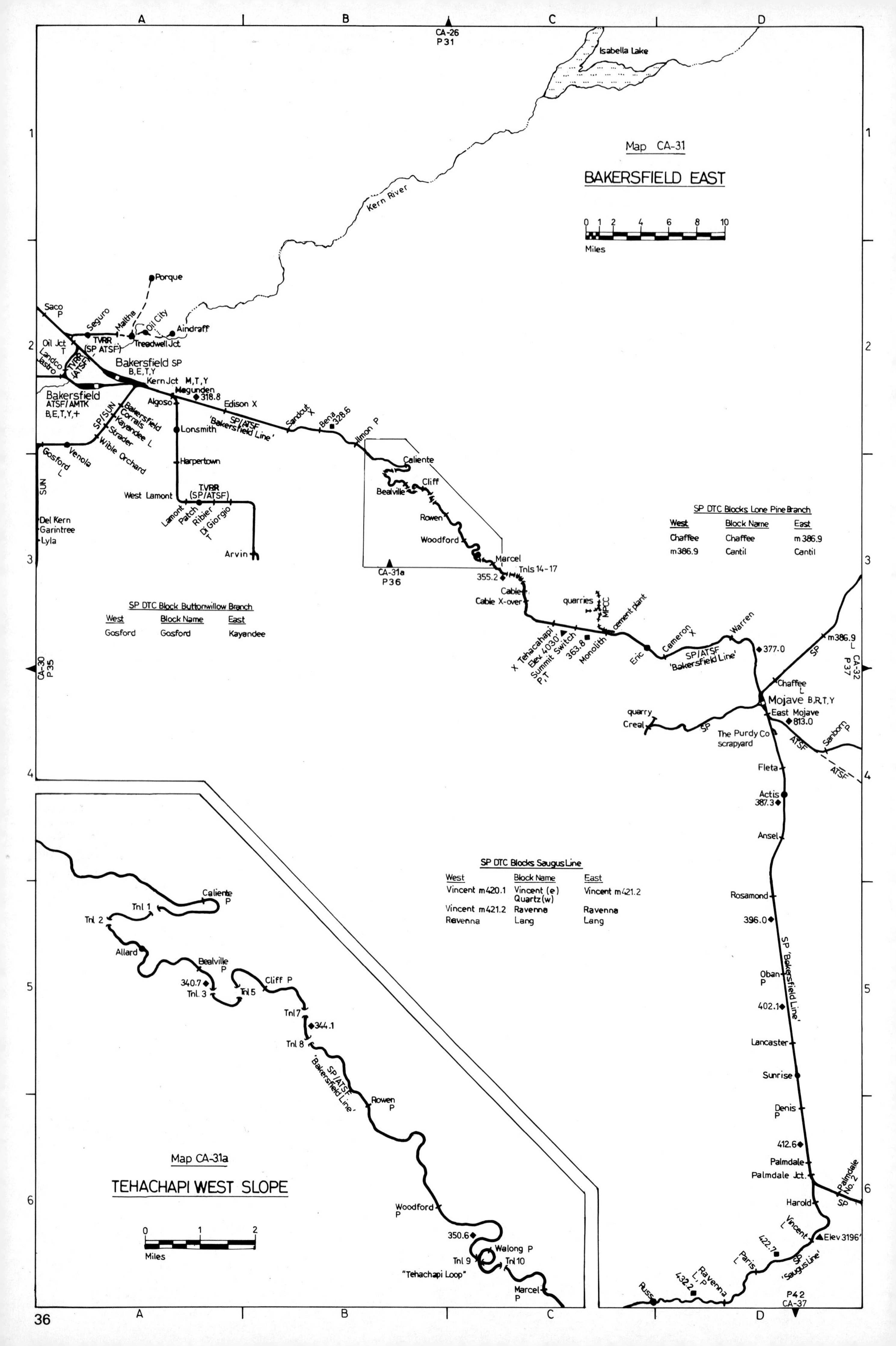

Map CA-31
BAKERSFIELD EAST
0 1 2 4 6 8 10
Miles
CA-26
P31
Isabella Lake
Kern River
Porque
Saco P
Seguro
Maltha
Oil City
Aindraff
Treadwell Jct
Oil Jct T
TVRR (SP ATSF)
Landco
Lastro
TVRR (ATSF)
Bakersfield SP
B,E,T,Y
Kern Jct M,T,Y
Magunden
318.8
Bakersfield
ATSF/AMTK
B,E,T,Y,+
Algoso
Edison X
SP/ATSF
'Bakersfield Line'
Sandcut X
Bena
328.6
Ilmon P
Lonsmith
SP/SUN
Bakersfield Corrals
Kayandee L
Strader
Wible Orchard
Venola
Gosford L
SUN
Harpertown
West Lamont
TVRR (SP/ATSF)
Lamont
Patch
Ribier
Di Giorgio T
Arvin
Del Kern
Garintree
Lyla
Caliente
Cliff
Bealville
Rowen
Woodford
Marcel
355.2
Tnls 14-17
CA-31a
P36
Cable
Cable X-over
quarries
MPCC
cement plant
X Tehacahapi
Elev. 4030'
Summit Switch
P,T
363.8
Monolith
Eric
Cameron X
SP/ATSF
'Bakersfield Line'
Warren
377.0
m386.9 L
SP
CA-32
P37
Chaffee L
Mojave B,R,T,Y
East Mojave
813.0
Sanborn P
ATSF
quarry
Creal
SP
The Purdy Co
scrapyard
Fleta
Actis
387.3
Ansel
CA-30
P35
SP DTC Blocks Lone Pine Branch
West | Block Name | East
Chaffee | Chaffee | m386.9
m386.9 | Cantil | Cantil
SP DTC Block Buttonwillow Branch
West | Block Name | East
Gosford | Gosford | Kayandee
SP DTC Blocks Saugus Line
West | Block Name | East
Vincent m420.1 | Vincent (e) Quartz (w) | Vincent m421.2
Vincent m421.2 | Ravenna | Ravenna
Ravenna | Lang | Lang
Rosamond
396.0
SP 'Bakersfield Line'
Oban P
402.1
Lancaster
Sunrise
Denis P
412.6
Palmdale
Palmdale Jct.
Palmdale No. 2
SP
Harold
Vincent L
Elev 3196'
422.7
SP 'Saugus Line'
Paris L
Ravenna L P
432.2
Russ
P42
CA-37
Map CA-31a
TEHACHAPI WEST SLOPE
0 1 2
Miles
Caliente P
Tnl 1
Tnl 2
Allard
Bealville P
340.7
Tnl. 3
Tnl 5
Cliff P
Tnl 7
344.1
Tnl 8
SP/ATSF
'Bakersfield Line'
Rowen P
Woodford P
350.6
Walong P
Tnl 9
Tnl 10
"Tehachapi Loop"
Marcel P
A B C D
1 2 3 4 5 6

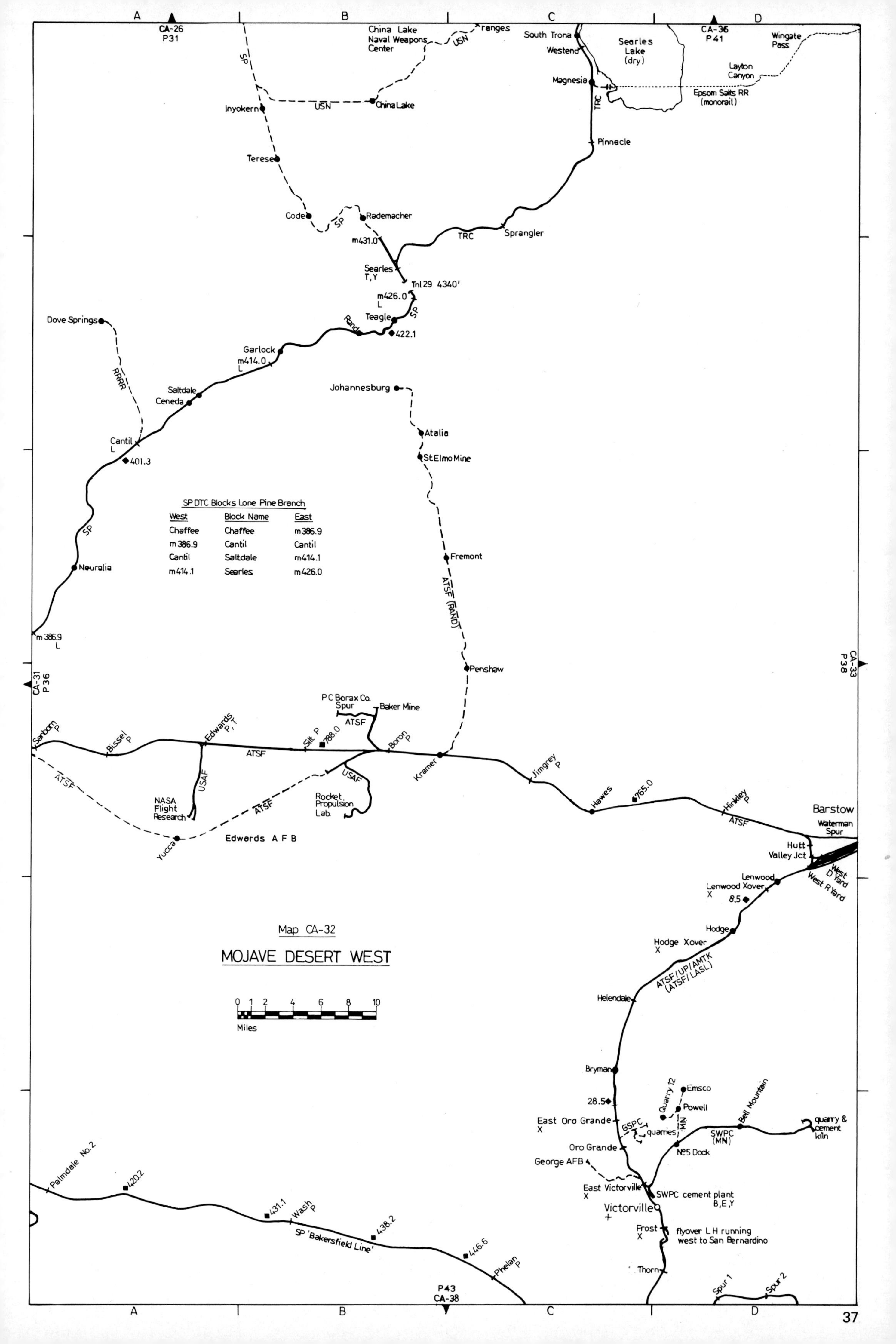
Map CA-32
MOJAVE DESERT WEST
0 1 2 4 6 8 10
Miles
SP DTC Blocks Lone Pine Branch
West Block Name East
Chaffee Chaffee m386.9
m 386.9 Cantil Cantil
Cantil Saltdale m414.1
m414.1 Searles m426.0
A
B
C
D
CA-26
P31
CA-36
P41
CA-31
P 36
CA-33
P38
P43
CA-38
China Lake
Naval Weapons
Center
ranges
USN
South Trona
Westend
Searles
Lake
(dry)
Wingate
Pass
Layton
Canyon
Magnesia
Epsom Salts RR
(monorail)
TRC
Pinnacle
SP
Inyokern
USN
China Lake
Terese
Code
SP
Rademacher
m431.0
TRC
Sprangler
Searles
T, Y
Tnl 29 4340'
m426.0
L
SP
Teagle
Rand
422.1
Dove Springs
Garlock
m414.0
L
RRRR
Saltdale
Ceneda
Johannesburg
Atalia
St Elmo Mine
Cantil
L
401.3
SP
Neuralia
Fremont
ATSF (RAND)
m 386.9
L
Penshaw
P C Borax Co.
Spur
Baker Mine
ATSF
Sanborn P
Bissel P
Edwards P, T
Silt P
788.0
Boron P
Kramer
Jimgrey P
Hawes
765.0
Hinkley P
Barstow
ATSF
ATSF
USAF
USAF
ATSF
NASA
Flight
Research
Rocket
Propulsion
Lab.
Yucca
Edwards A F B
Waterman
Spur
Hutt
Valley Jct
West
D Yard
West R Yard
Lenwood
Lenwood Xover
X
8.5
Hodge
Hodge Xover
X
ATSF/UP/AMTK
(ATSF/LASL)
Helendale
Bryman
28.5
Emsco
Quarry 12
Powell
MN
Bell Mountain
East Oro Grande
X
GSPC
quarries
SWPC
(MN)
quarry &
cement
kiln
Oro Grande
No 5 Dock
George AFB
East Victorville
X
SWPC cement plant
B, E, Y
Victorville
Frost
X
flyover L H running
west to San Bernardino
Thorn
Spur 1
Spur 2
Palmdale No. 2
420.2
431.1
Wash P
438.2
SP 'Bakersfield Line'
446.6
Phelan P

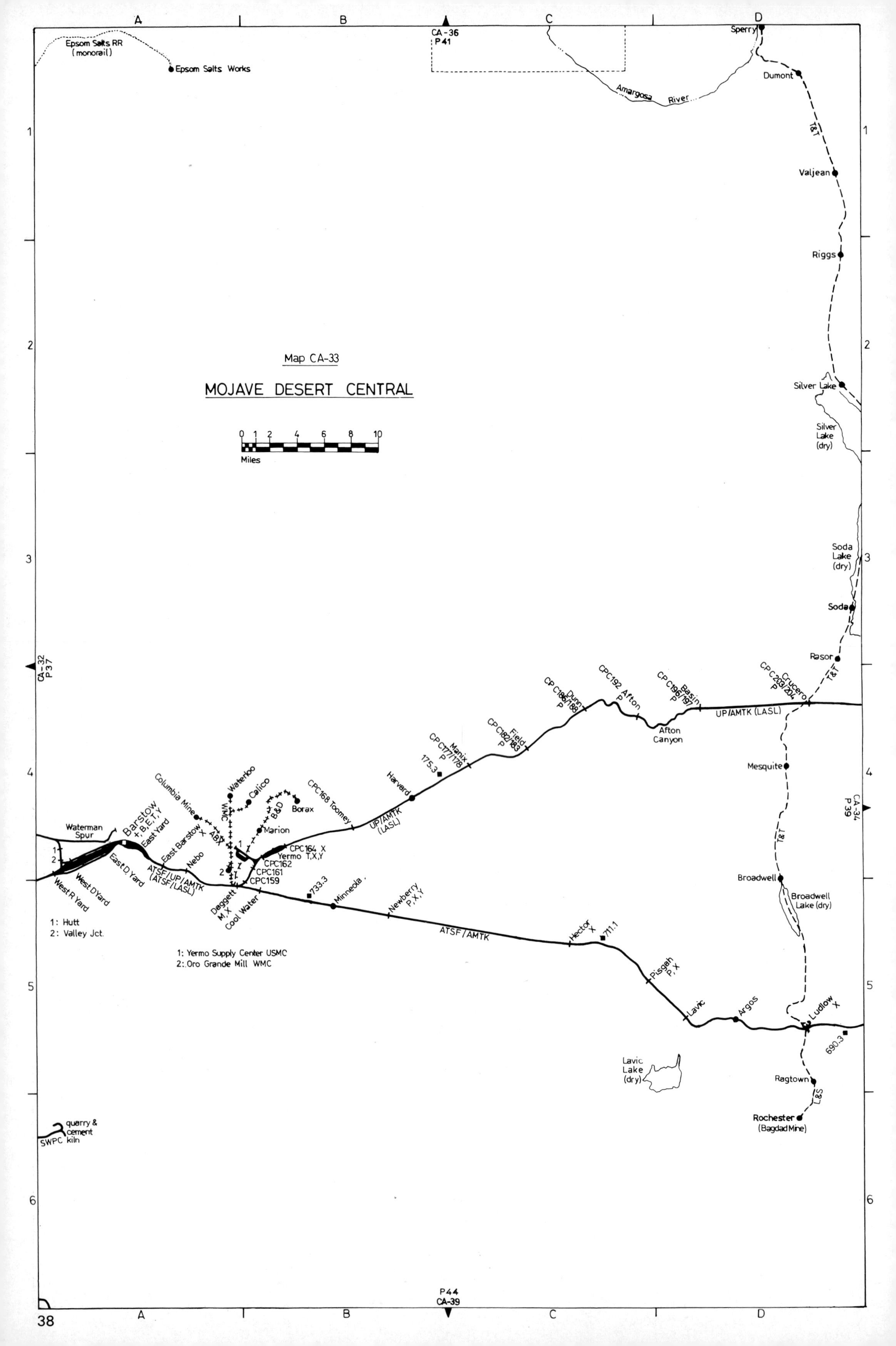

Map CA-33
MOJAVE DESERT CENTRAL
Miles
Epsom Salts RR (monorail)
Epsom Salts Works
CA-36 P41
Sperry
Dumont
Amargosa River
T&T
Valjean
Riggs
Silver Lake
Silver Lake (dry)
Soda Lake (dry)
Soda
Rasor
CA-32 P37
CA-34 P39
Crucero CP C203/204 P
Basin CP C196/197 P
CPC192 Afton P
Dunn CP C186/188 P
Field CP C182/183 P
Manix CP C177/178 P
UP/AMTK (LASL)
Afton Canyon
Mesquite
175.3
Harvard
CPC168 Toomey
UP/AMTK (LASL)
Columbia Mine
Waterloo
Calico
B&D
Borax
WMC
Marion
ABX
CPC164 X
Yermo T,X,Y
CPC162
CPC161
CPC159
Barstow +,B,E,T,Y
East Yard
Waterman Spur
East Barstow X
Nebo
ATSF/UP/AMTK (ATSF/LASL)
East D Yard
West D Yard
West R Yard
Daggett M,X
Cool Water
733.3
Minneola
Newberry P,X,Y
ATSF/AMTK
Hector X
711.1
Pisgah P,X
Lavic
Argos
Ludlow X
690.3
Broadwell
Broadwell Lake (dry)
Lavic Lake (dry)
Ragtown
L&S
Rochester (Bagdad Mine)
1: Hutt
2: Valley Jct.
1: Yermo Supply Center USMC
2: Oro Grande Mill WMC
quarry & cement kiln
SWPC
P44 CA-39

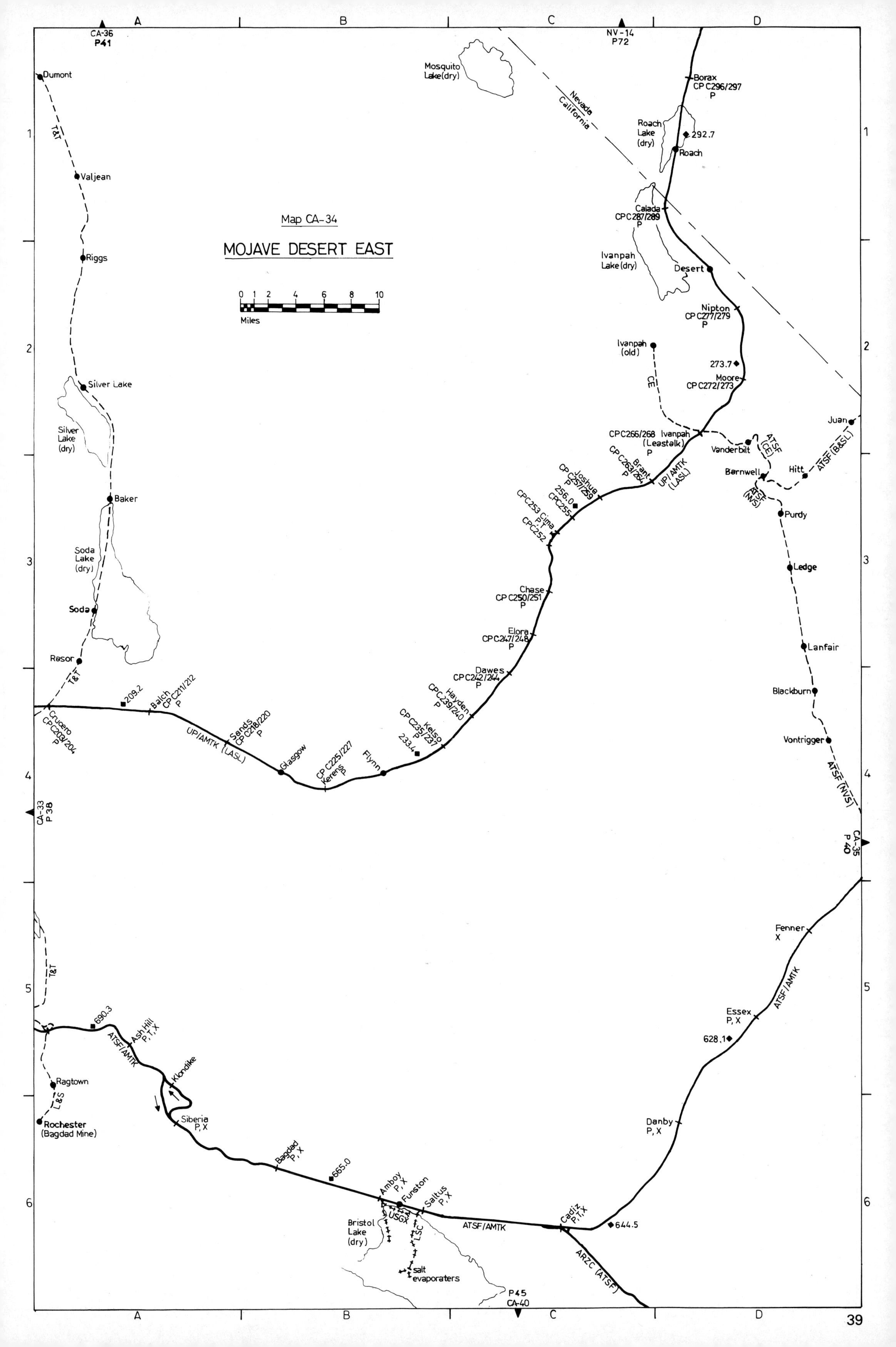

Map CA-34
MOJAVE DESERT EAST
Miles
0 1 2 4 6 8 10
CA-36 P41
NV-14 P72
CA-33 P38
CA-35 P40
P45 CA-40
Dumont
Valjean
Riggs
Silver Lake
Silver Lake (dry)
Baker
Soda Lake (dry)
Soda
Resor
T&T
Crucero CP C203/204 P
209.2
Balch CP C211/212 P
Sands CP C218/220 P
UP/AMTK (LASL)
Glasgow
CP C225/227 Kerens P
Flynn
233.4
Kelso CP C235/237 P
Hayden CP C239/240 P
Dawes CP C242/244 P
Elora CP C247/248 P
Chase CP C250/251 P
CP C252
Cima CP C253 P,T
CP C255
256.0
Joshua CP C257/259 P
Brant CP C263/264 P
CP C266/268 Ivanpah (Leastalk) P
Ivanpah (old)
CE
Moore CP C272/273
273.7
Nipton CP C277/279 P
Desert
Ivanpah Lake (dry)
Calada CP C287/289 P
Roach
292.7
Roach Lake (dry)
Borax CP C296/297 P
Mosquito Lake (dry)
Nevada
California
Vanderbilt
ATSF (CE)
Juan
ATSF (B&SL)
Hitt
Barnwell
ATSF (NVS)
Purdy
Ledge
Lanfair
Blackburn
Vontrigger
690.3
Ash Hill P,T,X
ATSF/AMTK
Klondike
Siberia P,X
Ragtown
L&S
Rochester (Bagdad Mine)
Bagdad P,X
665.0
Amboy P,X
Furston
USGX
Saltus P,X
LSC
Bristol Lake (dry)
salt evaporaters
Cadiz P,T,X
644.5
ARZC (ATSF)
Danby P,X
628.1
Essex P,X
Fenner X

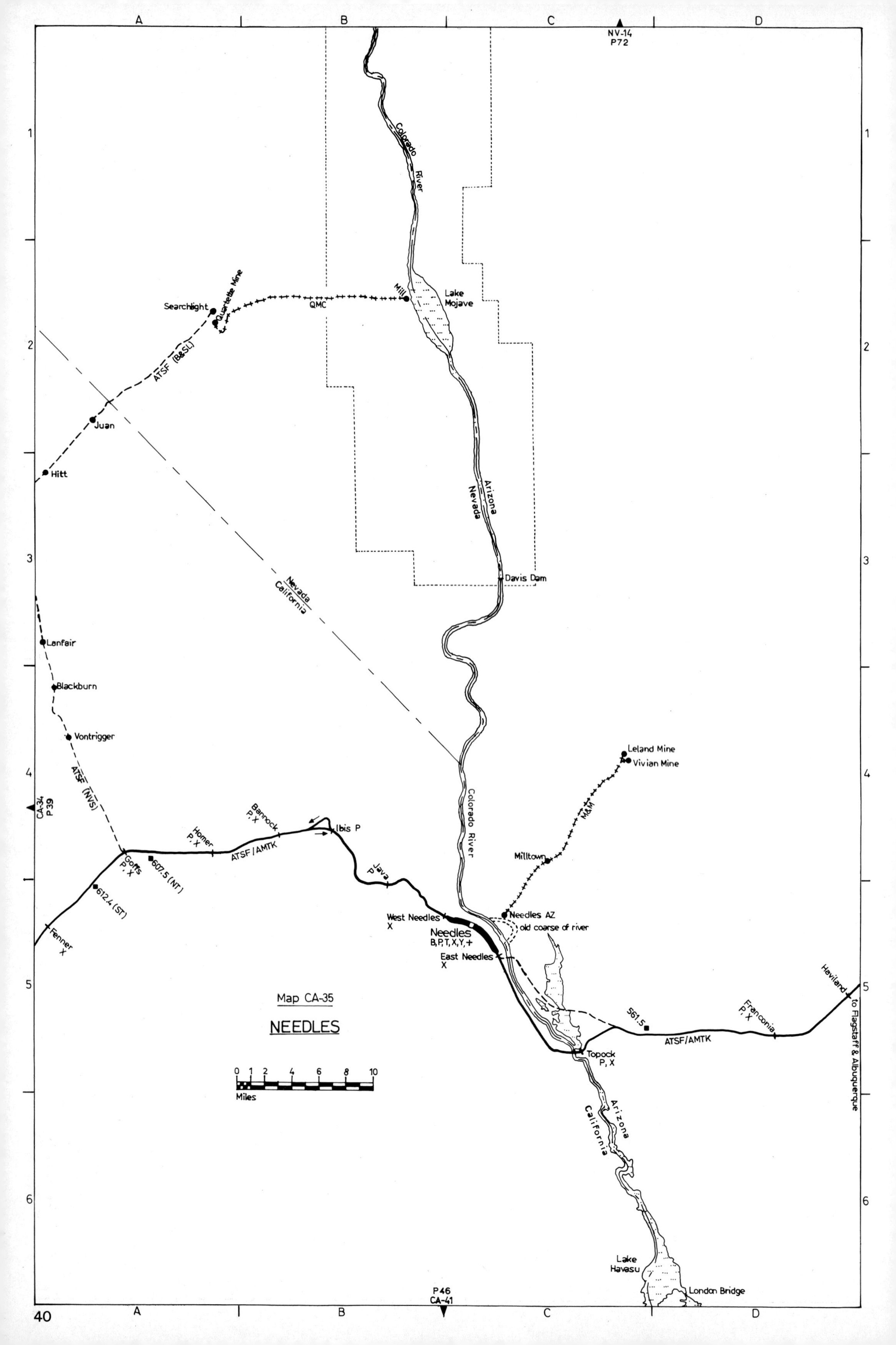

A
B
C
D
NV-14
P72
1
2
3
4
5
6
Colorado
River
Lake
Mojave
Mill
QMC
Searchlight
Quartette Mine
ATSF (B&SL)
Juan
Hitt
Arizona
Nevada
Davis Dam
Nevada
California
Lanfair
Blackburn
Vontrigger
ATSF (NVS)
CA-34
P39
Homer
P, X
Bannock
P, X
Ibis P
ATSF/AMTK
Goffs
P, X
607.5 (NT)
612.4 (ST)
Fenner
X
Java
P
Colorado River
Leland Mine
Vivian Mine
M&M
Milltown
Needles AZ
old coarse of river
West Needles
X
Needles
B,P,T,X,Y,+
East Needles
X
Map CA-35
NEEDLES
0 1 2 4 6 8 10
Miles
561.5
Franconia
P, X
Haviland
to Flagstaff & Albuquerque
ATSF/AMTK
Topock
P, X
Arizona
California
Lake
Havasu
London Bridge
P46
CA-41

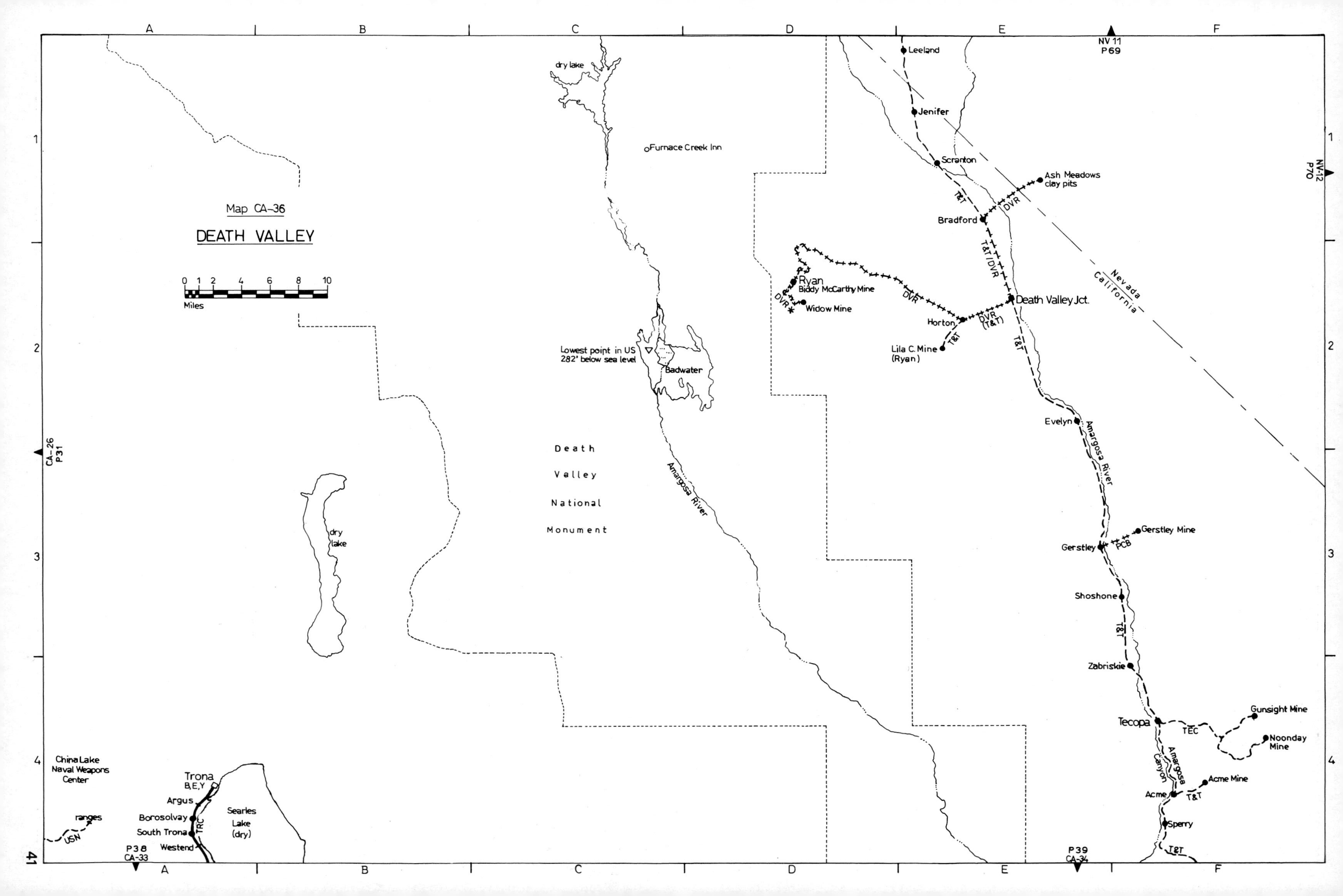
Map CA-36
DEATH VALLEY
0 1 2 4 6 8 10
Miles
dry lake
Furnace Creek Inn
Lowest point in US
282' below sea level
Badwater
Death
Valley
National
Monument
Amargosa River
dry
lake
China Lake
Naval Weapons
Center
ranges
USN
Trona
B,E,Y
Argus
Borosolvay
South Trona
Westend
TRC
Searles
Lake
(dry)
P38
CA-33
CA-26
P31
Leeland
Jenifer
Scranton
Ash Meadows
clay pits
DVR
T&T
Bradford
T&T/DVR
Nevada
California
Ryan
Biddy McCarthy Mine
Widow Mine
Horton
DVR
(T&T)
Death Valley Jct.
Lila C. Mine
(Ryan)
Evelyn
Gerstley
PCB
Gerstley Mine
Shoshone
Zabriskie
Tecopa
TEC
Gunsight Mine
Noonday
Mine
Amargosa
Canyon
Acme
Acme Mine
Sperry
NV 11
P69
NV-12
P70
P39
CA-34
A
B
C
D
E
F
1
2
3
4

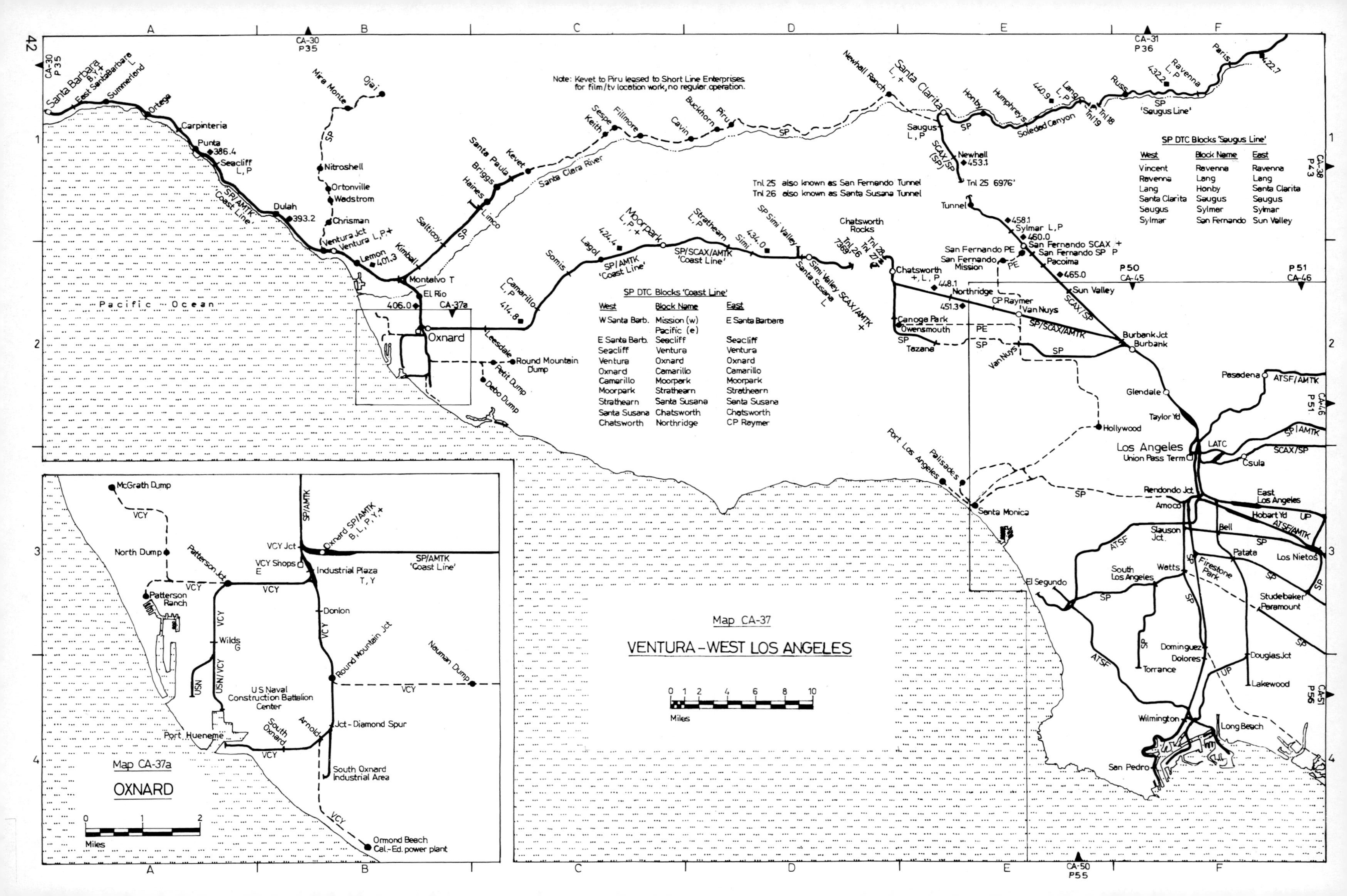

SP DTC Blocks 'Coast Line'

West	Block Name	East
W Santa Barb.	Mission (w)	E Santa Barbara
	Pacific (e)	
E Santa Barb.	Seacliff	Seacliff
Seacliff	Ventura	Ventura
Ventura	Oxnard	Oxnard
Oxnard	Camarillo	Camarillo
Camarillo	Moorpark	Moorpark
Moorpark	Strathearn	Strathearn
Strathearn	Santa Susana	Santa Susana
Santa Susana	Chatsworth	Chatsworth
Chatsworth	Northridge	CP Raymer

SP DTC Blocks 'Saugus Line'

West	Block Name	East
Vincent	Ravenna	Ravenna
Ravenna	Lang	Lang
Lang	Honby	Santa Clarita
Santa Clarita	Saugus	Saugus
Saugus	Sylmar	Sylmar
Sylmar	San Fernando	Sun Valley

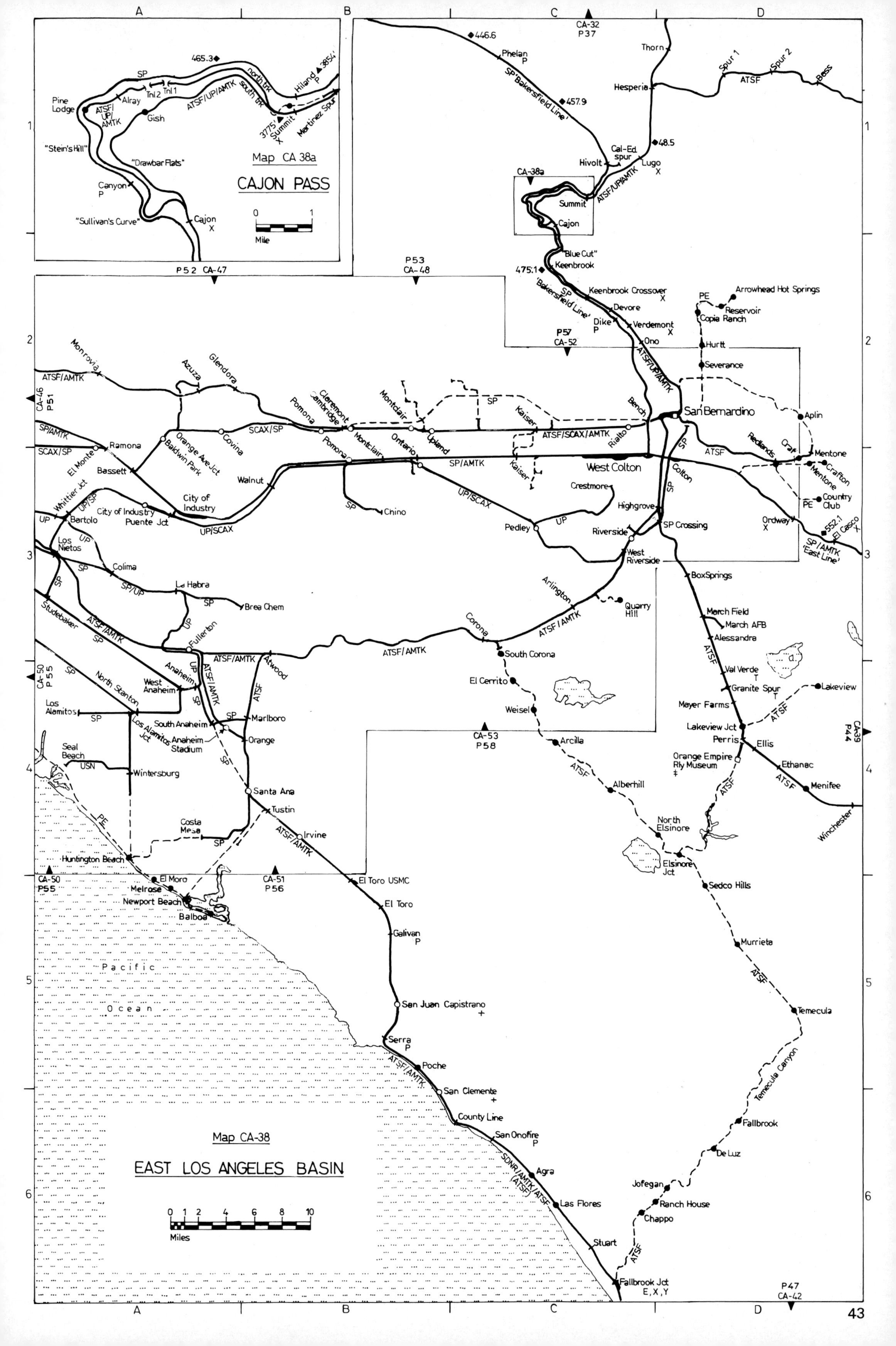
Map CA 38a
CAJON PASS
Mile
Pine Lodge
Alray
Tnl 2
Tnl 1
SP
Gish
ATSF/UP/AMTK
north trk
south trk
Hiland P
Summit
Martinez Spur
"Stein's Hill"
"Drawbar Flats"
Canyon P
"Sullivan's Curve"
Cajon X
465.3
Phelan P
SP 'Bakersfield Line'
Thorn
Hesperia
ATSF
Spur 1
Spur 2
Bess
Hivolt
Cal-Ed spur
Lugo X
Summit
Cajon
"Blue Cut"
Keenbrook
Keenbrook Crossover X
Devore
Dike P
Verdemont X
Ono
Arrowhead Hot Springs
Reservoir
Copia Ranch
Hurtt
Severance
San Bernardino
Aplin
Redlands
Craft
Mentone
Crafton
Country Club
PE
Ordway X
El Casco X
SP/AMTK 'East Line'
Monrovia
Azusa
Glendora
ATSF/AMTK
SP/AMTK
SCAX/SP
Ramona
El Monte
Bassett
Orange Ave Jct
Baldwin Park
Covina
Pomona
Claremont
Cambridge
Montclair
Upland
Ontario
Kaiser
Rialto
Bench
ATSF/SCAX/AMTK
SP/AMTK
West Colton
Colton
Crestmore
Highgrove
SP Crossing
Riverside
West Riverside
Walnut
City of Industry
City of Industry
Puente Jct
UP/SCAX
Chino
Pedley
Whittier Jct
Bartolo
Los Nietos
Colima
La Habra
Brea Chem
SP/UP
Studebaker
Fullerton
Arlington
Quarry Hill
Corona
South Corona
El Cerrito
Weisel
Arcilla
Alberhill
North Elsinore
Elsinore Jct
Box Springs
March Field
March AFB
Alessandra
Val Verde T
Granite Spur T
Mayer Farms
Lakeview
Lakeview Jct
Perris
Ellis
Ethanac
Menifee
Winchester
Orange Empire Rly Museum
Anaheim
West Anaheim
Atwood
Marlboro
Orange
South Anaheim
Anaheim Stadium
North Stanton
Los Alamitos
Los Alamitos Jct
Seal Beach
USN
Wintersburg
Santa Ana
Tustin
Irvine
Costa Mesa
Huntington Beach
El Moro
Melrose
Newport Beach
Balboa
El Toro USMC
El Toro
Galivan P
Sedco Hills
Murrieta
Temecula
Temecula Canyon
Pacific Ocean
San Juan Capistrano
Serra P
Poche
San Clemente
County Line
San Onofre P
Agra
SDNR/AMTK/ATSF (ATSF)
Las Flores
Stuart
Fallbrook
De Luz
Jofegan
Ranch House
Chappo
Fallbrook Jct E, X, Y
Map CA-38
EAST LOS ANGELES BASIN
Miles

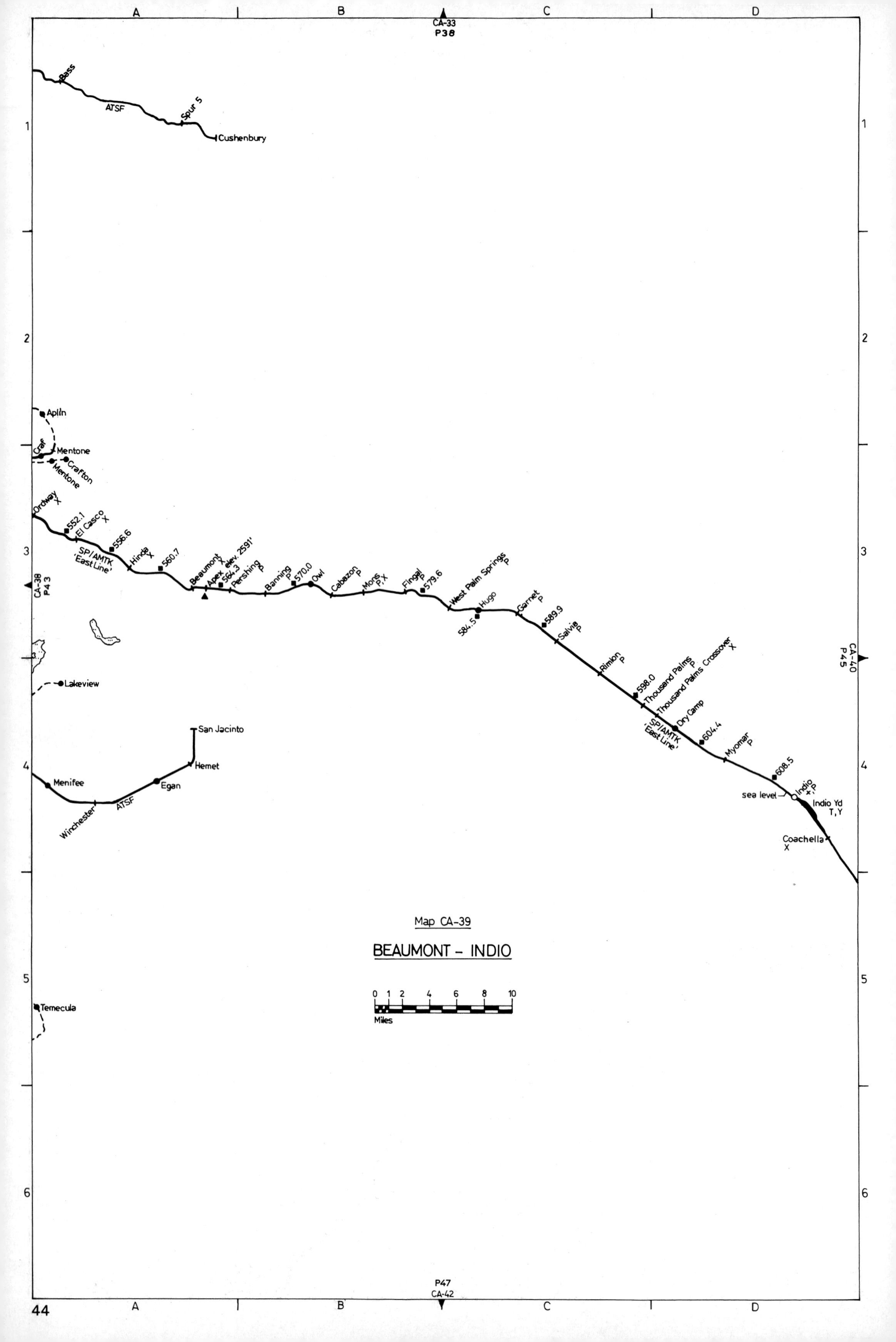

Map CA-39

BEAUMONT – INDIO

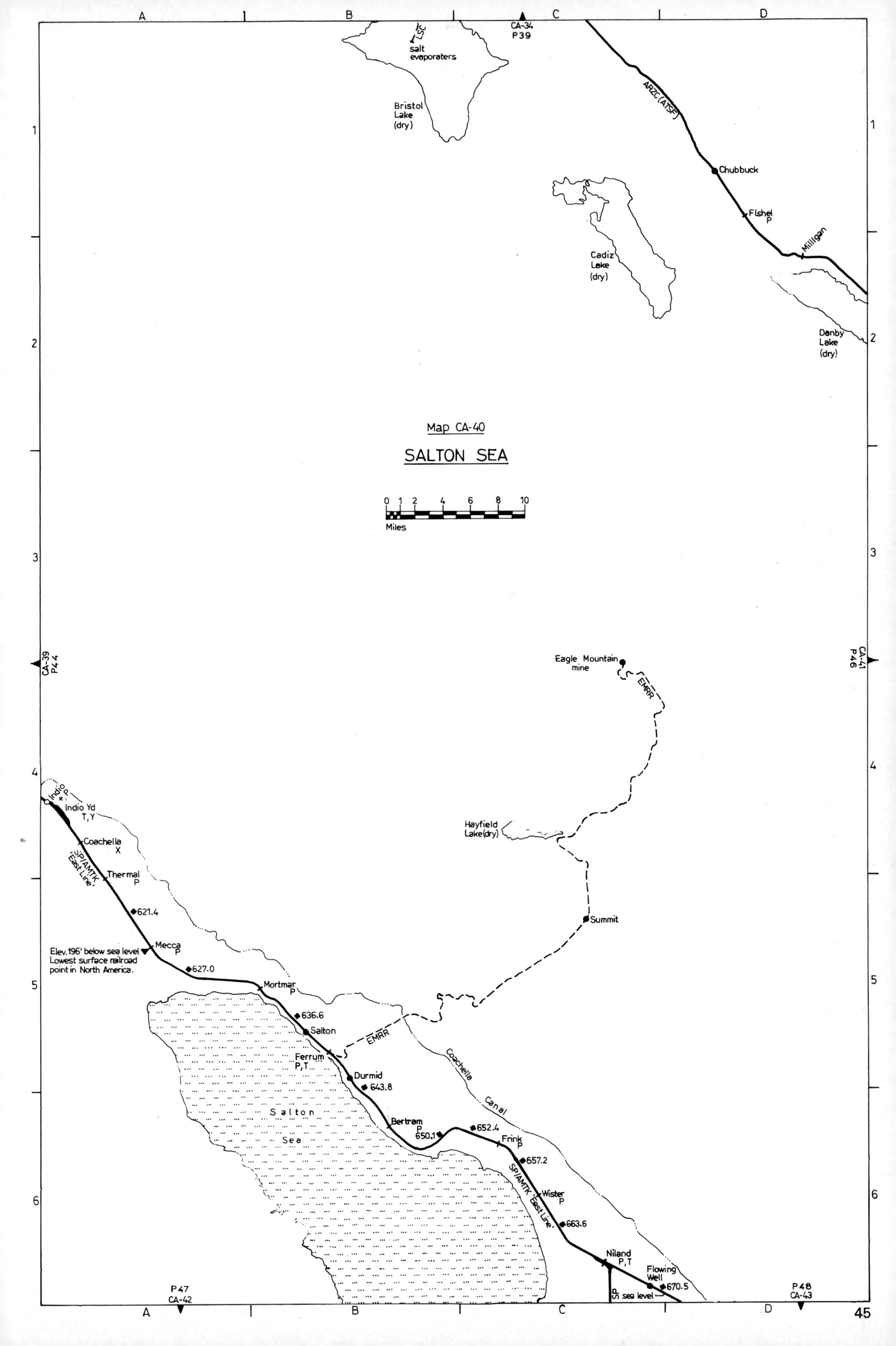

Map CA-40
SALTON SEA
0 1 2 4 6 8 10
Miles
LSC
salt evaporaters
Bristol Lake (dry)
CA-34 P39
ARZC (ATSF)
Chubbuck
Fishel P
Milligan
Cadiz Lake (dry)
Danby Lake (dry)
CA-39 P44
CA-41 P46
Eagle Mountain mine
EMRR
Hayfield Lake(dry)
Summit
Indio P
Indio Yd T, Y
Coachella X
SP/AMTK 'East Line'
Thermal P
621.4
Mecca P
Elev.196' below sea level Lowest surface railroad point in North America.
627.0
Mortmar P
636.6
Salton
Ferrum P,T
Durmid
643.8
Coachella Canal
Salton Sea
Bertram P
650.1
652.4
Frink P
657.2
Wister P
663.6
Niland P,T
Flowing Well
670.5
SP
sea level
P47 CA-42
P48 CA-43

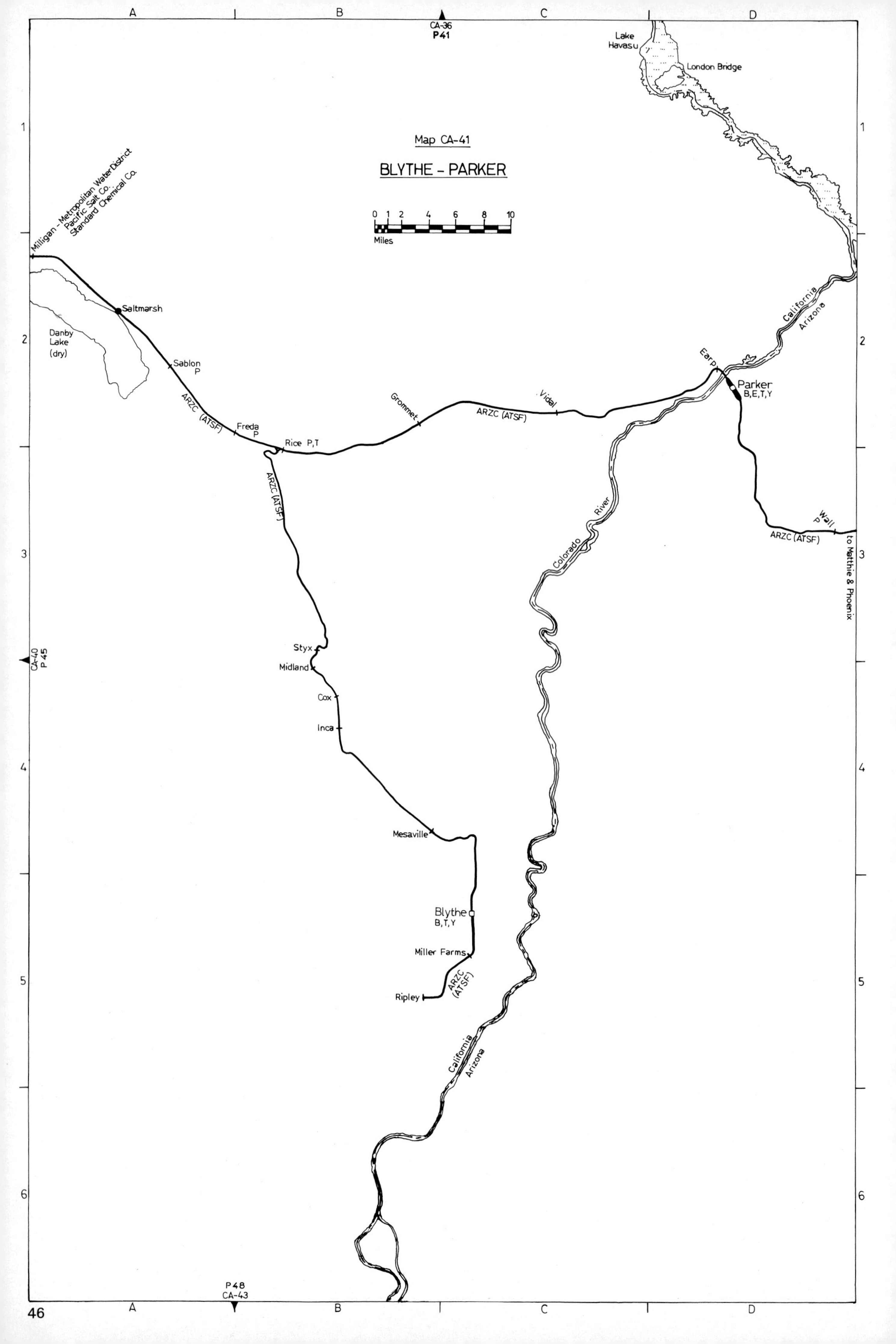

Map CA-41
BLYTHE - PARKER
0 1 2 4 6 8 10
Miles
CA-36
P41
Lake Havasu
London Bridge
Milligan - Metropolitan Water District
Pacific Salt Co.
Standard Chemical Co.
Saltmarsh
Danby Lake (dry)
Sablon P
ARZC (ATSF)
Freda P
Rice P,T
Grommet
Vidal
Earp
Parker B,E,T,Y
California
Arizona
Wall P
to Matthie & Phoenix
Colorado River
Styx
Midland
Cox
Inca
Mesaville
Blythe B,T,Y
Miller Farms
Ripley
CA-40 P45
P48 CA-43
A B C D
1 2 3 4 5 6

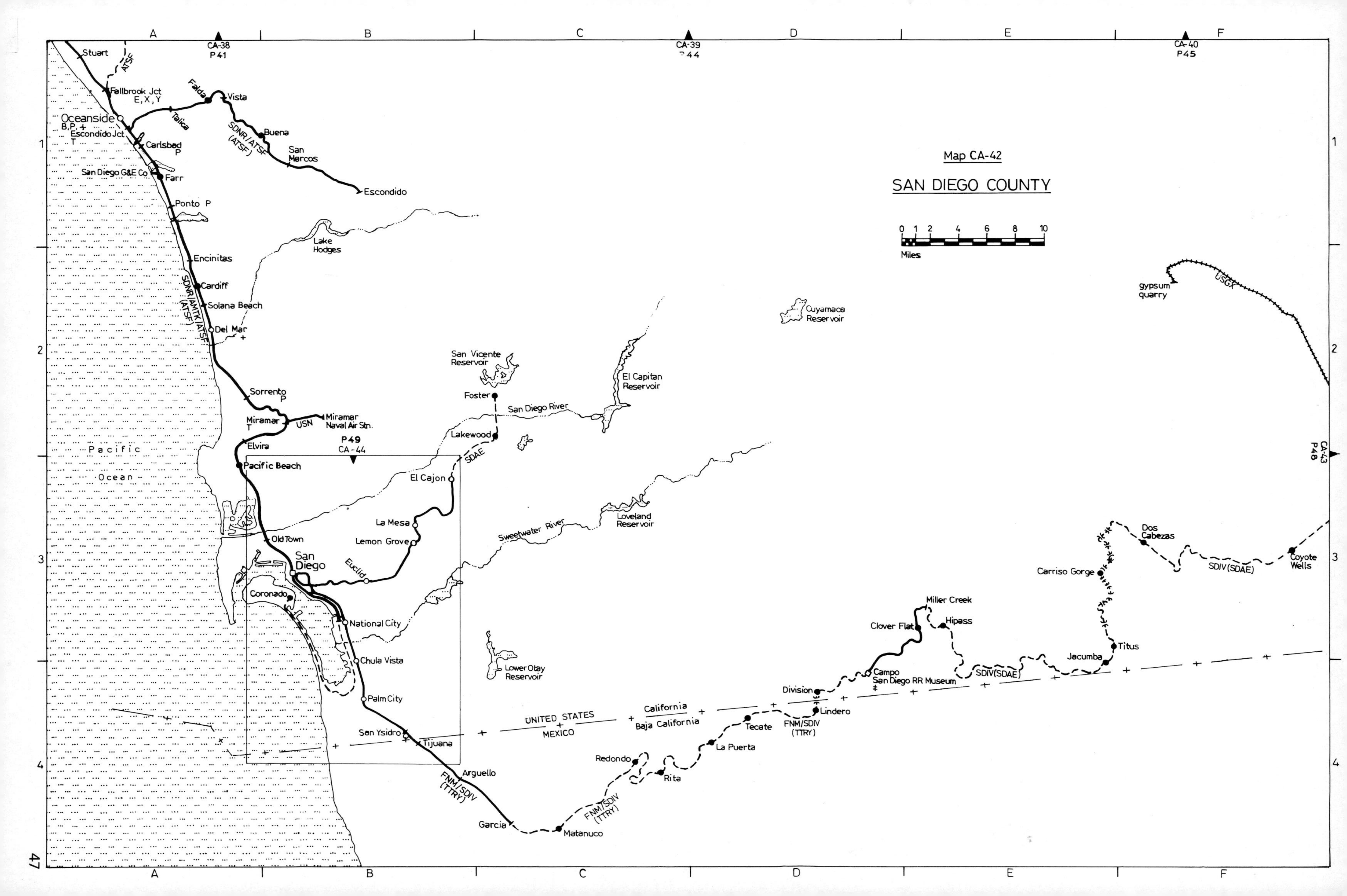

Map CA-42
SAN DIEGO COUNTY
0 1 2 4 6 8 10
Miles
CA-38
P41
CA-39
P44
CA-40
P45
CA-43
P48
P49
CA-44
A
B
C
D
E
F
1
2
3
4
Stuart
ATSF
Fallbrook Jct
E, X, Y
Oceanside
B, P, +
Escondido Jct.
T
Carlsbad
P
San Diego G&E Co
Farr
Talica
Falda
Vista
SDNR/ATSF
(ATSF)
Buena
San Marcos
Escondido
Ponto P
Lake Hodges
Encinitas
Cardiff
SDNR/AMTK/ATSF
(ATSF)
Solana Beach
Del Mar
Sorrento
P
Miramar
T
USN
Miramar
Naval Air Stn.
Elvira
Pacific
Ocean
Pacific Beach
Old Town
San Diego
Coronado
Euclid
Lemon Grove
La Mesa
El Cajon
SDAE
Lakewood
Foster
San Vicente
Reservoir
San Diego River
El Capitan
Reservoir
Cuyamaca
Reservoir
Sweetwater River
Loveland
Reservoir
Lower Otay
Reservoir
National City
Chula Vista
Palm City
San Ysidro
Tijuana
Arguello
FNM/SDIV
(TTRY)
Garcia
Matanuco
FNM/SDIV
(TTRY)
Redondo
Rita
La Puerta
Tecate
UNITED STATES
MEXICO
California
Baja California
Division
Lindero
FNM/SDIV
(TTRY)
Campo
San Diego RR Museum
Clover Flat
Miller Creek
Hipass
SDIV(SDAE)
Jecumba
Titus
Carriso Gorge
Dos
Cabezas
SDIV(SDAE)
Coyote
Wells
gypsum
quarry
USGX

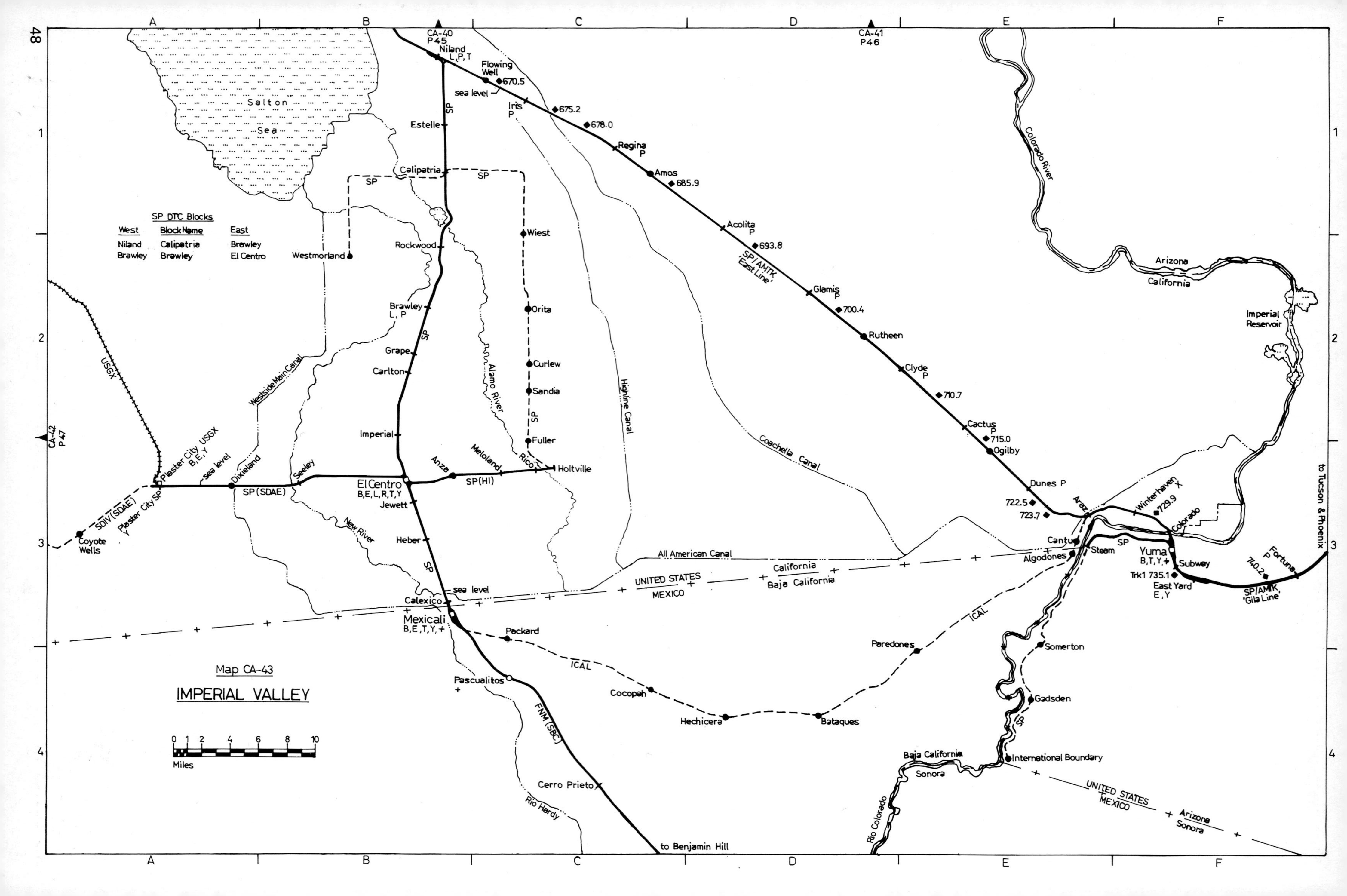
Map CA-43
IMPERIAL VALLEY
0 1 2 4 6 8 10
Miles
SP DTC Blocks
West Niland Brawley
Block Name Calipatria Brawley
East Brawley El Centro
CA-40 P45
CA-41 P46
CA-42 P47
Salton Sea
Niland L, P, T
Flowing Well
670.5
sea level
Iris P
675.2
678.0
Regina P
Amos
685.9
Acolita P
693.8
SP/AMTK 'East Line'
Glamis P
700.4
Rutheen
Clyde P
710.7
Cactus P
715.0
Ogilby
Dunes P
722.5
723.7
Araz
Winterhaven X
729.9
Colorado
Cantu
Algodones
Steam
SP
Yuma B, T, Y, +
Subway
Trk1 735.1
East Yard E, Y
Fortuna P
740.2
SP/AMTK 'Gila Line'
to Tucson & Phoenix
Colorado River
Arizona
California
Imperial Reservoir
Estelle
Calipatria
Rockwood
Westmorland
Wiest
Orita
Curlew
Sandia
Fuller
Holtville
Rico
Meloland
Anza
SP(HI)
Brawley L, P
Grape
Carlton
Imperial
El Centro B, E, L, R, T, Y
Jewett
Heber
Calexico
sea level
Mexicali B, E, T, Y, +
Seeley
Dixieland
SP (SDAE)
Plaster City USGX B, E, Y
Plaster City SP Y
SDIV (SDAE)
USGX
Coyote Wells
Westside Main Canal
New River
Alamo River
Highline Canal
Coachella Canal
All American Canal
UNITED STATES
MEXICO
California
Baja California
Packard
ICAL
Pascualitos
Cocopah
Hechicera
Bataques
Paredones
FNM (SBC)
Cerro Prieto
Rio Hardy
to Benjamin Hill
Somerton
Gadsden
International Boundary
Baja California
Sonora
Rio Colorado
Arizona
Sonora

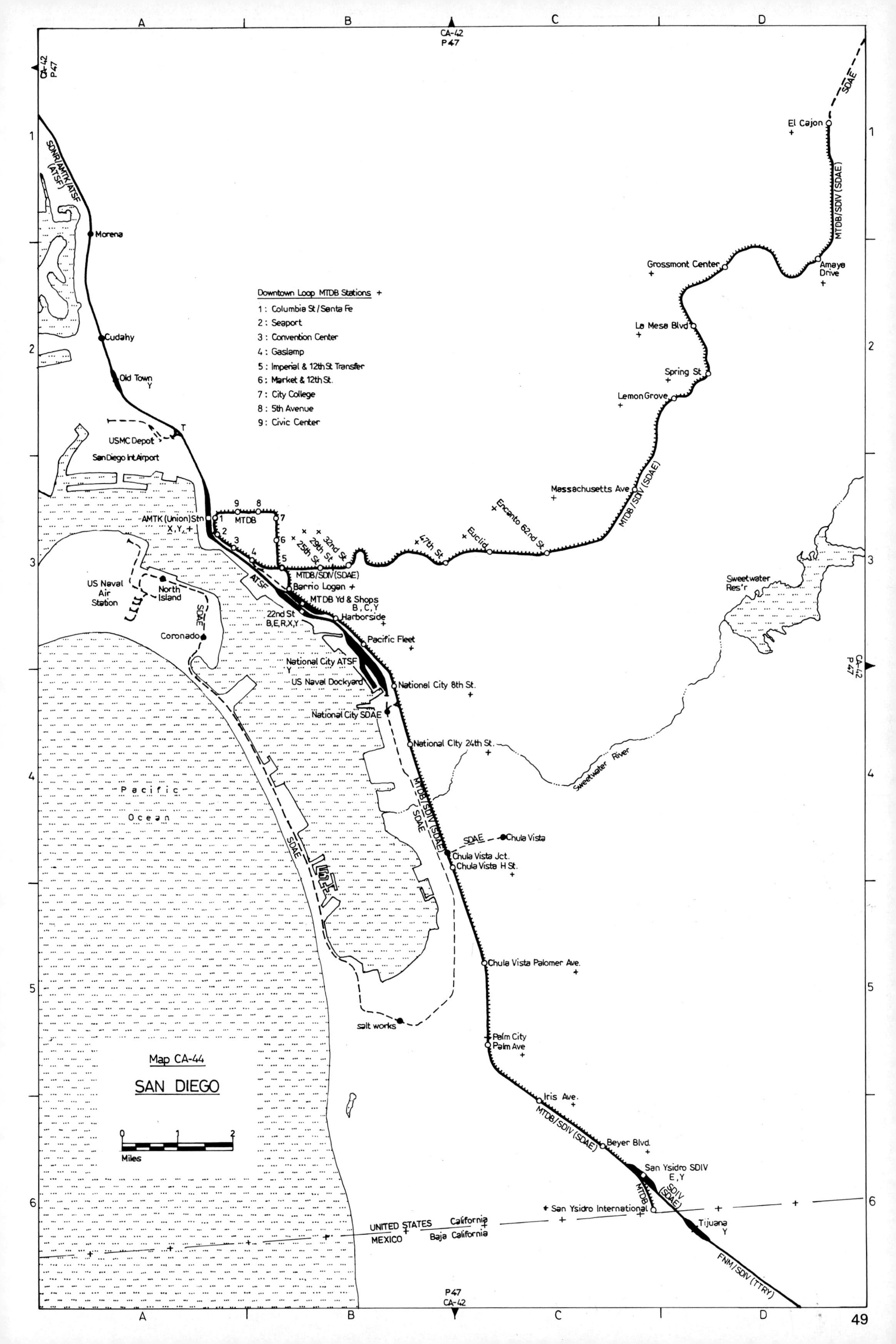
Map CA-44
SAN DIEGO
Downtown Loop MTDB Stations +
1 : Columbia St / Santa Fe
2 : Seaport
3 : Convention Center
4 : Gaslamp
5 : Imperial & 12th St Transfer
6 : Market & 12th St.
7 : City College
8 : 5th Avenue
9 : Civic Center
SDNR/AMTK/ATSF (ATSF)
Morena
Cudahy
Old Town Y
USMC Depot
San Diego Int Airport
AMTK (Union) Stn X, Y, +
MTDB
US Naval Air Station
North Island
Coronado
SDAE
ATSF
25th St
29th St
32nd St
47th St
Euclid
Encanto 62nd St
MTDB/SDIV (SDAE)
Barrio Logan +
MTDB Yd & Shops B, C, Y
22nd St B, E, R, X, Y
Harborside
Pacific Fleet
National City ATSF Y
US Naval Dockyard
National City 8th St.
National City SDAE
National City 24th St.
Sweetwater River
Sweetwater Res'r
Massachusetts Ave
Lemon Grove
Spring St
La Mesa Blvd
Grossmont Center
Amaya Drive
El Cajon
Pacific Ocean
Chula Vista
Chula Vista Jct.
Chula Vista H St.
Chula Vista Palomar Ave.
salt works
Palm City Palm Ave
Iris Ave.
Beyer Blvd.
San Ysidro SDIV E, Y
MTDB
SDIV (SDAE)
San Ysidro International
Tijuana Y
FNM/SDIV (TTRY)
UNITED STATES
MEXICO
California
Baja California
Miles
0 1 2
CA-42 P47
P47 CA-42
A B C D
1 2 3 4 5 6

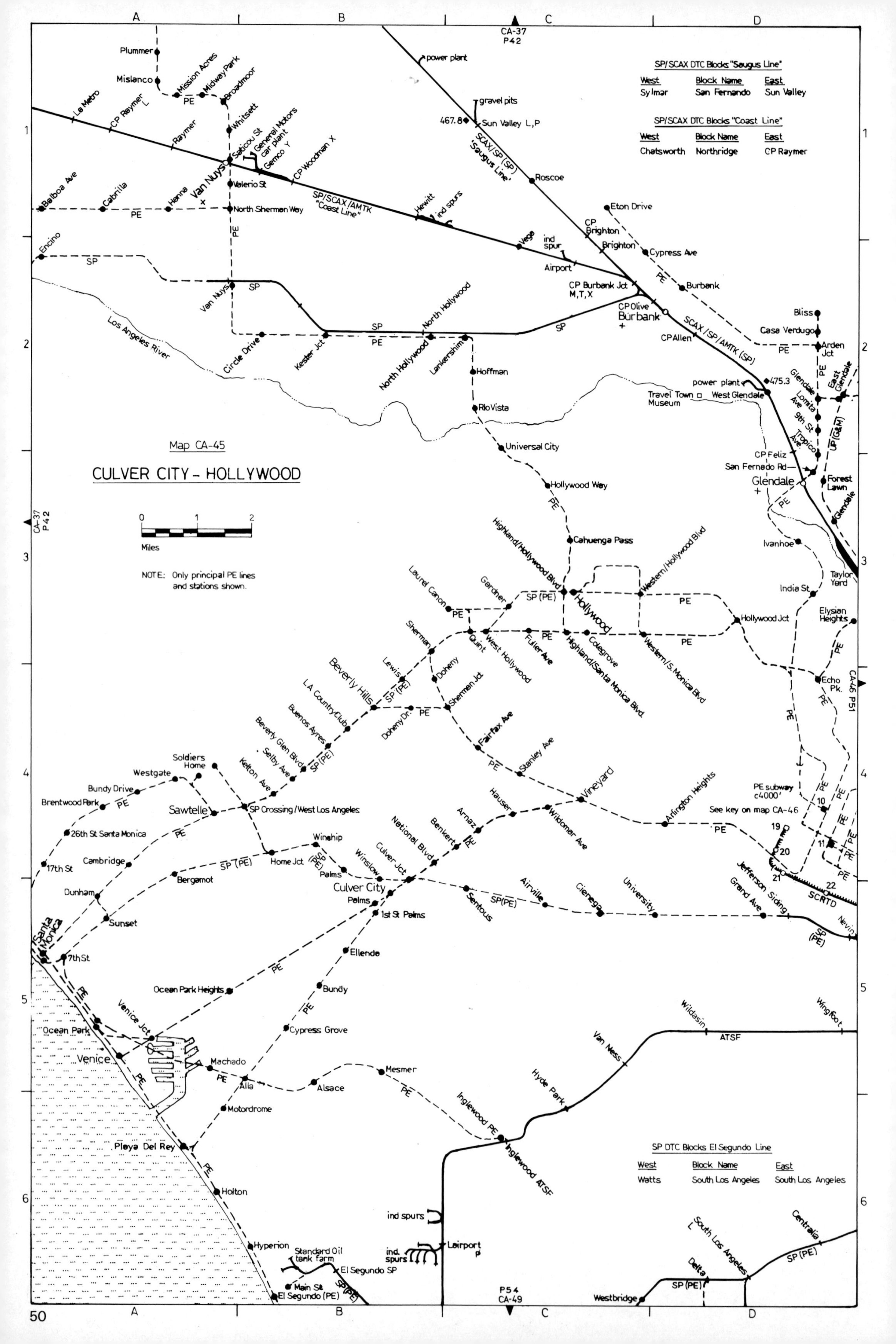
Map CA-45
CULVER CITY - HOLLYWOOD
Miles
NOTE: Only principal PE lines and stations shown.
SP/SCAX DTC Blocks "Saugus Line"
West | Block Name | East
Sylmar | San Fernando | Sun Valley
SP/SCAX DTC Blocks "Coast Line"
West | Block Name | East
Chatsworth | Northridge | CP Raymer
SP DTC Blocks El Segundo Line
West | Block Name | East
Watts | South Los Angeles | South Los Angeles
CA-37 P42
CA-46 P51
P54 CA-49
Plummer
Mislanco
Mission Acres
Midway Park
Broadmoor
Whitsett
Sabicou St
General Motors car plant
Gemco Y
CP Woodman X
Le Metro
CP Raymer
Raymer
Van Nuys
Valerio St
North Sherman Way
Balboa Ave
Cabrilla
Hanna
SP/SCAX/AMTK "Coast Line"
Hewitt
ind spurs
Vega
ind spur
Airport
power plant
gravel pits
467.8
Sun Valley L,P
SCAX/SP (SP) 'Saugus Line'
Roscoe
Eton Drive
CP Brighton
Brighton
Cypress Ave
Burbank
CP Burbank Jct M,T,X
CP Olive
Burbank
CP Allen
SCAX/SP/AMTK (SP)
Bliss
Casa Verdugo
Arden Jct
Glendale
East Glendale
Lomita Ave
9th St
Tropico Ave
UP (G&M)
power plant
475.3
Travel Town Museum
West Glendale
CP Feliz
San Fernando Rd
Glendale
Forest Lawn
Glendale
Ivanhoe
Taylor Yard
Encino
SP
PE
Van Nuys
Los Angeles River
Circle Drive
Kester Jct
North Hollywood
Lankershim
Hoffman
Rio Vista
Universal City
Hollywood Way
Cahuenga Pass
Highland/Hollywood Blvd
Western/Hollywood Blvd
Hollywood
Laurel Canon
Gardner
SP (PE)
India St
Hollywood Jct
Elysian Heights
Sherman
Quint
West Hollywood
Fuller Ave
Highland/Santa Monica Blvd
Colegrove
Western/S.Monica Blvd
Echo Pk.
Beverly Hills
Lewis
Doheny
Sherman Jct.
LA Country Club
Doheny Dr.
Buenos Ayres
Fairfax Ave
Stanley Ave
Beverly Glen Blvd
Selby Ave
Kelton Ave
Soldiers Home
Westgate
Bundy Drive
Brentwood Park
Sawtelle
SP Crossing/West Los Angeles
Vineyard
Arlington Heights
PE subway c4000'
See key on map CA-46
Hauser
Wildomar Ave
Arnaz
Benkert
National Blvd
26th St Santa Monica
17th St
Cambridge
Bergamot
Home Jct
Winship
Palms
Winslow
Culver Jct
Culver City
Palms
1st St Palms
Sentous
Airvile
Cienega
University
Jefferson Siding
Grand Ave
SCRTD
Nevin
19
20
21
22
10
11
Dunham
Sunset
Santa Monica
7th St
Ellenda
Bundy
Ocean Park Heights
Ocean Park
Venice Jct
Venice
Cypress Grove
Machado
Alla
Alsace
Mesmer
Motordrome
Playa Del Rey
Holton
Hyperion
Standard Oil tank farm
El Segundo SP
Main St
El Segundo (PE)
Inglewood PE
Inglewood ATSF
Hyde Park
Van Ness
Wildasin
ATSF
Wingfoot
ind spurs
Lairport
ind. spurs
Westbridge
Delta
SP (PE)
South Los Angeles
Centralia
A
B
C
D
1
2
3
4
5
6

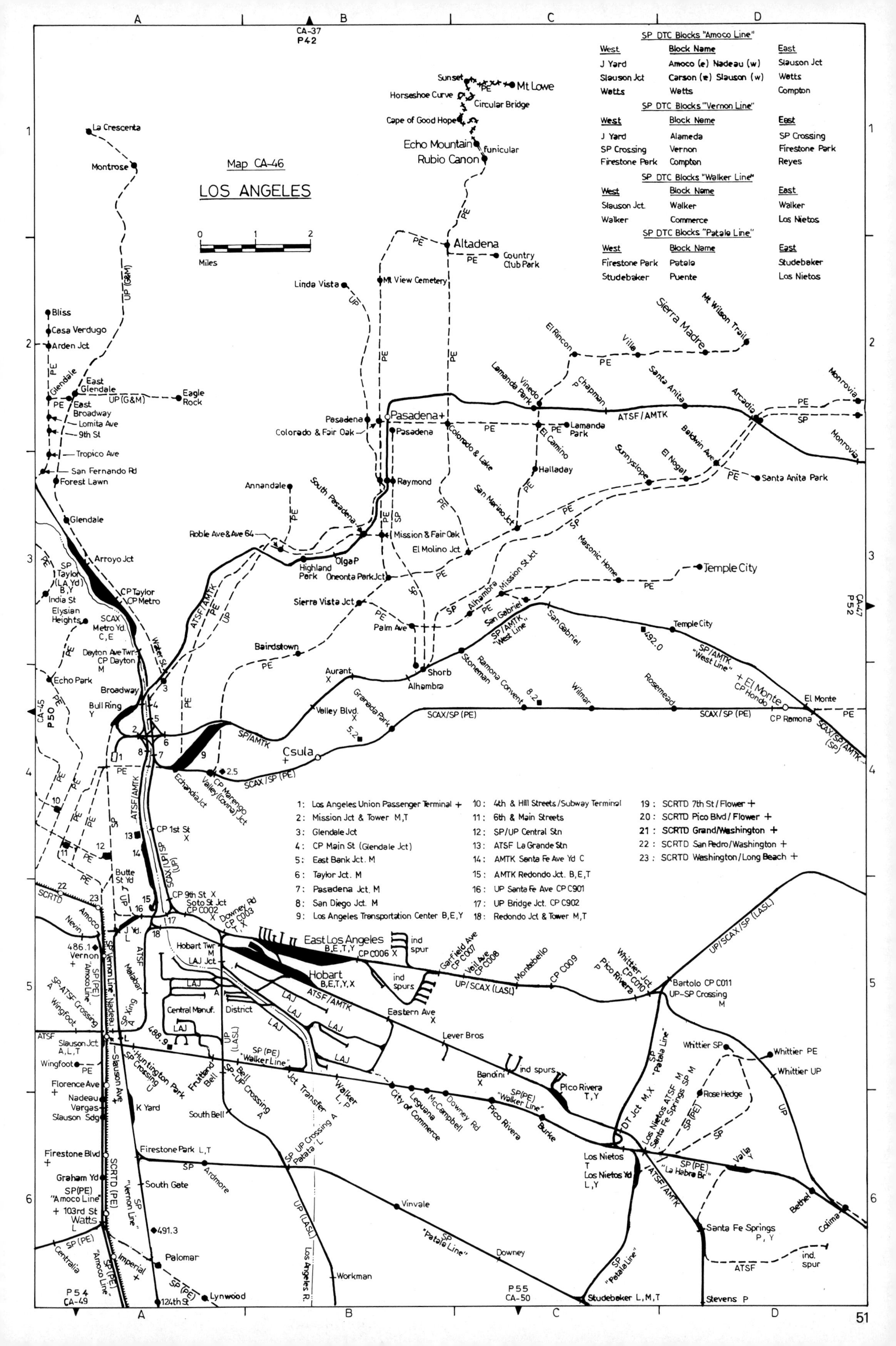

Map CA-46
LOS ANGELES
0 1 2
Miles
SP DTC Blocks "Amoco Line"
West | Block Name | East
J Yard | Amoco (e) Nadeau (w) | Slauson Jct
Slauson Jct | Carson (e) Slauson (w) | Watts
Watts | Watts | Compton
SP DTC Blocks "Vernon Line"
West | Block Name | East
J Yard | Alameda | SP Crossing
SP Crossing | Vernon | Firestone Park
Firestone Park | Compton | Reyes
SP DTC Blocks "Walker Line"
West | Block Name | East
Slauson Jct. | Walker | Walker
Walker | Commerce | Los Nietos
SP DTC Blocks "Patala Line"
West | Block Name | East
Firestone Park | Patala | Studebaker
Studebaker | Puente | Los Nietos
1: Los Angeles Union Passenger Terminal +
2: Mission Jct & Tower M,T
3: Glendale Jct
4: CP Main St (Glendale Jct)
5: East Bank Jct. M
6: Taylor Jct. M
7: Pasadena Jct. M
8: San Diego Jct. M
9: Los Angeles Transportation Center B,E,Y
10: 4th & Hill Streets/Subway Terminal
11: 6th & Main Streets
12: SP/UP Central Stn
13: ATSF La Grande Stn
14: AMTK Santa Fe Ave Yd C
15: AMTK Redondo Jct. B,E,T
16: UP Santa Fe Ave CP C901
17: UP Bridge Jct. CP C902
18: Redondo Jct & Tower M,T
19: SCRTD 7th St/Flower +
20: SCRTD Pico Blvd/Flower +
21: SCRTD Grand/Washington +
22: SCRTD San Pedro/Washington +
23: SCRTD Washington/Long Beach +
CA-37
P42
CA-45
P50
CA-47
P52
P54
CA-49
P55
CA-50
Sunset
Mt Lowe
Horseshoe Curve
Circular Bridge
Cape of Good Hope
Echo Mountain
funicular
Rubio Canon
La Crescenta
Montrose
UP (G&M)
Altadena
Country Club Park
Linda Vista
Mt View Cemetery
Mt Wilson Trail
Sierra Madre
El Rincon
Ville
Bliss
Casa Verdugo
Arden Jct
Glendale
East Glendale
UP (G&M)
Eagle Rock
East Broadway
Lomita Ave
9th St
Tropico Ave
San Fernando Rd
Forest Lawn
Lamanda Park
Vinedo
Chapman
Santa Anita
Arcadia
Monrovia
ATSF/AMTK
Pasadena
Pasadena +
Colorado & Fair Oak
Colorado & Lake
El Camino
Lamanda Park
Halladay
Baldwin Ave
El Nogal
Sunnyslope
Santa Anita Park
Raymond
Annandale
South Pasadena
San Marino Jct
Glendale
Roble Ave & Ave 64
Mission & Fair Oak
El Molino Jct
Arroyo Jct
Highland Park
Olga P
Oneonta Park Jct
Masonic Home
Temple City
SP Taylor (LA Yd) B,Y
India St
CP Taylor
CP Metro
Elysian Heights
SCAX Metro Yd. C,E
Sierra Vista Jct
Mission St Jct
Alhambra
San Gabriel
Dayton Ave Twr CP Dayton M
Palm Ave
SP/AMTK "West Line"
San Gabriel
492.0
Temple City
Bairdstown
Water St
Echo Park
Broadway
Aurant X
Shorb
Alhambra
Stoneman
Ramona Convent
8.2
Wilmar
Rosemead
SP/AMTK "West Line"
El Monte
CP Hondo
El Monte
Bull Ring Y
Valley Blvd. X
Granada Park
5.2
SCAX/SP (PE)
CP Ramona
SCAX/SP/AMTK (SP)
SP/AMTK
Csula
Echandia Jct
CP Marengo
Valley (Covina) Jct
2.5
SCAX/SP (PE)
ATSF/AMTK
CP 1st St X
SCAX/UP/SP (UP)
Butte St Yd
CP 9th St X
Soto St Jct CP C002 X
Downey Rd CP C003 T, X
SCRTD
Amoco
Nevin
486.1
Vernon
SP (PE) "Amoco Line"
Vernon Line
Nadeau
SP-ATSF Crossing A
Wingfoot
J Yd. L
ATSF
Malabar
SP Xing A
Hobart Twr M
LAJ Jct
East Los Angeles B,E,T,Y
CP C006 X
ind spur
Hobart B,E,T,Y,X
ind spurs
Garfield Ave CP C007
Veil Ave CP C008
Montebello
CP C009
UP/SCAX (LASL)
Pico Rivera P
Whittier Jct CP C010
Bartolo CP C011
UP-SP Crossing M
UP/SCAX/SP (LASL)
Central Manuf.
District
ATSF/AMTK
Eastern Ave X
Lever Bros
Slauson Jct A,L,T
Wingfoot PE
Florence Ave +
Nadeau
Vergas
Slauson Sdg
488.9
Slauson Ave
Huntington Park
SP Crossing U
Fruitland
Bell
SP-UP Crossing A
UP (LASL)
SP (PE) "Walker Line"
Jct Transfer
Walker L,P
Bandini X
ind spurs
Pico Rivera T,Y
Whittier SP
Whittier PE
Whittier UP
Rose Hedge
K Yard
South Bell
City of Commerce
Leguana
McCampbell
Downey Rd
Pico Rivera
SP(PE) "Walker Line"
Burke
DT Jct M,X
Los Nietos ATSF M
Santa Fe Springs SP M
SP "Patala Line"
Firestone Blvd +
Firestone Park L,T
SP
Ardmore
SP-UP Crossing A
Patala L
Los Nietos T
Los Nietos Yd L,Y
SP (PE) "La Habra Br"
Valla Y
Graham Yd
SP(PE) "Amoco Line"
+ 103rd St
Watts L
SCRTD (PE)
South Gate
SP "Vernon Line"
491.3
Vinvale
SP "Patala Line"
UP (LASL)
ATSF/AMTK
Santa Fe Springs P,Y
Bethel
Colima
SP (PE)
Centralia
SP (PE) "Amoco Line"
Imperial +
Palomar
Downey
ind. spur
ATSF
Workman
Los Angeles R.
SP (PE)
124th St
Lynwood
SP "Patala Line"
Studebaker L,M,T
Stevens P
PE
SP
UP

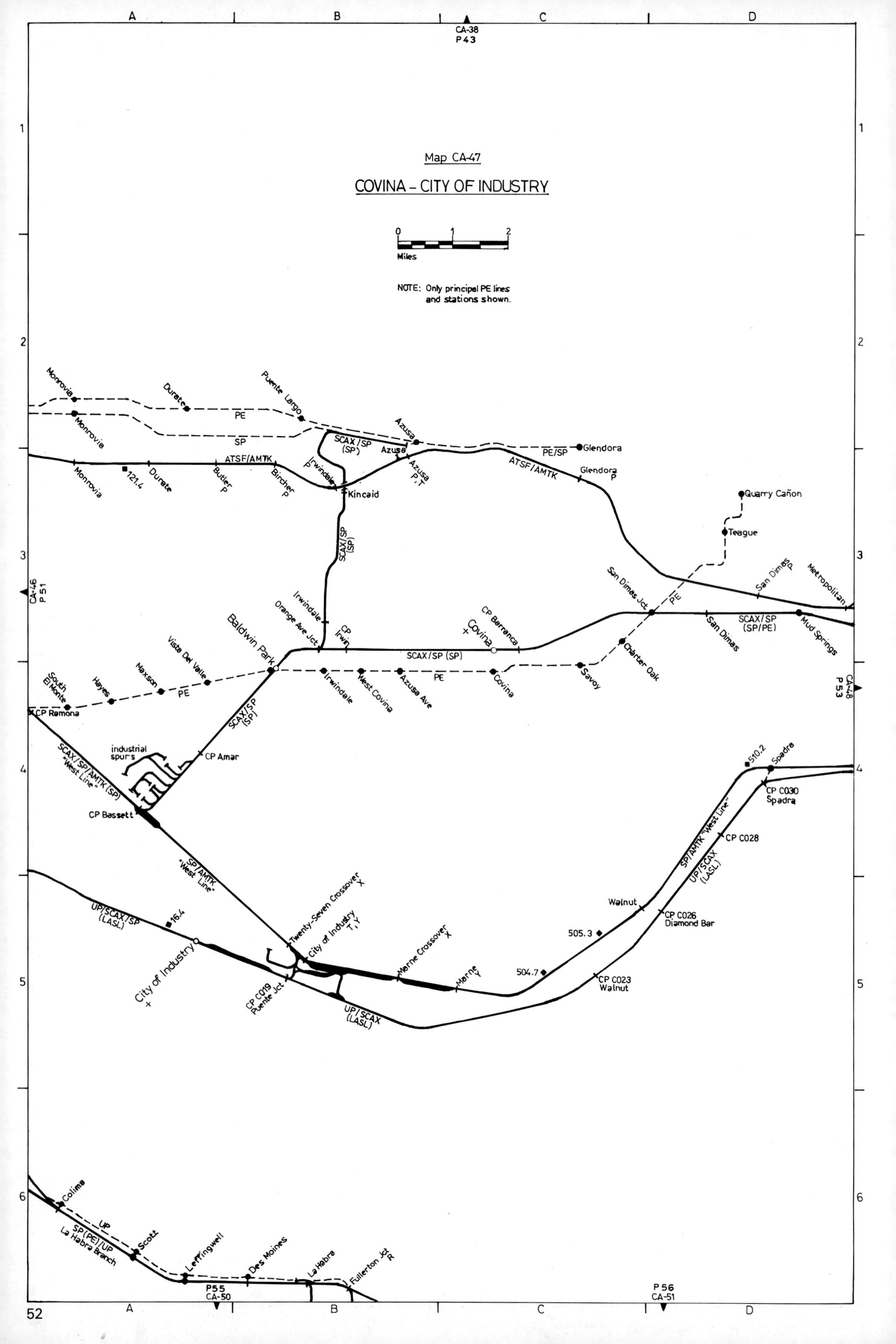

Map CA-47
COVINA – CITY OF INDUSTRY
0
1
2
Miles
NOTE: Only principal PE lines and stations shown.
CA-38
P43
CA-46
P51
CA-48
P53
P55
CA-50
P56
CA-51
Monrovia
Monrovia
Duarte
Puente Largo
Azusa
Glendora
PE
SP
SCAX/SP (SP)
Azusa
PE/SP
ATSF/AMTK
Monrovia
121.4
Duarte
Butler P
Bircher P
Irwindale P
Azusa P, T
Kincaid
ATSF/AMTK
Glendora P
Quarry Cañon
Teague
SCAX/SP (SP)
San Dimas Jct
PE
San Dimas P
Metropolitan
Irwindale
Orange Ave Jct
CP Irwin
Covina
CP Barranca
SCAX/SP (SP)
San Dimas
SCAX/SP (SP/PE)
Mud Springs
Baldwin Park
Vista Del Valle
Maxson
Hayes
South El Monte
CP Ramona
PE
Irwindale
West Covina
Azusa Ave
PE
Covina
Savoy
Charter Oak
SCAX/SP (SP)
CP Amar
industrial spurs
SCAX/SP/AMTK (SP) "West Line"
CP Bassett
510.2
Spadra
CP C030 Spadra
CP C028
SP/AMTK "West Line"
UP/SCAX (LASL)
SP/AMTK "West Line"
UP/SCAX/SP (LASL)
16.4
Twenty-Seven Crossover X
City of Industry T, Y
Marne Crossover X
Walnut
CP C026 Diamond Bar
505.3
504.7
Marne Y
CP C023 Walnut
City of Industry
CP C019 Puente Jct
UP/SCAX (LASL)
Colima
UP
SP(PE)/UP La Habra Branch
Scott
Leffingwell
Des Moines
La Habra
Fullerton Jct Y
A
B
C
D
1
2
3
4
5
6

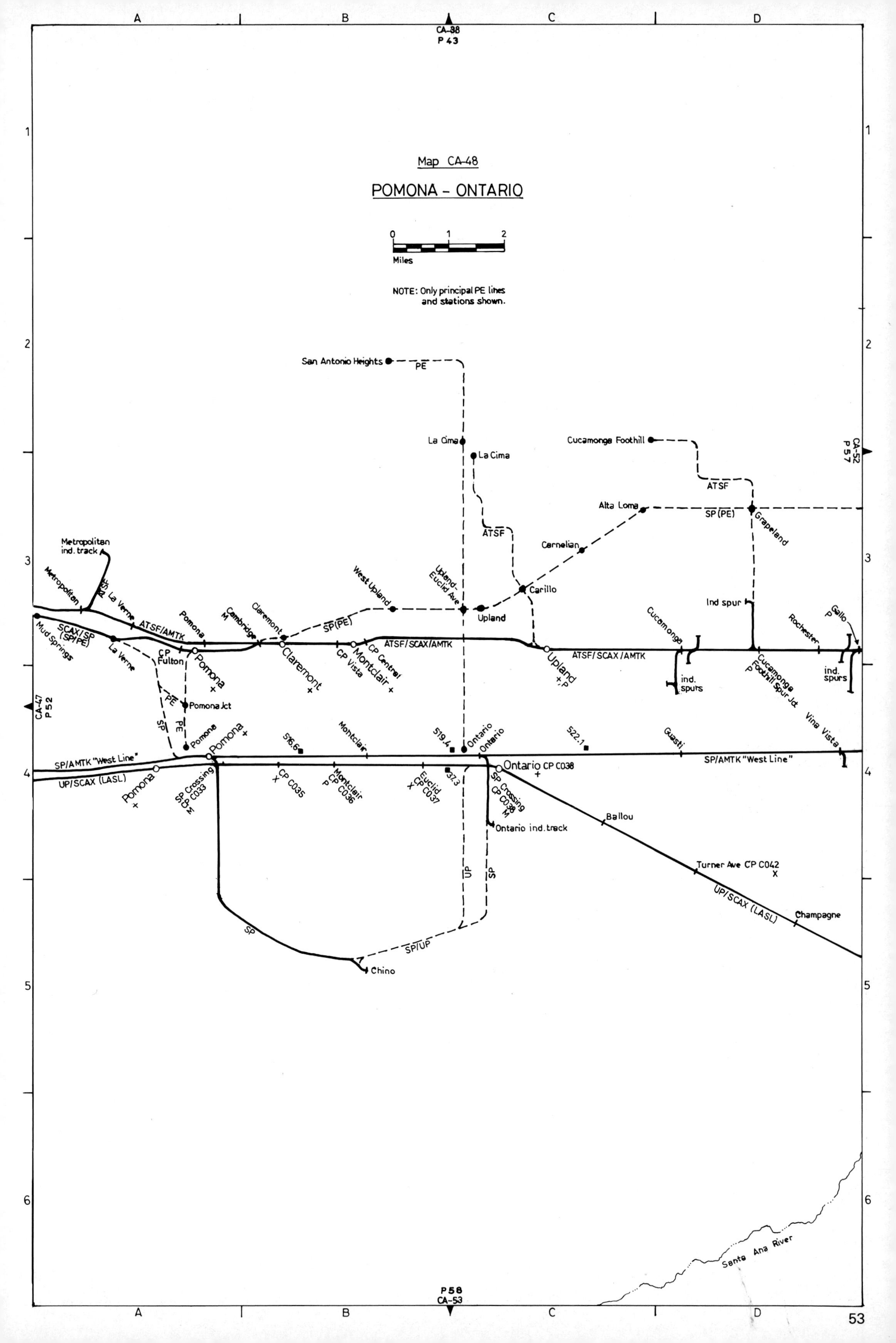
Map CA-48
POMONA - ONTARIO
Miles
NOTE: Only principal PE lines and stations shown.
CA-38 P 43
CA-52 P 57
CA-47 P 52
P 58 CA-53
San Antonio Heights
La Cima
Cucamonga Foothill
ATSF
SP (PE)
Alta Loma
Grapeland
Carnelian
Carillo
Upland
West Upland
Upland-Euclid Ave
Metropolitan ind. track
Metropolitan
La Verne
ATSF/AMTK
Pomona
Cambridge
Claremont
SCAX/SP (SP/PE)
Mud Springs
CP Fulton
Montclair
CP Vista
CP Central
ATSF/SCAX/AMTK
Cucamonga
Ind spur
Rochester
Gallo
ind. spurs
Cucamonga Foothill Spur Jct
Vina Vista
Pomona Jct
PE
SP
516.6
519.4
522.1
Ontario
Guasti
SP/AMTK "West Line"
UP/SCAX (LASL)
SP Crossing CP C033
CP C035
CP C036
Euclid CP C037
Ontario CP C038
SP Crossing CP C038
Ontario ind. track
Ballou
Turner Ave CP C042
Champagne
UP
SP/UP
Chino
Santa Ana River

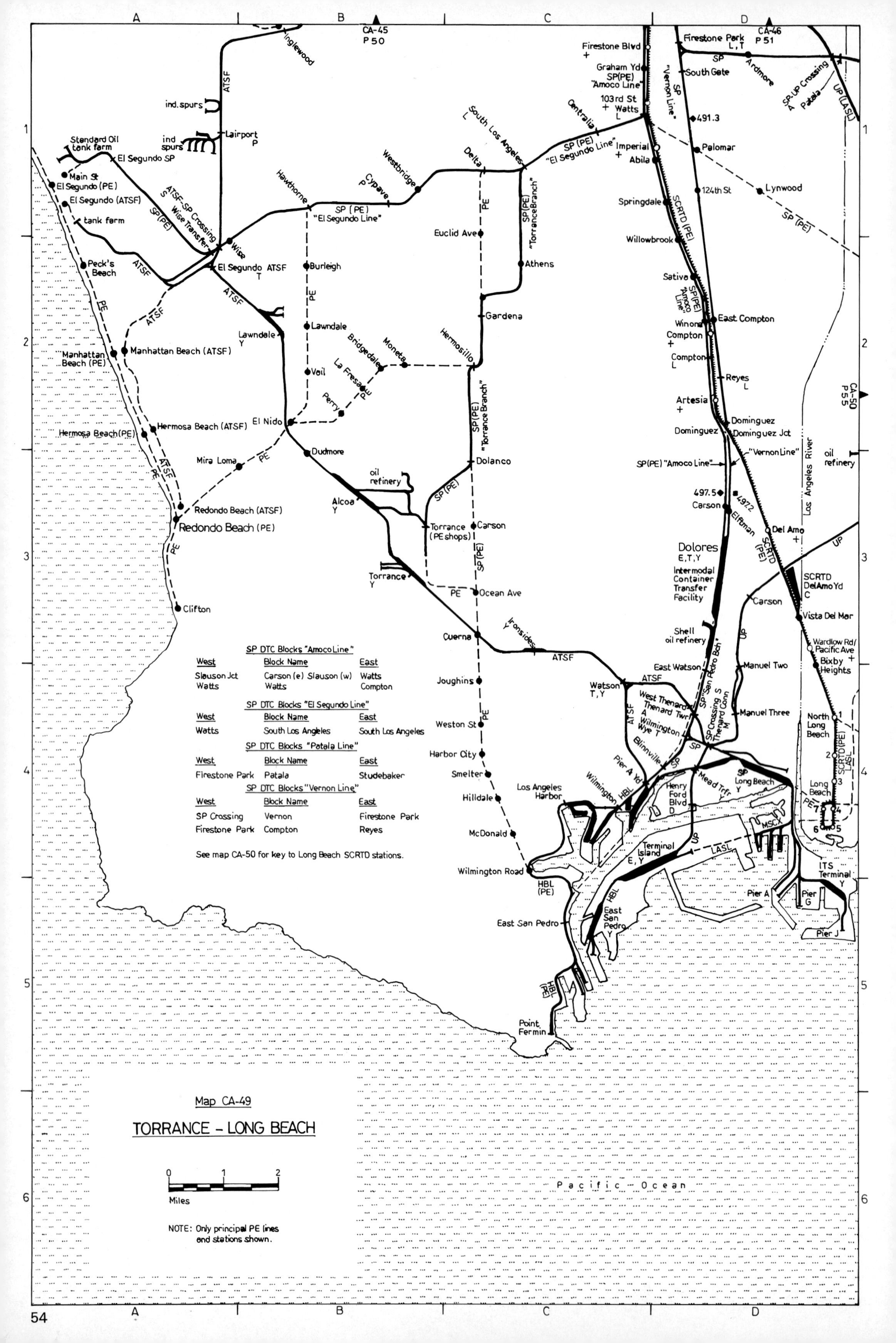
A
B
C
D
CA-45
P50
CA-46
P51
CA-50
P55
Inglewood
ATSF
ind. spurs
ind
spurs
Lairport
P
Standard Oil
tank farm
El Segundo SP
Main St
El Segundo (PE)
El Segundo (ATSF)
tank farm
ATSF-SP Crossing
S
Wise Transfer
SP(PE)
Wise
Peck's
Beach
ATSF
El Segundo ATSF
T
PE
Manhattan
Beach (PE)
Manhattan Beach (ATSF)
Lawndale
Y
Hermosa Beach (PE)
Hermosa Beach (ATSF)
Mira Loma
Redondo Beach (ATSF)
Redondo Beach (PE)
Clifton
Hawthorne
SP (PE)
"El Segundo Line"
Burleigh
Lawndale
Veil
El Nido
Bridgedale
Moneta
La Fresa
P
Perry
Dudmore
oil
refinery
Alcoa
Y
Torrance
Y
Torrance
(PE shops)
Cypave
P
Westbridge
Delta
South Los Angeles
L
Centralia
SP (PE)
"El Segundo Line"
Euclid Ave
SP(PE)
"Torrance Branch"
Athens
Gardena
Hermosillo
Dolanco
Carson
Ocean Ave
Cuerna
Ironsides
Y
Joughins
Weston St
Harbor City
Smelter
Hilldale
McDonald
Wilmington Road
HBL
(PE)
East San Pedro
Point
Fermin
Firestone Blvd
Graham Yd
SP(PE)
"Amoco Line"
103rd St
Watts
L
Imperial
Abila
Springdale
Willowbrook
Sativa
SCRTD (PE)
SP(PE)
"Amoco Line"
Winona
Compton
Compton
L
East Compton
Reyes
L
Artesia
Dominguez
Dominguez
Dominguez Jct
"Vernon Line"
SP(PE) "Amoco Line"
497.5
497.2
Carson
Elftman
Dolores
E,T,Y
Intermodal
Container
Transfer
Facility
Shell
oil refinery
East Watson
Watson
T, Y
ATSF
West Thenard
Thenard Twr
A
Wilmington
Wye T
SP "San Pedro Bch"
SP Crossing
S
Thenard Conn
M
Blinnville
Pier A Yd
Wilmington
HBL
Los Angeles
Harbor
Henry
Ford
Blvd
D
Mead Trfr
SP
Long Beach
Y
Terminal
Island
E, Y
LASL
MSCX
East
San
Pedro
Y
Pier A
Pier G
Pier J
ITS
Terminal
Y
Firestone Park
L, T
SP
"Vernon Line"
South Gate
Ardmore
SP-UP Crossing
A
Patala
UP (LASL)
491.3
Palomar
124th St
Lynwood
SP (PE)
Los Angeles River
oil
refinery
Del Amo
UP
SCRTD
Del Amo Yd
C
Carson
Vista Del Mar
Wardlow Rd/
Pacific Ave
Bixby
Heights
Manuel Two
Manuel Three
North
Long
Beach
SCRTD(PE)
LASL
Long
Beach
PE
Pacific Ocean
SP DTC Blocks "Amoco Line"
West | Block Name | East
Slauson Jct | Carson (e) Slauson (w) | Watts
Watts | Watts | Compton
SP DTC Blocks "El Segundo Line"
West | Block Name | East
Watts | South Los Angeles | South Los Angeles
SP DTC Blocks "Patala Line"
West | Block Name | East
Firestone Park | Patala | Studebaker
SP DTC Blocks "Vernon Line"
West | Block Name | East
SP Crossing | Vernon | Firestone Park
Firestone Park | Compton | Reyes
See map CA-50 for key to Long Beach SCRTD stations.
Map CA-49
TORRANCE - LONG BEACH
0
1
2
Miles
NOTE: Only principal PE lines and stations shown.

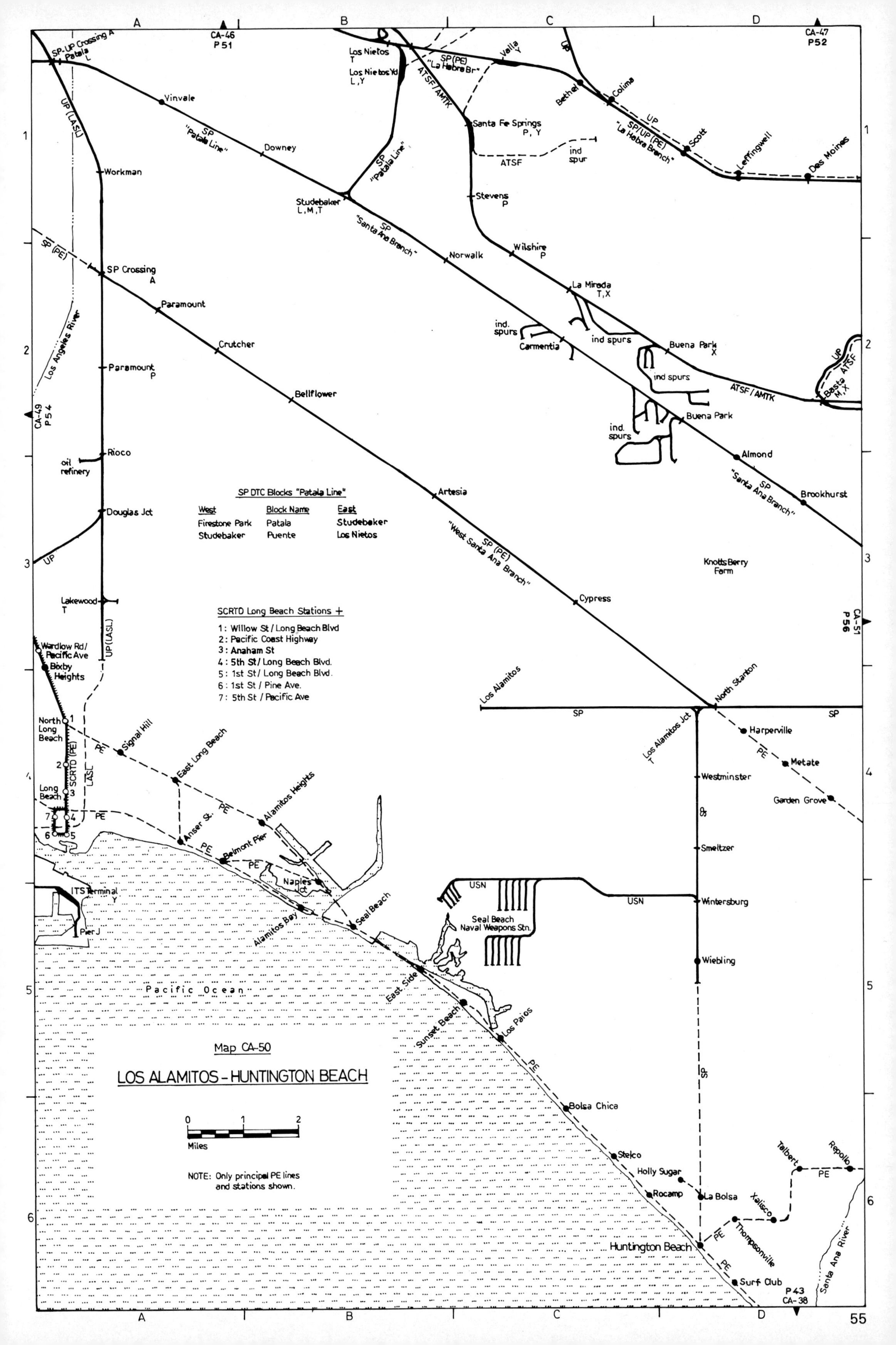

Map CA-50
LOS ALAMITOS - HUNTINGTON BEACH
SP DTC Blocks "Patala Line"
West | Block Name | East
Firestone Park | Patala | Studebaker
Studebaker | Puente | Los Nietos
SCRTD Long Beach Stations +
1: Willow St / Long Beach Blvd
2: Pacific Coast Highway
3: Anaham St
4: 5th St / Long Beach Blvd.
5: 1st St / Long Beach Blvd.
6: 1st St / Pine Ave.
7: 5th St / Pacific Ave
NOTE: Only principal PE lines and stations shown.
Miles
0
1
2
CA-46 P51
CA-47 P52
CA-49 P54
CA-51 P56
P43 CA-38
SP-UP Crossing A
Patala L
Vinvale
SP "Patala Line"
Downey
Workman
UP (LASL)
Los Nietos T
Los Nietos Yd L, Y
SP (PE) "La Habra Br"
Valla Y
ATSF/AMTK
Santa Fe Springs P, Y
ATSF
ind spur
Bethel
Colima
UP
SP/UP (PE) "La Habra Branch"
Scott
Leffingwell
Des Moines
Studebaker L, M, T
SP "Santa Ana Branch"
Stevens P
Norwalk
Wilshire P
La Mirada T, X
SP (PE)
SP Crossing A
Paramount
Crutcher
Los Angeles River
Paramount P
Bellflower
ind. spurs
Carmentia
ind spurs
Buena Park X
ind spurs
ATSF/AMTK
Basta M, X
UP
ATSF
Buena Park
ind. spurs
Almond
Rioco
oil refinery
Artesia
Brookhurst
Douglas Jct
SP (PE) "West Santa Ana Branch"
Knotts Berry Farm
Lakewood T
Cypress
Wardlow Rd/ Pacific Ave
Bixby Heights
Los Alamitos
North Stanton
SP
North Long Beach
SCRTD (PE)
LASL
Signal Hill
PE
East Long Beach
Los Alamitos Jct T
Harperville
Metate
Westminster
Garden Grove
Long Beach
Anser St.
Alamitos Heights
Belmont Pier
Naples Jct
Smeltzer
USN
ITS Terminal Y
Pier J
Alamitos Bay
Seal Beach
Wintersburg
Seal Beach Naval Weapons Stn.
Wiebling
East Side
Pacific Ocean
Sunset Beach
Los Patos
Bolsa Chica
Stelco
Holly Sugar
Rocamp
La Bolsa
Talbert
Repollo
Xalisco
Thompsonville
Huntington Beach
Surf Club
Santa Ana River

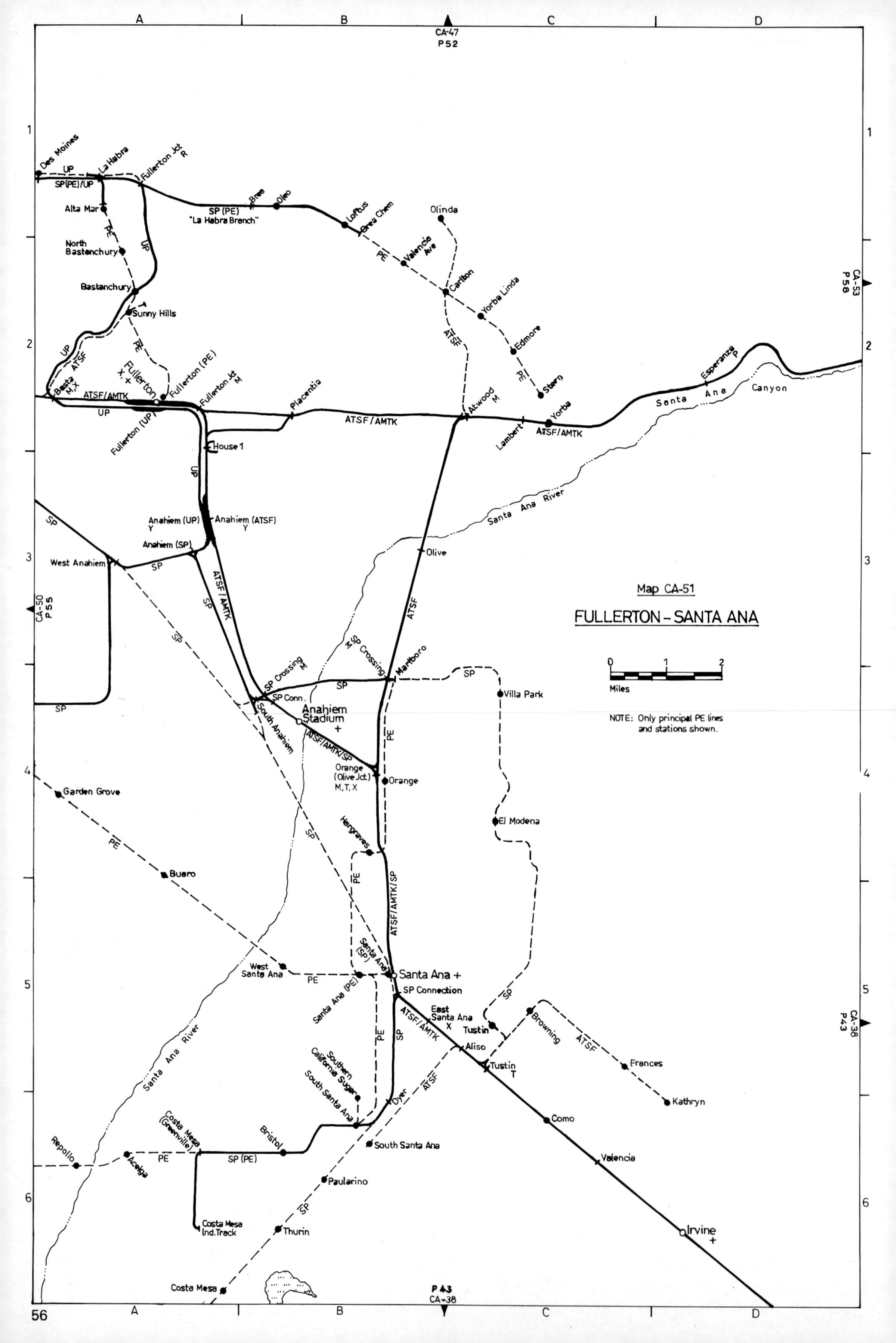
Map CA-51
FULLERTON - SANTA ANA
Miles
NOTE: Only principal PE lines and stations shown.
CA-47 P52
CA-53 P58
CA-50 P55
CA-38 P43
P43 CA-38
Des Moines
La Habra
Fullerton Jct R
SP(PE)/UP
Alta Mar
North Bastanchury
Bastanchury
Sunny Hills
SP (PE) "La Habra Branch"
Brea
Oleo
Loftus
Brea Chem
Olinda
Valencia Ave
Carlton
Yorba Linda
Edmore
Stern
Fullerton X, +
Fullerton (PE)
Fullerton Jct M
Basta M, X
Fullerton (UP)
Placentia
Atwood M
Lambert
Yorba
ATSF/AMTK
Esperanza P
Santa Ana Canyon
Santa Ana River
House 1
Anaheim (UP) Y
Anaheim (ATSF) Y
Anaheim (SP)
West Anaheim
Olive
SP Crossing M
Marlboro
Villa Park
SP Conn.
Anaheim Stadium +
South Anaheim
ATSF/AMTK/SP
Orange (Olive Jct) M, T, X
Orange
El Modena
Garden Grove
Hargraves
Buaro
West Santa Ana
Santa Ana (SP)
Santa Ana +
SP Connection
Santa Ana (PE)
East Santa Ana X
Tustin
Browning
Aliso
Tustin T
Frances
Kathryn
Southern California Sugar
South Santa Ana
Dyer
Como
Bristol
Costa Mesa (Greenville)
SP (PE)
Repollo
Acelga
Valencia
Paularino
Costa Mesa Ind. Track
Thurin
Irvine +
Costa Mesa

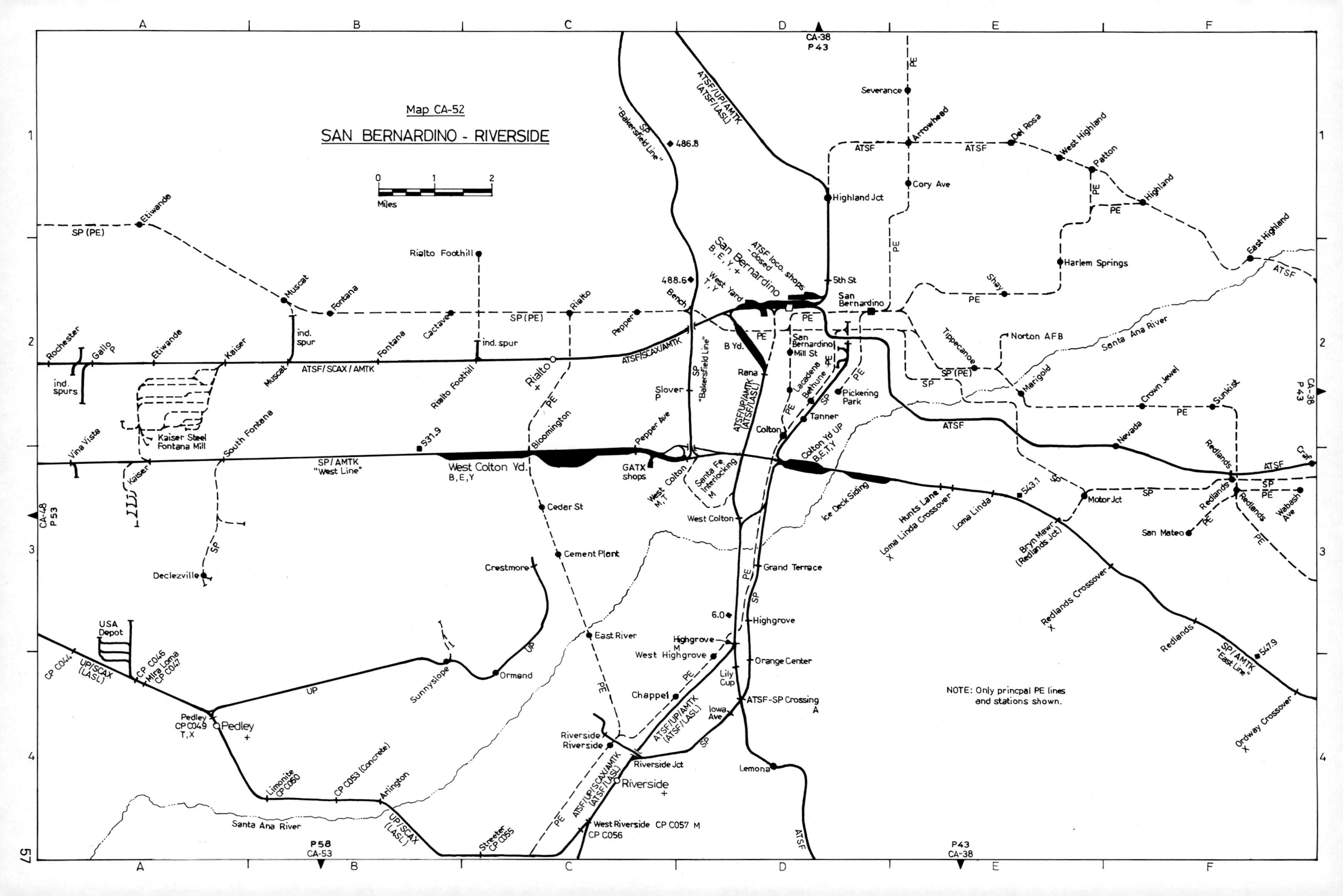
Map CA-52
SAN BERNARDINO - RIVERSIDE
0 1 2
Miles
NOTE: Only principal PE lines and stations shown.
CA-38 P 43
CA-48 P 53
P58 CA-53
P43 CA-38
SP (PE)
Etiwanda
Muscat
Fontana
Cactave
Rialto Foothill
ind. spur
Rialto
Pepper
Bench
488.6
486.8
SP "Bakersfield Line"
ATSF/UP/AMTK (ATSF/LASL)
Rochester
Gallo P
ind. spurs
Kaiser
ATSF/SCAX/AMTK
Kaiser Steel Fontana Mill
Vina Vista
South Fontana
531.9
SP/AMTK "West Line"
West Colton Yd. B, E, Y
Bloomington
Pepper Ave
GATX shops
Slover P
West Colton M, T
Santa Fe Interlocking M
Ceder St
Cement Plent
Declezville
Crestmore
San Bernardino B, E, Y, +
ATSF loco. shops - closed
West Yard T, Y
B Yd.
Rana
5th St
Highland Jct
San Bernardino
San Bernardino Mill St
Lacadena
Bethune
Tanner
Colton
Pickering Park
Colton Yd UP B, E, T, Y
Severance
Arrowhead
ATSF
Cory Ave
Del Rosa
West Highland
Patton
Highland
PE
Harlem Springs
Shay
East Highland
Tippecanoe
SP (PE)
Norton AFB
Marigold
Santa Ana River
Crown Jewel
Sunkist
Nevada
Redlands
Craft
Wabash Ave
Redlands
San Mateo
Motor Jct
543.1
Hunts Lane
Loma Linda Crossover X
Loma Linda
Ice Deck Siding
Bryn Mawr (Redlands Jct)
Redlands Crossover X
SP/AMTK "East Line"
547.9
Ordway Crossover X
West Colton
Grand Terrace
Highgrove
6.0
Highgrove M
West Highgrove
Orange Center
Lily Cup
ATSF-SP Crossing A
Iowa Ave
Chappel
Lemona
East River
Riverside
Riverside
Riverside Jct
Riverside +
West Riverside CP C057 M
CP C056
ATSF/UP/SCAX/AMTK (ATSF/LASL)
Streeter CP C055
Arlington
CP C053 (Concrete)
Limonite CP C050
UP/SCAX (LASL)
Santa Ana River
Pedley CP C049 T, X
Pedley +
UP
Sunnyslope
Ormand
USA Depot
CP C046
Mira Loma CP C047
CP C044
UP/SCAX (LASL)
A
B
C
D
E
F
1
2
3
4

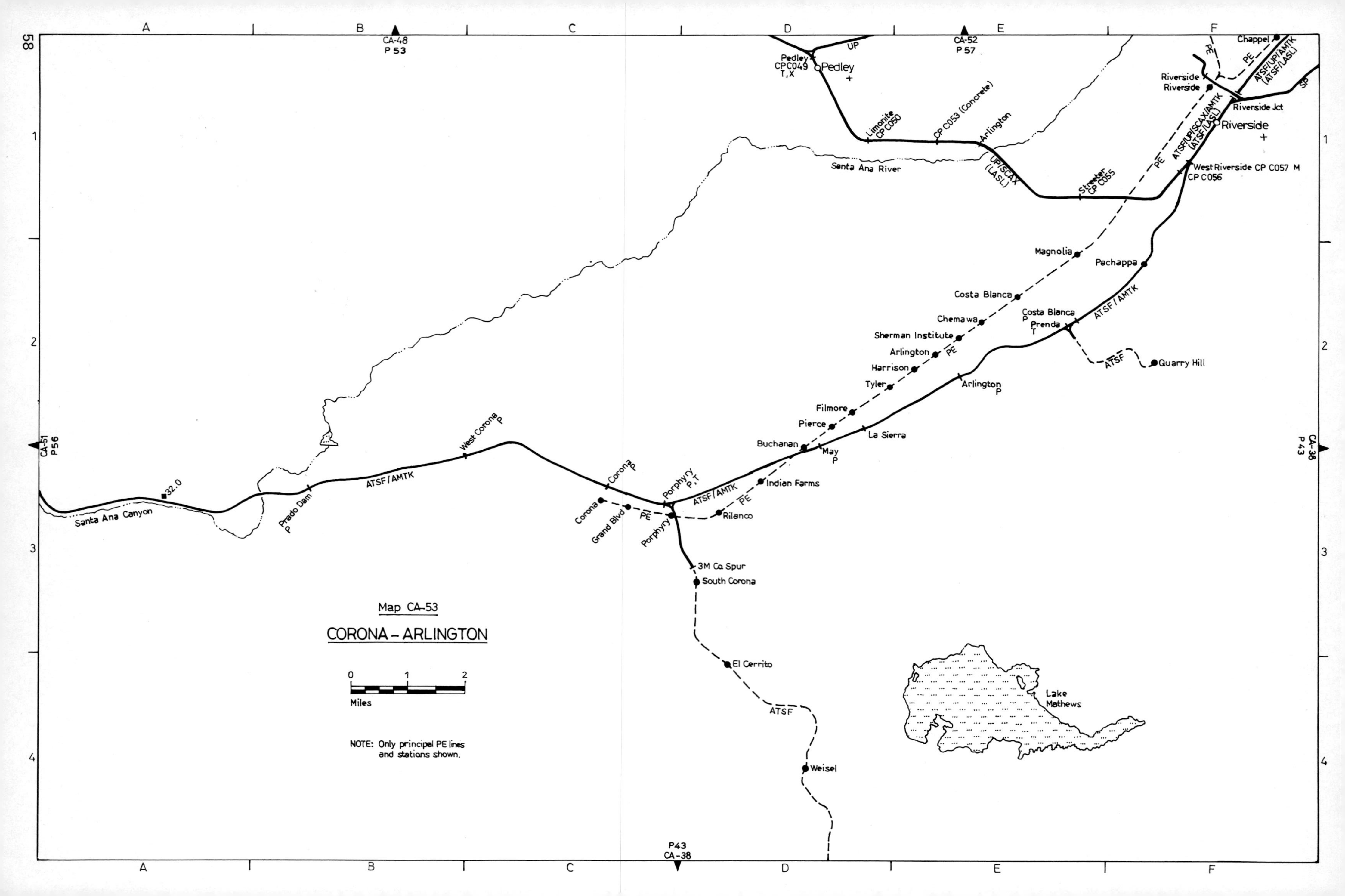

Map CA-53
CORONA - ARLINGTON
0 1 2
Miles
NOTE: Only principal PE lines and stations shown.
CA-48 P 53
CA-52 P 57
CA-51 P56
CA-38 P 43
P43 CA-38
Pedley CPC049 T,X
Pedley
UP
Limonite CP C050
CP C053 (Concrete)
Arlington
UP/SCAX (LASL)
Santa Ana River
Streeter CP C055
Chappel
PE
ATSF/UP/AMTK (ATSF/LASL)
SP
Riverside
Riverside
Riverside Jct
Riverside
ATSF/UP/SCAX/AMTK (ATSF/LASL)
West Riverside CP C057 M
CP C056
Magnolia
Pachappa
Costa Blanca
Chemawa
Costa Blanca P
Prenda T
ATSF/AMTK
Sherman Institute
Arlington
Harrison
Tyler
ATSF
Quarry Hill
Arlington P
Filmore
Pierce
La Sierra
Buchanan
May P
Indian Farms
Porphyry P,T
Rilanco
Corona P
Corona
Grand Blvd
Porphyry
3M Co Spur
South Corona
El Cerrito
Weisel
Lake Mathews
West Corona P
32.0
Prado Dam P
Santa Ana Canyon

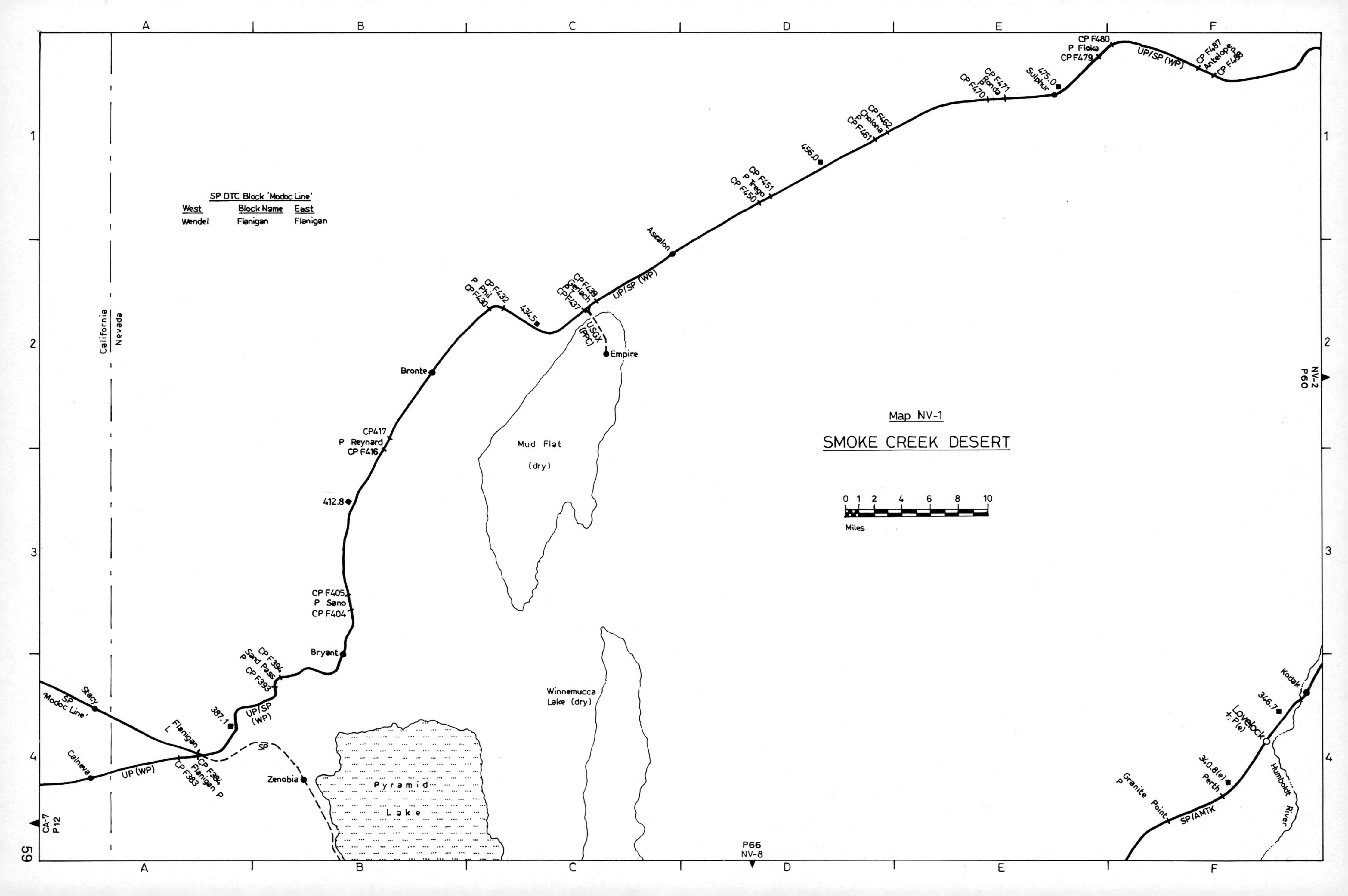
Map NV-1
SMOKE CREEK DESERT
0 1 2 4 6 8 10
Miles
SP DTC Block 'Modoc Line'
West | Block Name | East
Wendel | Flanigan | Flanigan
California
Nevada
Mud Flat (dry)
Winnemucca Lake (dry)
Pyramid Lake
Humboldt River
UP/SP (WP)
UP (WP)
SP 'Modoc Line'
SP/AMTK
SP
USGX (PPC)
Empire
Stacy
Calneva
Flanigan L
CP F384
Flanigan P
CP F383
Zenobia
387.1
CP F394
P Sand Pass
CP F393
Bryant
CP F405
P Sano
CP F404
412.8
CP417
P Reynard
CP F416
Bronte
CP F432
P Phil
CP F430
434.5
CP F438
Gerlach
P L
CP F437
Ascalon
CP F451
P Trego
CP F450
456.0
CP F462
Cholona
P
CP F461
CP F471
Ronda
P
CP F470
475.0
Sulphur
CP F480
P Floka
CP F479
CP F487
Antelope
CP F488
Kodak
346.7
Lovelock
+, P(e)
340.8(e)
Perth
Granite Point
P
CA-7
P12
NV-2
P60
P66
NV-8

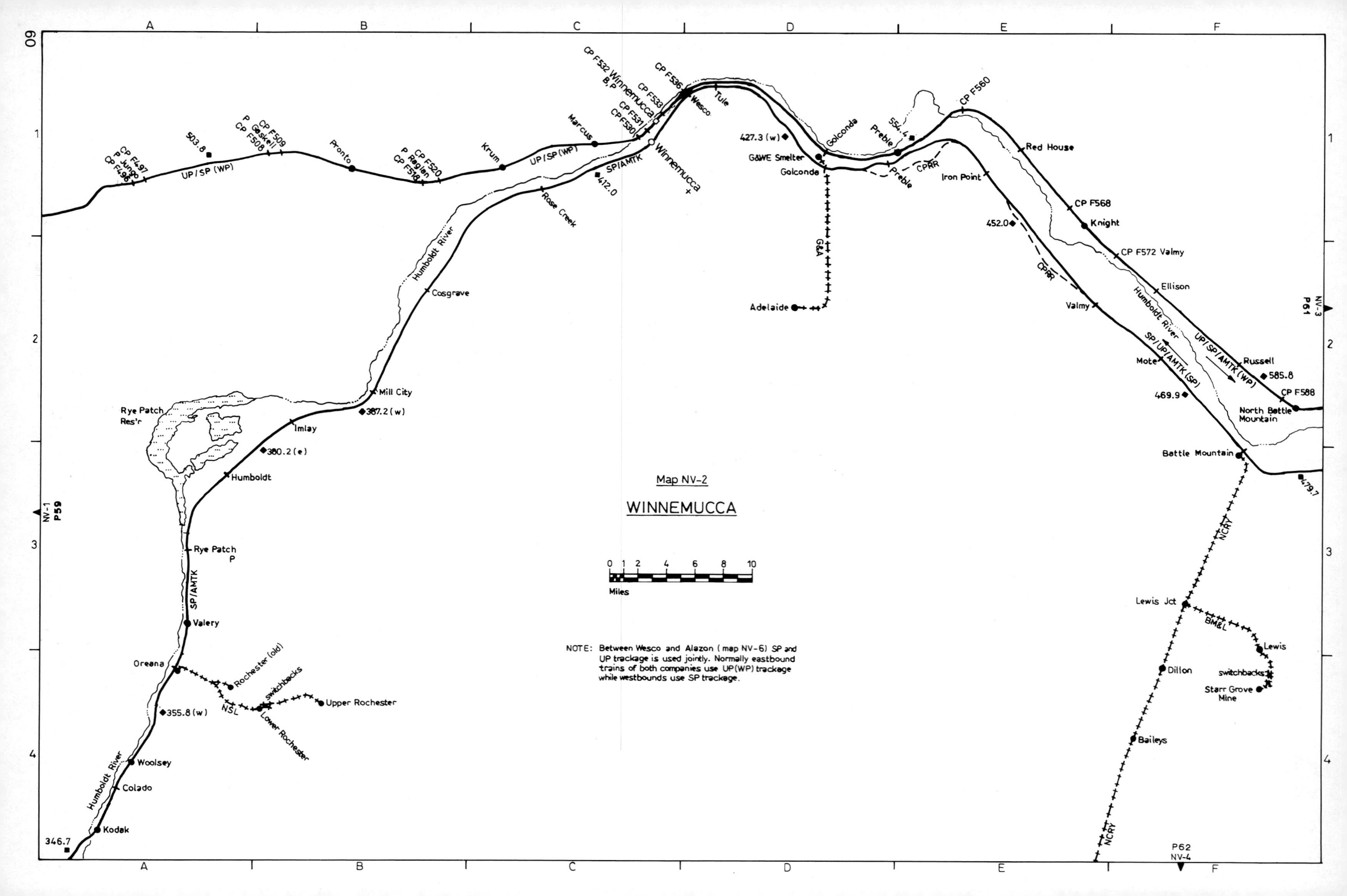

Map NV-2
WINNEMUCCA
0 1 2 4 6 8 10
Miles
NOTE: Between Wesco and Alazon (map NV-6) SP and UP trackage is used jointly. Normally eastbound trains of both companies use UP(WP) trackage while westbounds use SP trackage.
NV-3
P61
NV-1
P59
P62
NV-4
CP F497
P Jungo
CP F496
503.8
CP F509
P Gaskell
CP F508
UP/SP (WP)
Pronto
CP F520
P Raglan
CP F518
Krum
Marcus
UP/SP (WP)
CP F532 Winnemucca B,P
CP F533
CP F531
CP F530
CP F536
Wesco
Tule
Winnemucca
SP/AMTK
412.0
Rose Creek
427.3 (w)
Golconda
G&WE Smelter
Golconda
Preble
554.4
Preble
CPRR
CP F560
Red House
Iron Point
CP F568
Knight
452.0
CP F572 Valmy
CPRR
Ellison
Valmy
Humboldt River
SP/UP/AMTK (SP)
UP/SP/AMTK (WP)
Russell
585.8
Mote
469.9
CP F588
North Bottle Mountain
Battle Mountain
479.7
G&A
Adelaide
Humboldt River
Cosgrave
Mill City
387.2 (w)
Rye Patch Res'r
Imlay
380.2 (e)
Humboldt
Rye Patch
P
SP/AMTK
Valery
Oreana
Rochester (old)
switchbacks
Upper Rochester
355.8 (w)
NSL
Lower Rochester
Woolsey
Humboldt River
Colado
Kodak
346.7
NCRY
Lewis Jct
BM&L
Lewis
Dillon
switchbacks
Starr Grove Mine
Baileys
NCRY

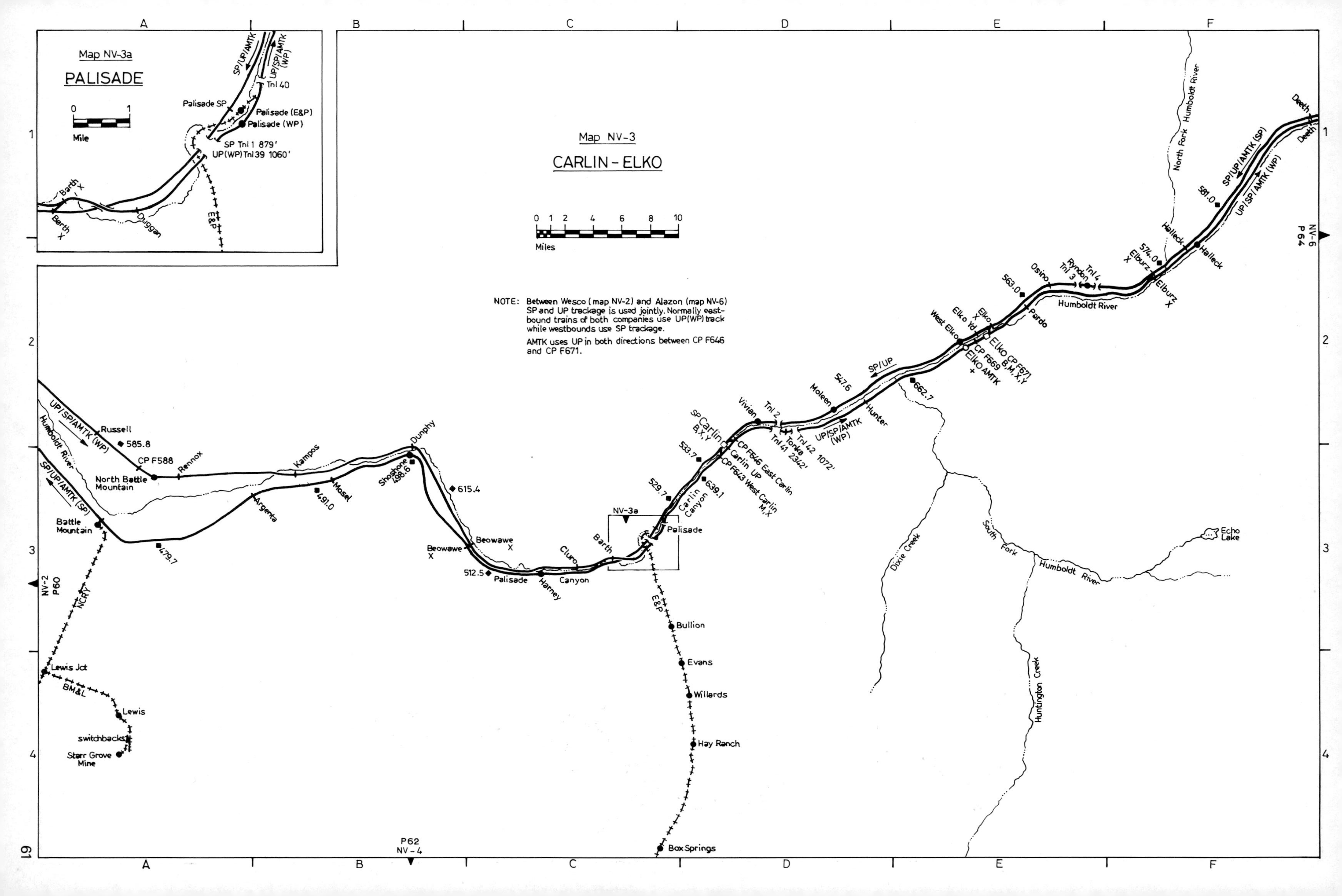

Map NV-3a
PALISADE
0
1
Mile
SP/UP/AMTK
UP/SP/AMTK (WP)
Tnl 40
Palisade SP
Palisade (E&P)
Palisade (WP)
SP Tnl 1 879'
UP(WP) Tnl 39 1060'
Barth X
Barth X
Duggan
E&P
Map NV-3
CARLIN - ELKO
0 1 2 4 6 8 10
Miles
NOTE: Between Wesco (map NV-2) and Alazon (map NV-6) SP and UP trackage is used jointly. Normally east-bound trains of both companies use UP(WP) track while westbounds use SP trackage.
AMTK uses UP in both directions between CP F646 and CP F671.
UP/SP/AMTK (WP)
Russell
585.8
CP F588
Rennox
North Battle Mountain
Humboldt River
SP/UP/AMTK (SP)
Battle Mountain
479.7
Argenta
491.0
Mosel
Kampos
Shoshone 498.6
Dunphy
615.4
Beowawe X
Beowawe X
512.5
Palisade
Harney
Canyon
Cluro
Barth
NV-3a
Palisade
529.7
Carlin Canyon
639.1
533.7
SP Carlin B,X,Y
CP F646 East Carlin
Carlin UP
CP F643 West Carlin M,X
Vivian
Tnl 2
Tnl 41 2342'
Tonka
Tnl 42 1072'
UP/SP/AMTK (WP)
Moleen
547.6
Hunter
SP/UP
662.7
West Elko
Elko Yd
Elko X
Elko CP F671 B,M,X,Y
CP F669
Elko AMTK +
563.0
Pardo
Osino
Tnl 3
Ryndon
Tnl 4
Humboldt River
Elburz X
Elburz X
574.0
Halleck
Halleck
581.0
SP/UP/AMTK (SP)
UP/SP/AMTK (WP)
Deeth
Deeth
North Fork Humboldt River
NV-6 P64
NV-2 P60
NCRY
Lewis Jct
BM&L
Lewis
switchbacks
Starr Grove Mine
P62 NV-4
E&P
Bullion
Evans
Willards
Hay Ranch
Box Springs
Dixie Creek
South Fork
Humboldt River
Huntington Creek
Echo Lake
A
B
C
D
E
F
1
2
3
4

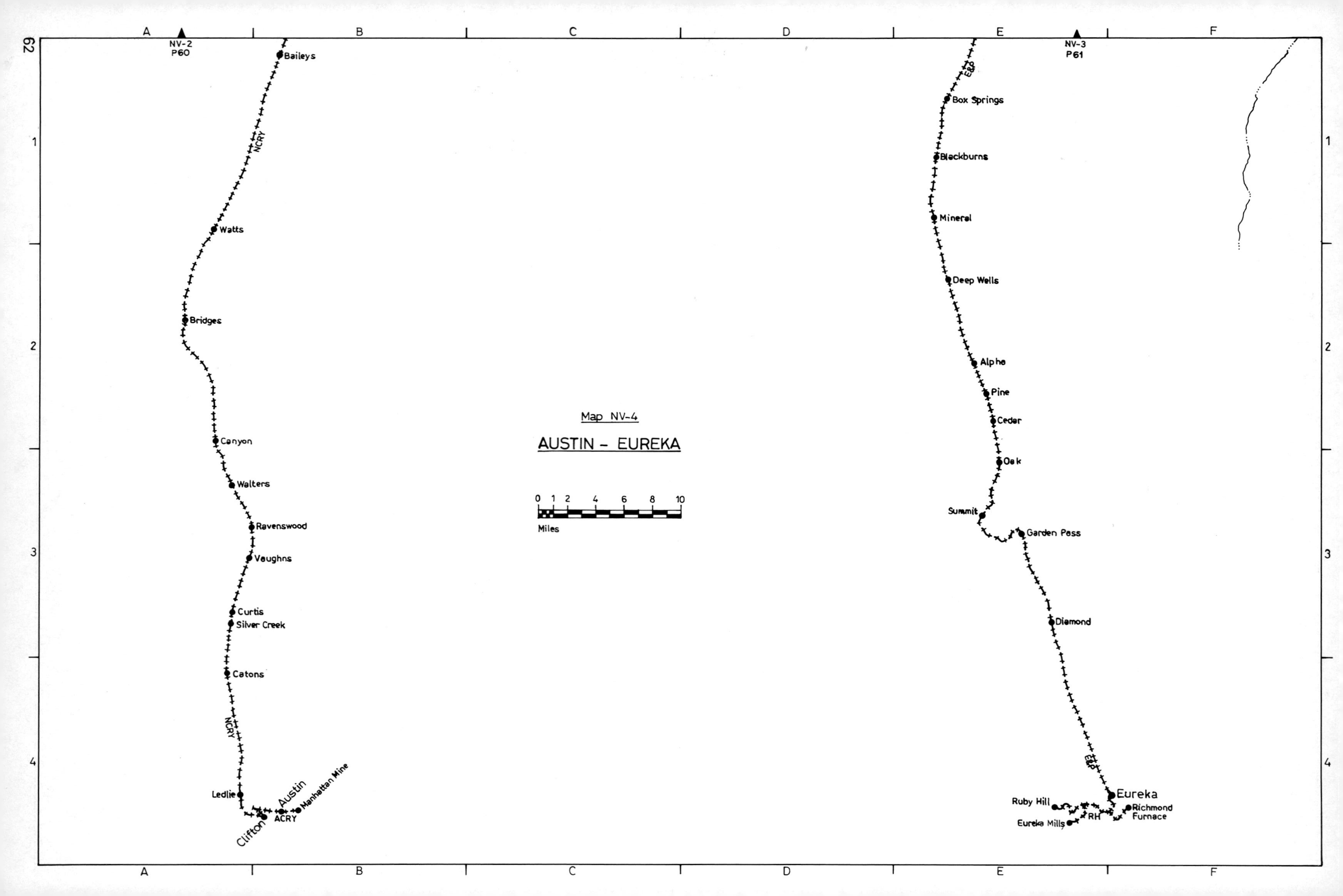
Map NV-4
AUSTIN - EUREKA
0 1 2 4 6 8 10
Miles
A
B
C
D
E
F
1
2
3
4
NV-2
P60
NV-3
P61
Baileys
NCRY
Watts
Bridges
Canyon
Walters
Ravenswood
Vaughns
Curtis
Silver Creek
Catons
Ledlie
Clifton
Austin
ACRY
Manhattan Mine
E&P
Box Springs
Blackburns
Mineral
Deep Wells
Alpha
Pine
Cedar
Oak
Summit
Garden Pass
Diamond
Eureka
Ruby Hill
Eureka Mills
RH
Richmond
Furnace

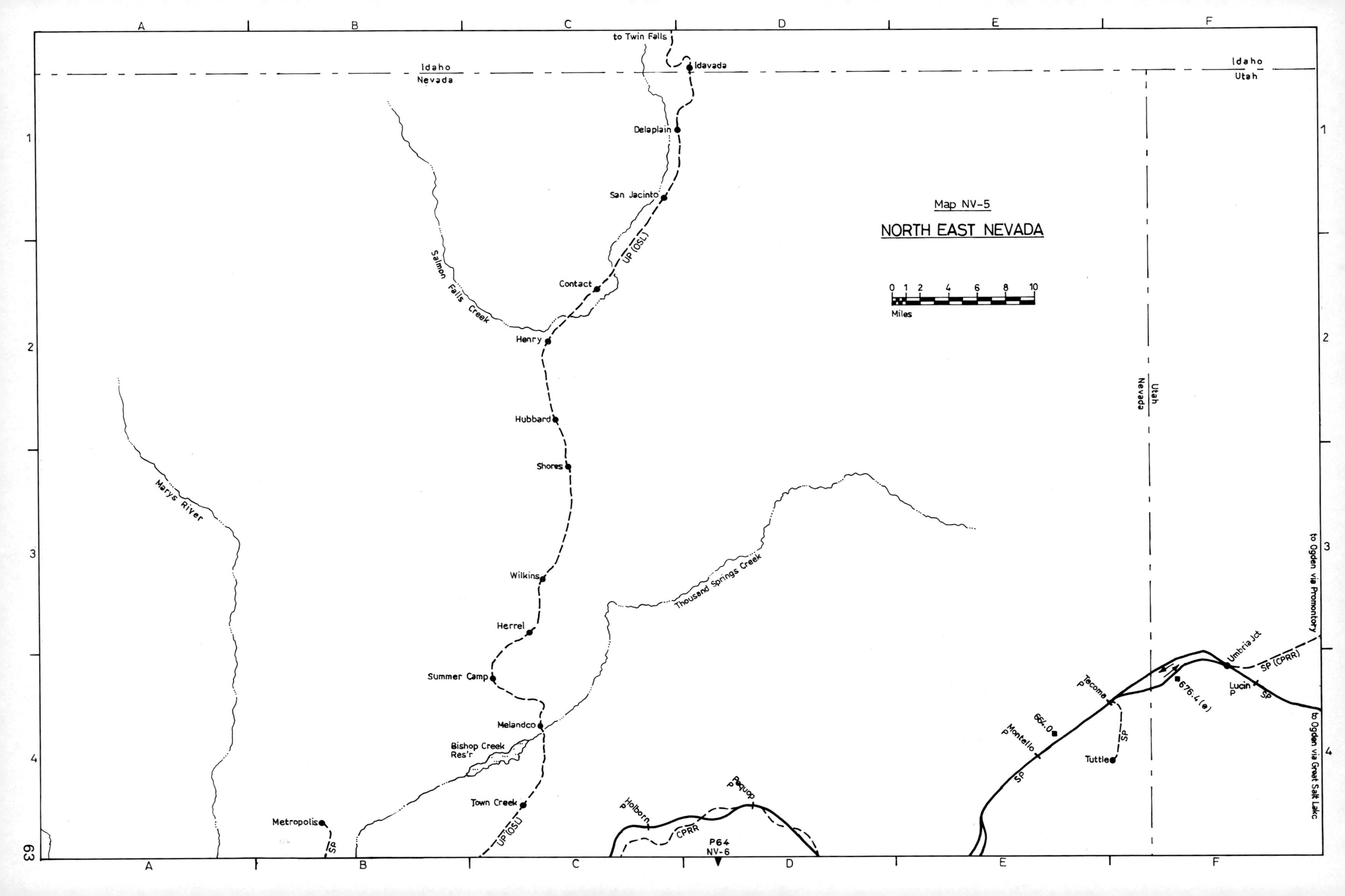
Map NV-5
NORTH EAST NEVADA
0 1 2 4 6 8 10
Miles
Idaho
Nevada
Idaho
Utah
Utah
Nevada
to Twin Falls
Idavada
Delaplain
San Jacinto
UP (OSL)
Contact
Salmon Falls Creek
Henry
Hubbard
Shores
Marys River
Wilkins
Herrel
Thousand Springs Creek
Summer Camp
Melandco
Bishop Creek
Res'r
Town Creek
UP (OSL)
Metropolis
SP
Holborn
CPRR
Pequop
P64
NV-6
Montello
SP
664.0
Tecoma
Tuttle
SP
676.4 (e)
Umbria Jct
SP (CPRR)
Lucin
SP
to Ogden via Promontory
to Ogden via Great Salt Lake
A
B
C
D
E
F
1
2
3
4

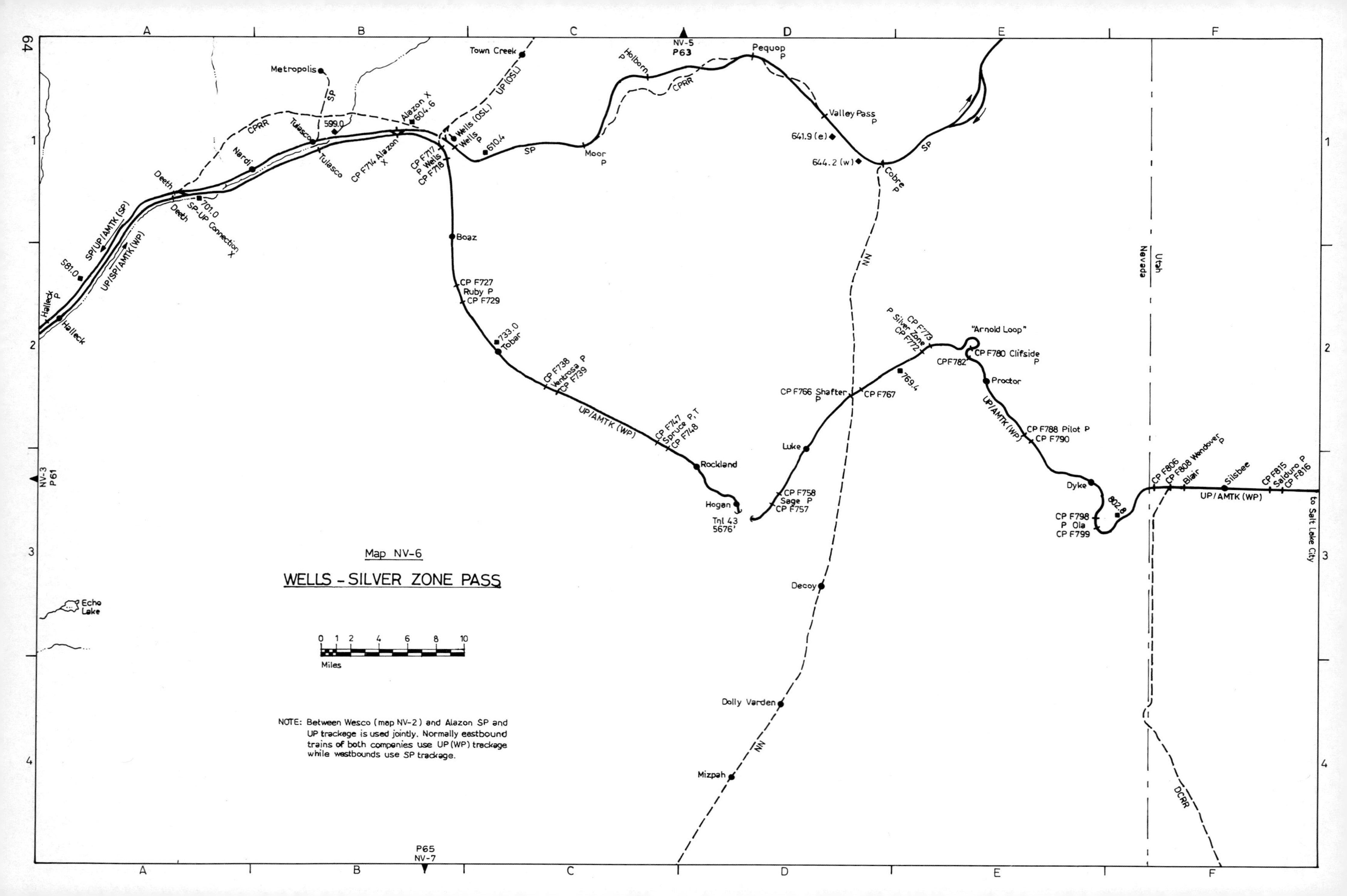

Map NV-6

WELLS - SILVER ZONE PASS

0 1 2 4 6 8 10
Miles

NOTE: Between Wesco (map NV-2) and Alazon SP and UP trackage is used jointly. Normally eastbound trains of both companies use UP (WP) trackage while westbounds use SP trackage.

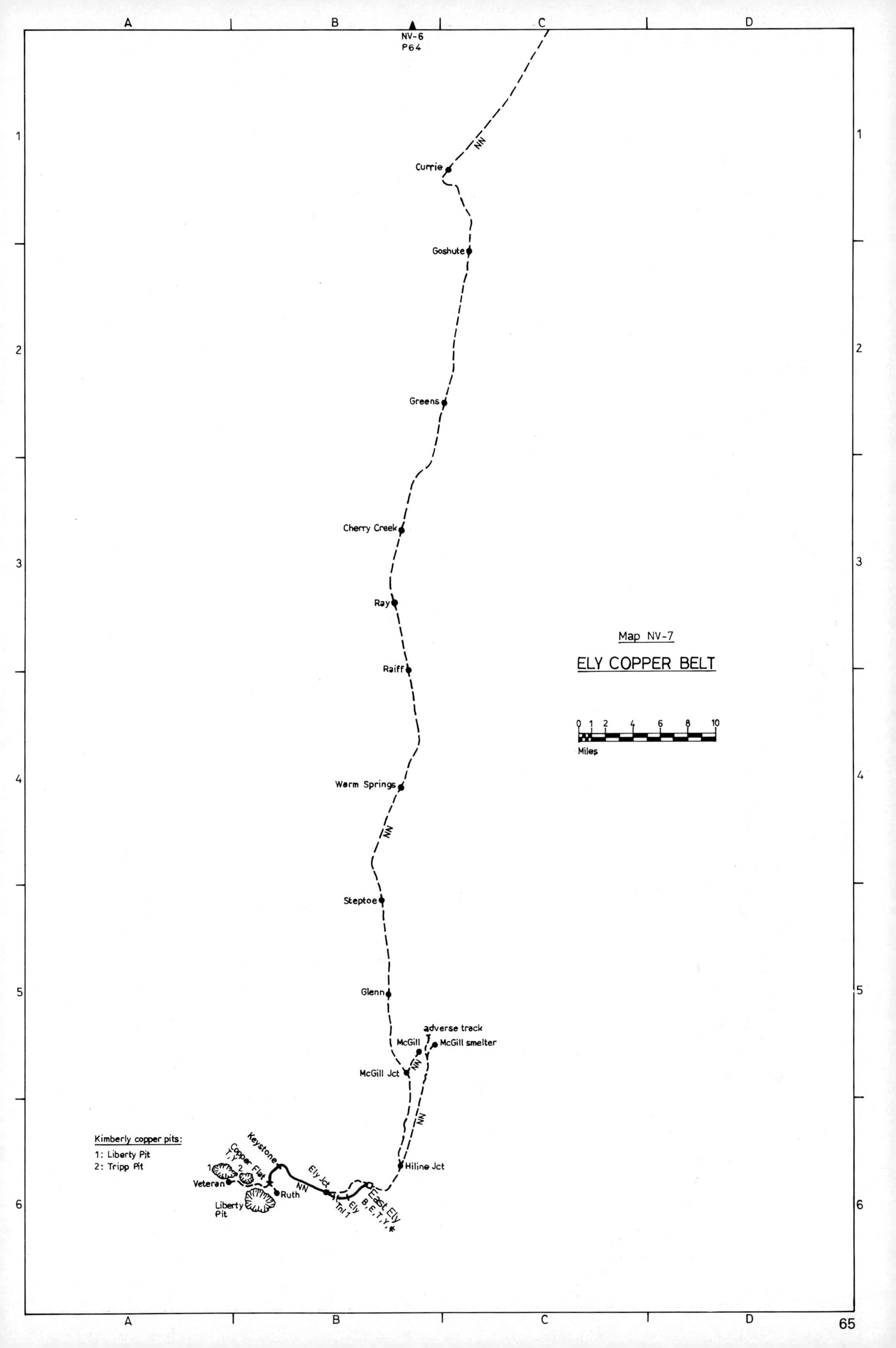

Map NV-7
ELY COPPER BELT
0 1 2 4 6 8 10
Miles
NV-6
P64
A
B
C
D
1
2
3
4
5
6
NN
Currie
Goshute
Greens
Cherry Creek
Ray
Raiff
Warm Springs
NN
Steptoe
Glenn
adverse track
McGill
McGill smelter
McGill Jct
NN
NN
Hiline Jct
Kimberly copper pits:
1: Liberty Pit
2: Tripp Pit
Keystone
Copper Flat
T,Y
1
2
Veteran
Liberty Pit
Ruth
NN
Ely Jct
Tnl 1
Ely
East Ely
B,E,T,Y,*

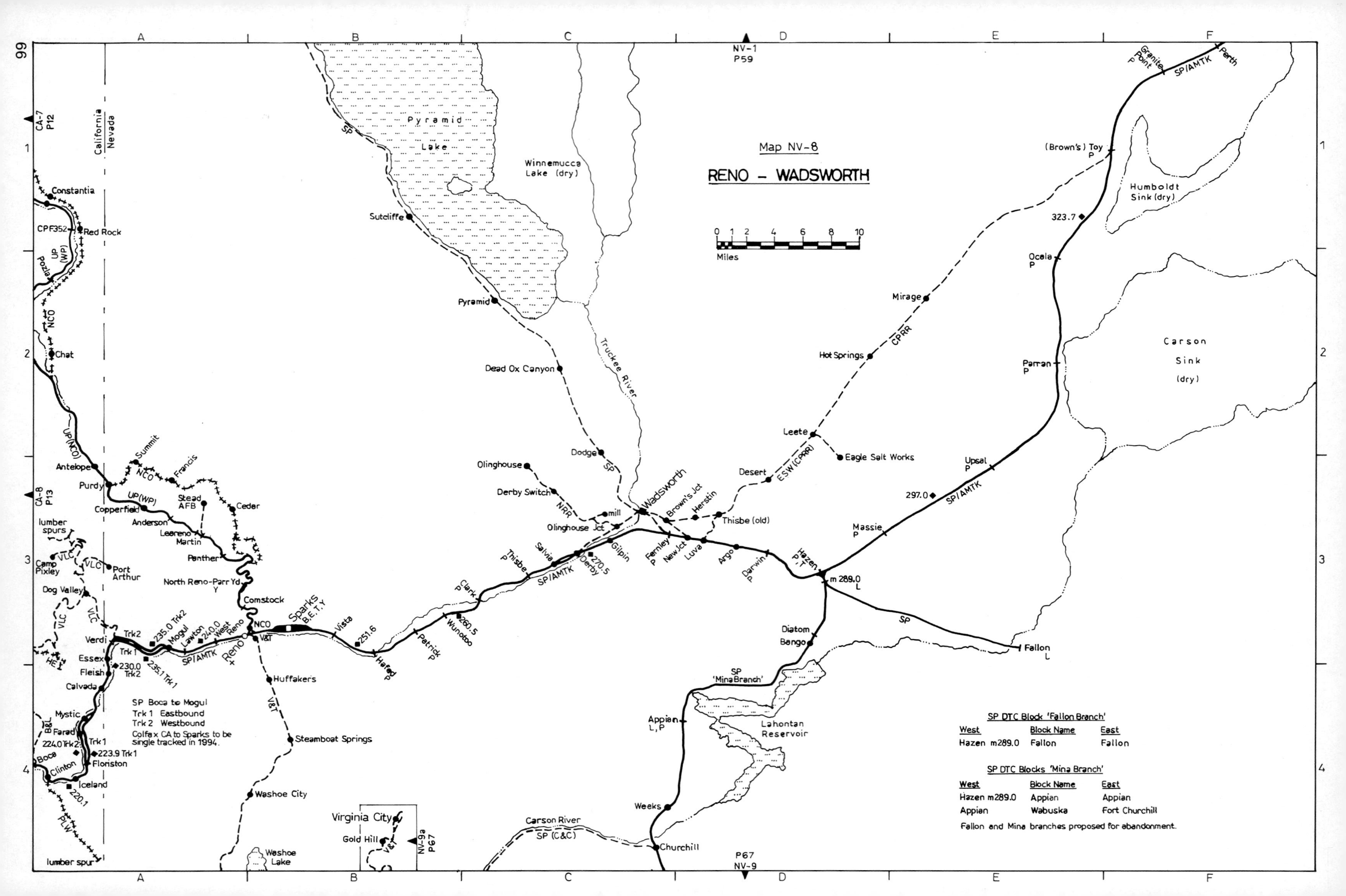

Map NV-8
RENO - WADSWORTH
0 1 2 4 6 8 10
Miles
NV-1
P59
P67
NV-9
CA-7
P12
CA-8
P13
NV-9a
P67
California
Nevada
Pyramid Lake
Winnemucca Lake (dry)
Humboldt Sink (dry)
Carson Sink (dry)
Lahontan Reservoir
Truckee River
Carson River
Washoe Lake
SP
SP/AMTK
CPRR
ESW (CPRR)
NRR
V&T
VLC
UP(NCO)
UP(WP)
NCO
PLW
HE
B&L
SP (C&C)
SP 'Mina Branch'
Perth
Granite Point P
(Brown's) Toy P
323.7
Ocala P
Parran P
Upsal P
297.0
Massie P
Hazen P,T
m 289.0 L
Fallon L
Diatom
Bango
Appian L,P
Weeks
Churchill
Mirage
Hot Springs
Leete
Eagle Salt Works
Desert
Thisbe (old)
Herstin
Brown's Jct
Wadsworth
Fernley P
New Jct
Luva
Argo
Darwin P
Gilpin
mill
Olinghouse Jct
Olinghouse
Derby Switch
Dodge
Dead Ox Canyon
Pyramid
Sutcliffe
270.5
Derby
Salvia
Thisbe P
Clark P
260.5
Wunotoo
Patrick P
Hafed P
251.6
Vista
Sparks B,E,T,Y
NCO
V&T
Comstock
Reno
West Reno
240.0
Lawton
Mogul
235.0 Trk2
235.1 Trk1
230.0 Trk2
Trk1
Trk2
Verdi
Essex
Fleish
Calvada
Mystic
Farad
224.0 Trk2
223.9 Trk1
Trk1
Floriston
Boca
Clinton
Iceland
220.1
lumber spur
lumber spurs
Camp Pixley
Dog Valley
Port Arthur
North Reno-Parr Yd Y
Panther
Leareno Martin
Anderson
Copperfield
Stead AFB
Cedar
Francis
Summit
Purdy
Antelope
Chat
Pozola
CPF352
Red Rock
Constantia
Huffakers
Steamboat Springs
Washoe City
Virginia City
Gold Hill
SP Boca to Mogul
Trk 1 Eastbound
Trk 2 Westbound
Colfax CA to Sparks to be single tracked in 1994.
SP DTC Block 'Fallon Branch'
West | Block Name | East
Hazen m289.0 | Fallon | Fallon
SP DTC Blocks 'Mina Branch'
West | Block Name | East
Hazen m289.0 | Appian | Appian
Appian | Wabuska | Fort Churchill
Fallon and Mina branches proposed for abandonment.

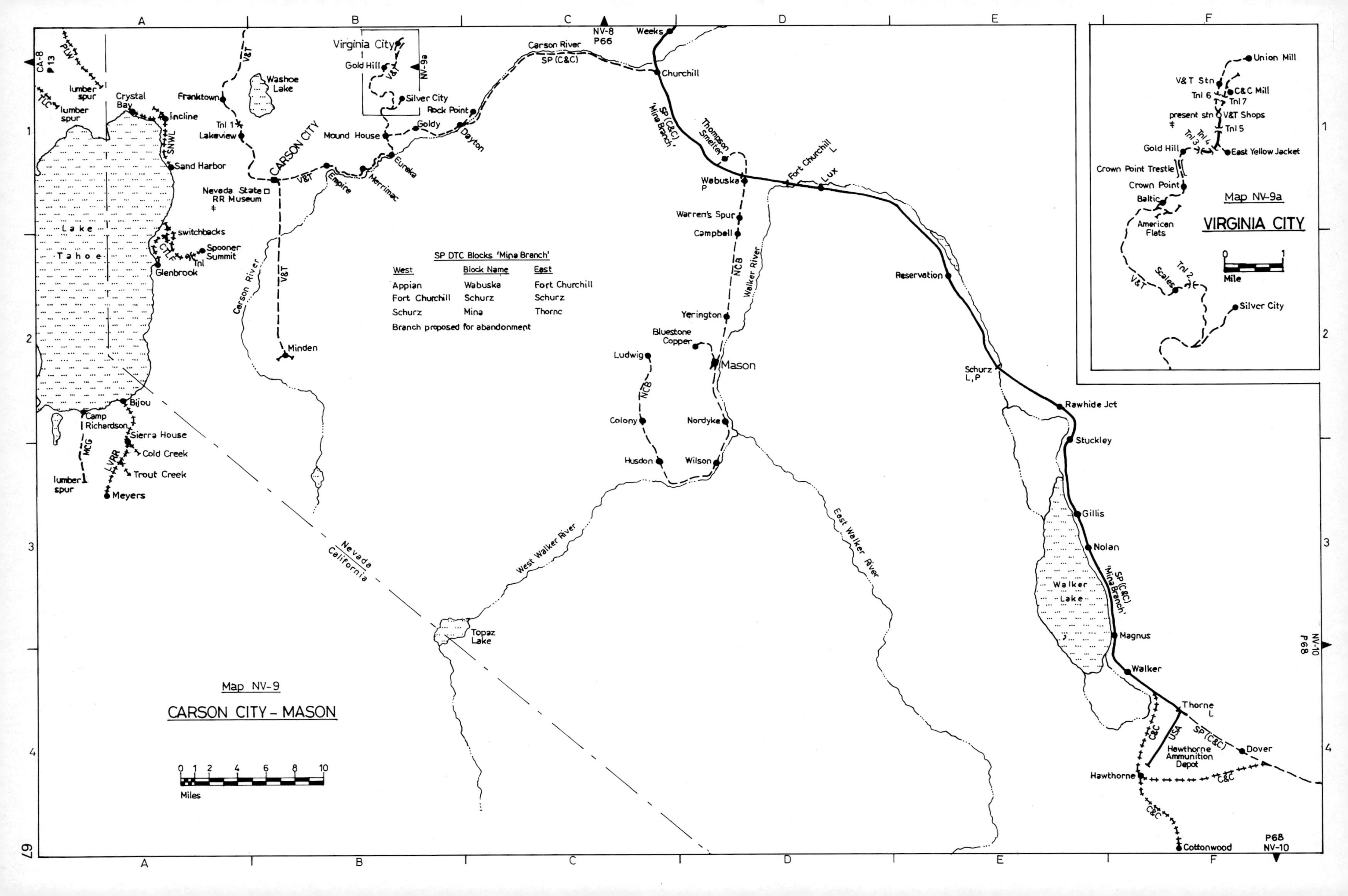

SP DTC Blocks 'Mina Branch'

West	Block Name	East
Appian	Wabuska	Fort Churchill
Fort Churchill	Schurz	Schurz
Schurz	Mina	Thorne

Branch proposed for abandonment

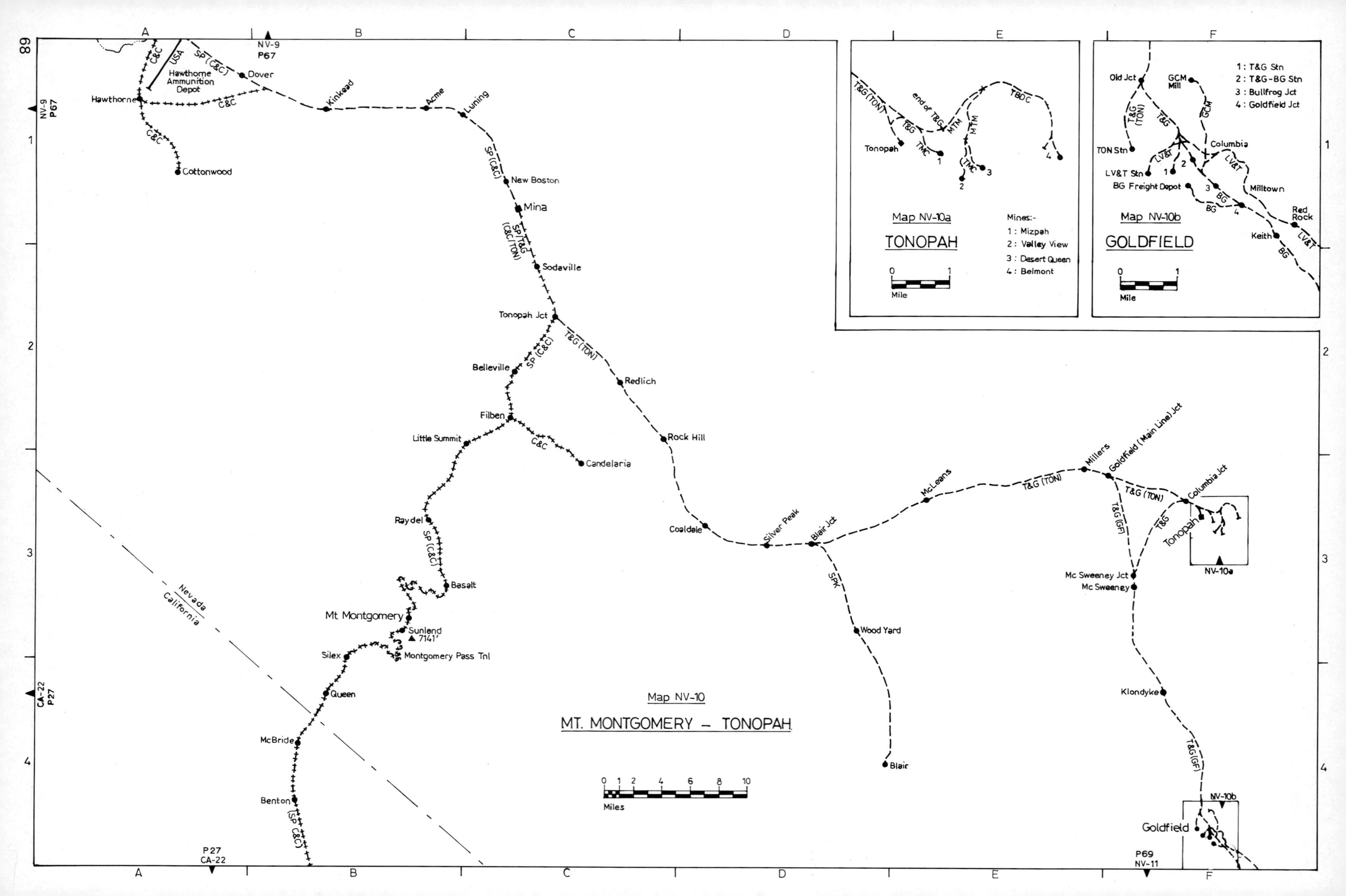

Map NV-10
MT. MONTGOMERY – TONOPAH
0 1 2 4 6 8 10
Miles
Hawthorne
Hawthorne Ammunition Depot
USA
C&C
SP (C&C)
Dover
NV-9
P67
Cottonwood
Kinkead
Acme
Luning
New Boston
Mina
SP/T&G (C&C/TON)
Sodaville
Tonopah Jct
T&G (TON)
Belleville
SP (C&C)
Filben
Little Summit
Candelaria
Redlich
Rock Hill
Raydel
Basalt
Mt Montgomery
Sunland
7141'
Montgomery Pass Tnl
Silex
Queen
McBride
Benton
(SP C&C)
Nevada
California
P27
CA-22
Coaldale
Silver Peak
Blair Jct
SPK
Wood Yard
Blair
McLeans
Millers
Goldfield (Main Line) Jct
Columbia Jct
T&G (GF)
T&G
Tonopah
NV-10a
Mc Sweeney Jct
Mc Sweeney
Klondyke
Goldfield
NV-10b
P69
NV-11
Map NV-10a
TONOPAH
0 1
Mile
Mines:-
1 : Mizpah
2 : Valley View
3 : Desert Queen
4 : Belmont
T&G (TON)
end of T&G
MTM
TMC
TBDC
Map NV-10b
GOLDFIELD
0 1
Mile
1 : T&G Stn
2 : T&G-BG Stn
3 : Bullfrog Jct
4 : Goldfield Jct
Old Jct
GCM Mill
GCM
TON Stn
LV&T Stn
BG Freight Depot
Columbia
LV&T
Milltown
BG
Red Rock
Keith

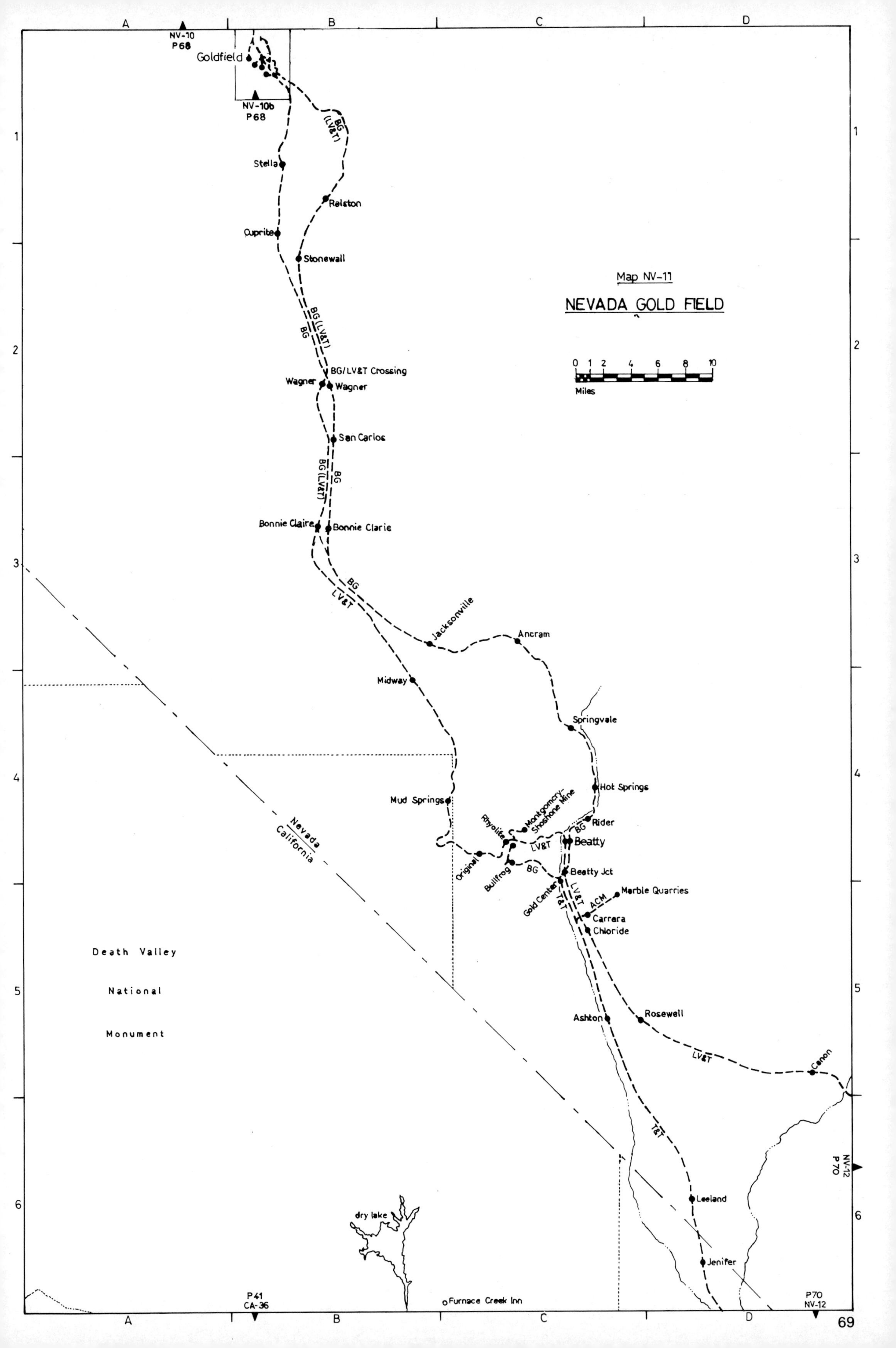
Map NV-11
NEVADA GOLD FIELD
0 1 2 4 6 8 10
Miles
Goldfield
NV-10
P68
NV-10b
P68
BG (LV&T)
Stella
Ralston
Cuprite
Stonewall
BG (LV&T)
BG
BG/LV&T Crossing
Wagner
Wagner
San Carlos
BG (LV&T)
BG
Bonnie Claire
Bonnie Clarie
BG
LV&T
Jacksonville
Ancram
Midway
Springvale
Hot Springs
Mud Springs
Rhyolite
Montgomery-Shoshone Mine
Rider
BG
LV&T
Beatty
Original
Bullfrog
BG
Beatty Jct
Gold Center
LV&T
T&T
ACM
Marble Quarries
Carrara
Chloride
Nevada
California
Death Valley
National
Monument
Ashton
Rosewell
LV&T
Canon
T&T
NV-12
P70
Leeland
dry lake
Jenifer
P41
CA-36
Furnace Creek Inn
P70
NV-12

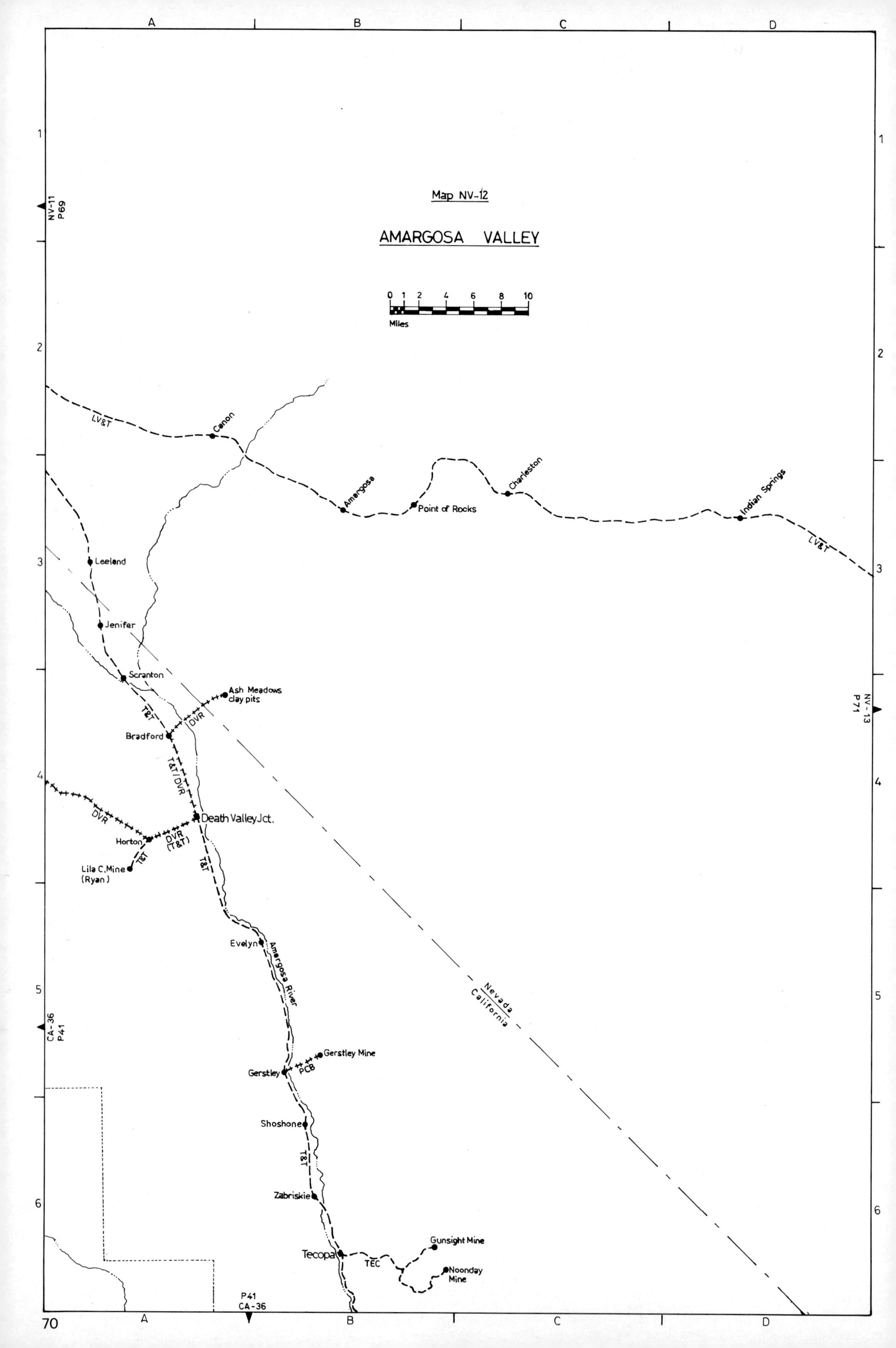
Map NV-12
AMARGOSA VALLEY
0 1 2 4 6 8 10
Miles
A
B
C
D
1
2
3
4
5
6
NV-11
P69
NV-13
P71
CA-36
P41
P41
CA-36
LV&T
Canon
Amargosa
Point of Rocks
Charleston
Indian Springs
LV&T
Leeland
Jenifer
Scranton
Ash Meadows
clay pits
DVR
T&T
Bradford
T&T/DVR
DVR
Death Valley Jct.
Horton
DVR
(T&T)
T&T
Lila C. Mine
(Ryan)
T&T
Evelyn
Amargosa River
Nevada
California
Gerstley Mine
Gerstley
PCB
Shoshone
T&T
Zabriskie
Gunsight Mine
Tecopa
TEC
Noonday
Mine

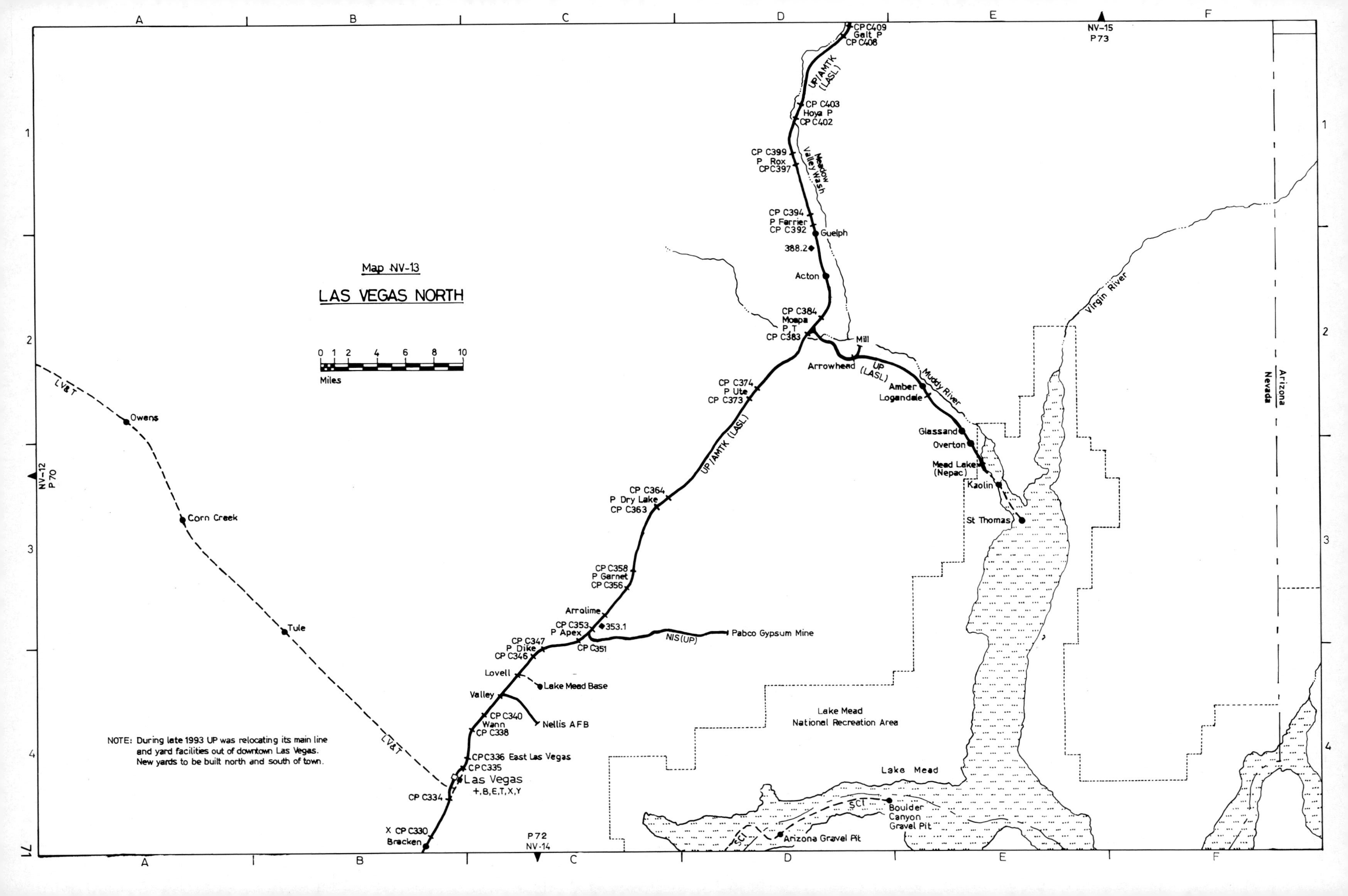
Map NV-13
LAS VEGAS NORTH
0 1 2 4 6 8 10
Miles
NV-15
P73
NV-12
P70
P72
NV-14
Arizona
Nevada
CP C409
Galt P
CP C408
UP/AMTK (LASL)
CP C403
Hoya P
CP C402
CP C399
P Rox
CP C397
Meadow Valley Wash
CP C394
P Farrier
CP C392
Guelph
388.2
Acton
CP C384
Moapa
P T
CP C383
Mill
Arrowhead
UP (LASL)
Muddy River
Amber
Logandale
Glassand
Overton
Mead Lake (Nepac)
Kaolin
St Thomas
Virgin River
CP C374
P Ute
CP C373
UP/AMTK (LASL)
CP C364
P Dry Lake
CP C363
CP C358
P Garnet
CP C356
Arrolime
CP C353
P Apex
353.1
CP C351
NIS (UP)
Pabco Gypsum Mine
CP C347
P Dike
CP C346
Lovell
Lake Mead Base
Valley
Nellis AFB
CP C340
Wann
CP C338
CP C336 East Las Vegas
CP C335
Las Vegas
+, B, E, T, X, Y
CP C334
X CP C330
Bracken
LV&T
Owens
Corn Creek
Tule
Lake Mead
National Recreation Area
Lake Mead
SCT
Boulder
Canyon
Gravel Pit
Arizona Gravel Pit
NOTE: During late 1993 UP was relocating its main line
and yard facilities out of downtown Las Vegas.
New yards to be built north and south of town.

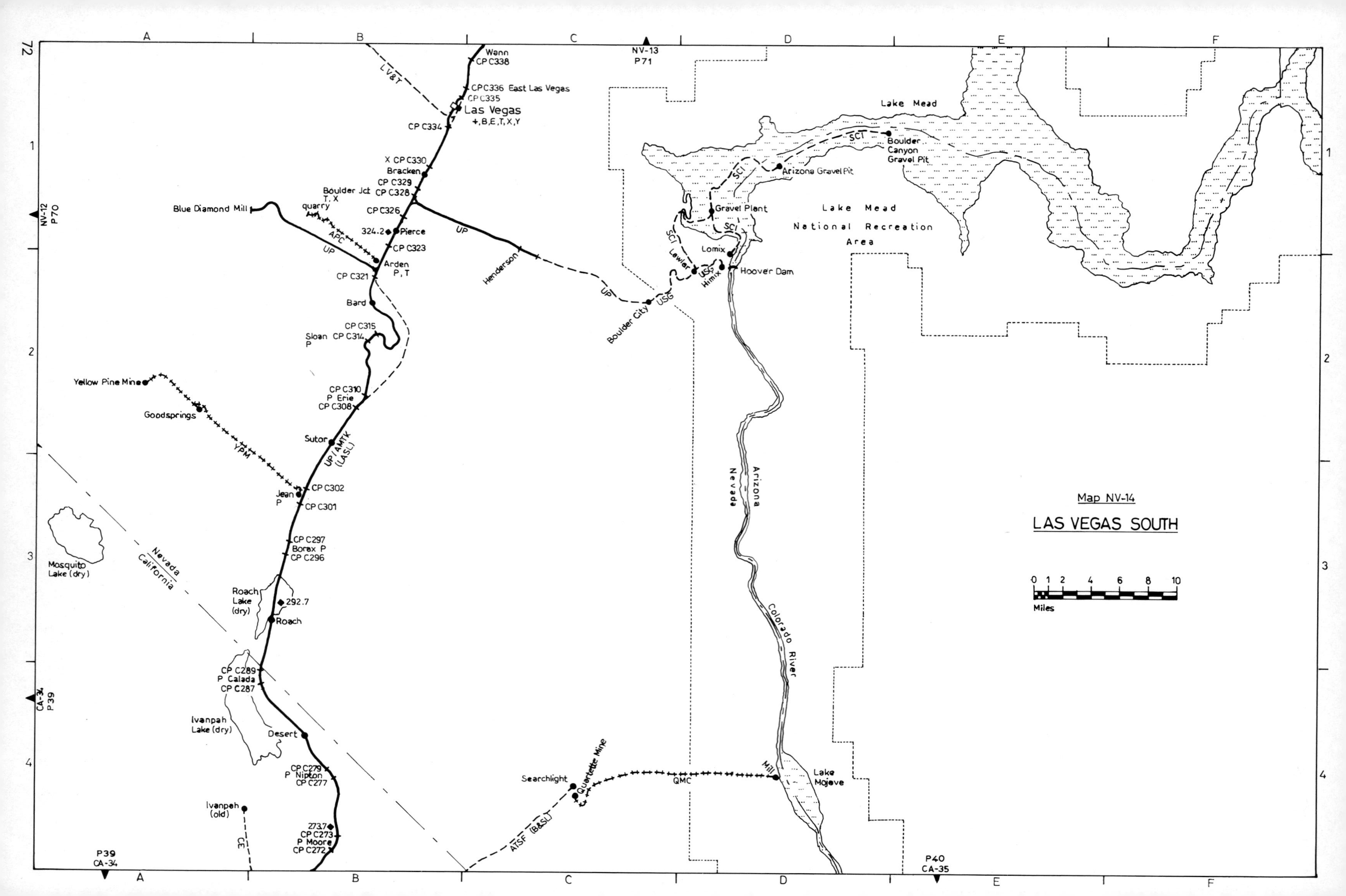
Map NV-14
LAS VEGAS SOUTH
0 1 2 4 6 8 10
Miles
Wann
CP C338
CP C336 East Las Vegas
CP C335
Las Vegas
+, B, E, T, X, Y
CP C334
LV&T
X CP C330
Bracken
CP C329
CP C328
Boulder Jct
T, X
quarry
Blue Diamond Mill
CP C326
324.2
Pierce
CP C323
APC
UP
Arden
P, T
CP C321
Bard
CP C315
Sloan CP C314
P
Henderson
Boulder City
USG
Lawler
Himix
Lomix
Hoover Dam
SCI
Gravel Plant
Arizona Gravel Pit
Boulder
Canyon
Gravel Pit
Lake Mead
Lake Mead
National Recreation
Area
Yellow Pine Mine
Goodsprings
YPM
CP C310
P Erie
CP C308
Sutor
UP/AMTK
(LASL)
Jean
P
CP C302
CP C301
CP C297
Borax P
CP C296
Mosquito
Lake (dry)
Nevada
California
Roach
Lake
(dry)
292.7
Roach
CP C289
P Calada
CP C287
Ivanpah
Lake (dry)
Desert
CP C279
P Nipton
CP C277
Ivanpah
(old)
CE
273.7
CP C273
P Moore
CP C272
Arizona
Nevada
Colorado River
Searchlight
Quartette Mine
QMC
Mill
Lake
Mojave
ATSF (B&SL)
NV-12
P70
NV-13
P71
CA-34
P39
P39
CA-34
P40
CA-35
A
B
C
D
E
F
1
2
3
4

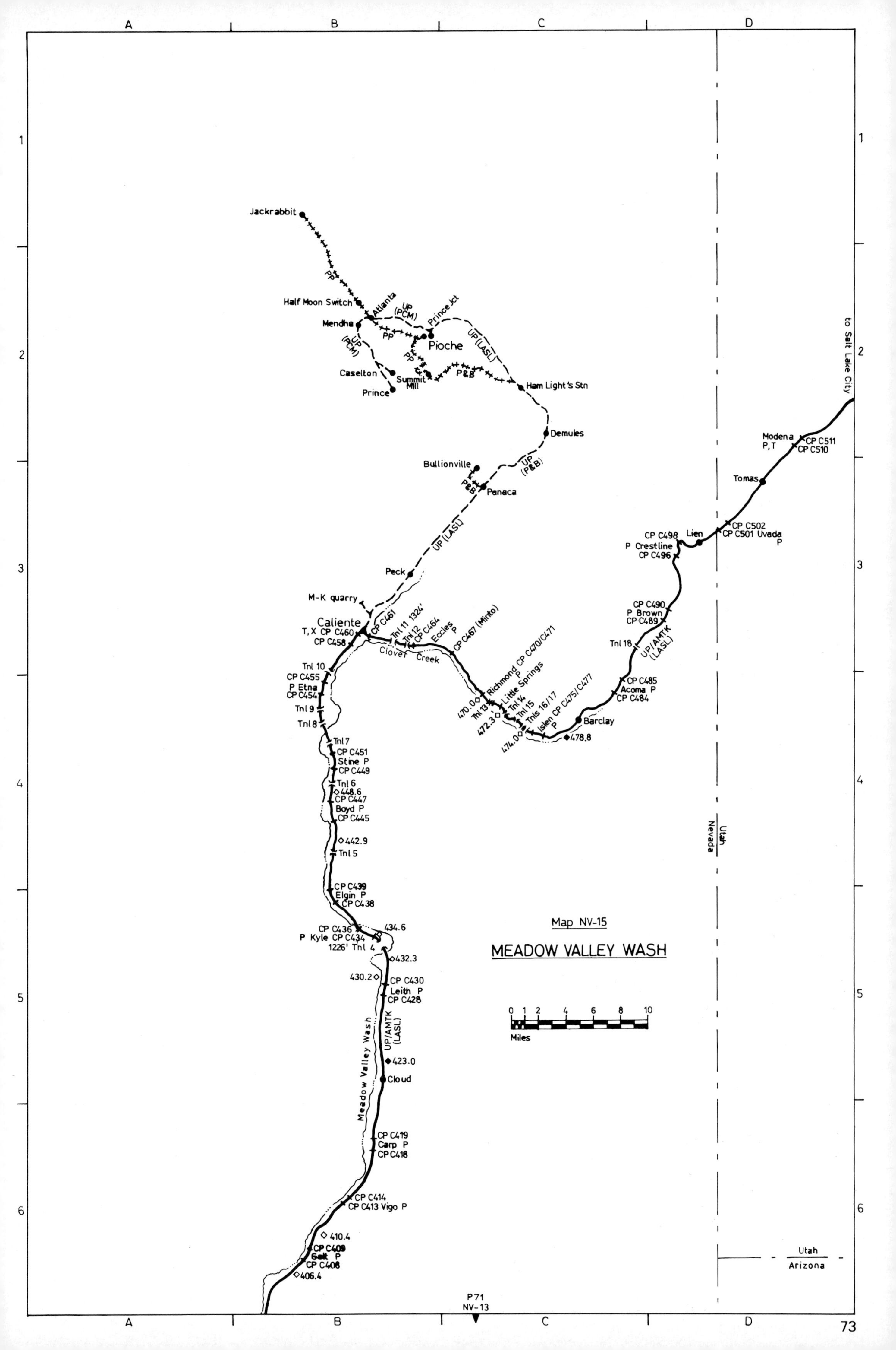
Map NV-15
MEADOW VALLEY WASH
Miles
Jackrabbit
Half Moon Switch
Atlanta
Mendha
Prince Jct
Pioche
Caselton
Summit Mill
Prince
Ham Light's Stn
Demules
Bullionville
Panaca
Peck
M-K quarry
Caliente
T, X CP C460
CP C458
CP C461
Tnl 11 1324'
Tnl 12
CP C464
Eccles P
CP C467 (Minto)
Clover Creek
Richmond CP C470/C471 P
Little Springs
Tnl 13
Tnl 14
Tnl 15
Tnls 16/17
Islen CP C475/C477 P
470.0
472.3
474.0
478.8
Barclay
CP C485
Acoma P
CP C484
Tnl 18
UP/AMTK (LASL)
CP C490
P Brown
CP C489
CP C498
P Crestline
CP C496
Lien
CP C502
CP C501 Uvada P
Tomas
Modena P, T
CP C511
CP C510
to Salt Lake City
Utah
Nevada
Arizona
Tnl 10
CP C455
P Etna
CP C454
Tnl 9
Tnl 8
Tnl 7
CP C451
Stine P
CP C449
Tnl 6
448.6
CP C447
Boyd P
CP C445
442.9
Tnl 5
CP C439
Elgin P
CP C438
CP C436
P Kyle CP C434
1226' Tnl 4
434.6
432.3
430.2
CP C430
Leith P
CP C428
Meadow Valley Wash
423.0
Cloud
CP C419
Carp P
CP C418
CP C414
CP C413 Vigo P
410.4
CP C409
Galt P
CP C408
406.4
P71
NV-13
UP (PCM)
PP
UP (LASL)
P&B
UP (P&B)

APPENDIX

Railroad Reporting & Identification Marks

Wherever possible the marks used in this Atlas to identify railroads are based on the system of Reporting Marks issued by the Association of American Railroads (AAR), exceptions are for long deceased companies or industrial, lumber and tourist operators not covered by the AAR system.

MARK	COMPANY TITLE	REMARKS
ABL	Alameda Belt Line	*ATSF-UP joint subsidiary*
ABX	American Borax Co.	*3' gauge*
ACM	American Carrara Marble Co.	
ACRY	Austin City Railway	*3' gauge*
AL	Almanor Railroad	
AMC	Amador Central Railroad	
AMR	Arcata & Mad River Railroad	
AMTK	National Railroad Passenger Corp. - "Amtrak"	
ARZC	Arizona & California Railroad	
ATSF	Atchison Topeka & Santa Fe Railway	
B&B	Bodie & Benton Railroad & Commercial Co.	*3' gauge*
B&D	Borate & Daggett Railroad	*3' gauge*
B&L	Boca & Loyalton Railroad	*later WP*
B&SL	Barnwell & Searchlight Railroad	*later ATSF*
BART	Bay Area Rapid Transit	*5'6" gauge 750V dc 3rd rail*
BER	Bucksport & Eel River Railway	
BG	Bullfrog Goldfield Railroad	
BHL	Bear Harbor Lumber Railroad	
BLLC	Big Lakes Lumber Co.	
BM&L	Battle Mountain & Lewis Railway	*3' gauge*
BN	Burlington Northern Inc.	
C&C	Carson & Colorado Railroad	*3' gauge, later N&C*
C&L	Colusa & Lake Railway	*3' gauge*
C&N	California & Nevada Railroad	*3' gauge*
CCFR	California Coal Fields Railroad	
CCMT	Crescent City Mill & Transportation Co. RR	
CCRR	California Central Railroad	*5' gauge later SP*
CCT	Central California Traction	*ATSF-SP-UP joint*
CDTX	Joint Powers Board - "CalTrain"	*formerly California DoT*
CE	California Eastern Railway	*later ATSF*
CFNR	California Northern Railroad	*ARZC affiliate*
CPLT	Camino Placerville & Lake Tahoe Railroad	
CPRR	Central Pacific Railroad	*later SP*
CSE	California Shasta & Eastern Railroad	
CSFE	Casper South Fork & Eastern Railroad	
CSRM	California State Railroad Museum	
CTLF	Carson Tahoe Lumber & Fuming Co.	*3' gauge*
CVL	Clover Valley Lumber Co.	
CWP	Crown Willamette Paper Co.	
CWR	California Western Railroad	
D&C	Diamond & Calder Railroad	*3' gauge*
DBT	Delta Bulk Terminal	
DCRR	Deep Creek Railroad	
DNSR	Del Norte Southern Railroad	
DVR	Death Valley Railroad	*3' gauge*
DVR*	Death Valley Railroad ("Baby Gauge" division)	*2' gauge*
E&F	Eureka & Freshwater Railway	
E&P	Eureka & Palisade Railroad	*3' gauge later E-N*
E-N	Eureka-Nevada Railway	*3' gauge*
EJD	E J Dodge Lumber Co.	
EMRR	Eagle Mountain Railroad (Kaiser Steel)	
ERC	Elk Redwood Company Railroad	*3' gauge*
ESW	Eagle Salt Works Railroad	
EUKA	Eureka Southern Railroad	*formerly NWP, later NCRR*
FBSE	Fort Bragg & Southeastern Railroad	
FCCR	Fresno Copper Company Railroad	
FI	Fresno Interurban Railroad	*later ATSF*
FNM	Ferrocarriles Nacionales de Mexico /National Railways of Mexico	
FRR	Feather River Railroad	
G&A	Golconda & Adelaide Railroad	*3' gauge*
G&M	Glendale & Montrose Railway	*later UP*
GATX	General American Tankcar Corp.	
GF	Goldfield Railroad	*later T&G*
GN	Great Northern Railway	*later BN*
GSPC	Golden State Portland Cement Co.	
GWR	Great Western Railway (N-C-O Division)	
HBL	Harbor Belt Line Railroad	*ATSF-SP-UP joint*
HE	Hobart Estates Railroad	*3' gauge formerly SNWL*
HH	Hetch-Hetchy Railroad	
HI	Holton Interurban Railway	*later SP*
HN	Humbolt Northern Railway	*later NWP*
HR	Humbolt Redwood Co.	
HRL	Hammond Redwood Lumber Co.	
HS	Hobart Southern Railroad	
ICAL	Inter-California Railroad	*SP subsidiary*
IM	Iron Mountain Railway	*3' gauge*
ITS	International Transportation Services	
IV	Indian Valley Railroad	
KLSR	Kings Lake Shore Railroad	
L&S	Ludlow & Southern Railway	
LAJ	Los Angeles Junction Railway	*ATSF subsidiary*
LASL	Los Angeles & Salt Lake Railroad	*later UP*
LAUPT	Los Angeles Union Passenger Terminal	*ATSF-SP-UP subsidiary later AMTK*
LBL	Long-Bell Lumber Co.	
LLB	Lassen Lumber & Box Company Railroad	
LSC	Leslie Salt Company	
LTRT	Lake Tahoe Railway & Transportation Co.	*3' gauge, later SP*
LV&T	Las Vegas & Tonopah Railroad	
LVRR	Lake Valley Railroad	*3' gauge*
M&M	Mohave & Milltown Railway	*3' gauge*
M&W	Minarettes & Western Railway	
MCL	Michigan-California Lumber Co.	*3' gauge*
MCR	McCloud Railway	
MET	Modesto & Empire Traction Co.	
MN	Mojave Northern Railroad	
MPCC	Monolith Portland Cement Co.	*3' gauge*
MSCX	Metropolitan Stevedore Corp.	
MSP	Madera Sugar Pine Railroad	
MSV	Monteray & Salinas Valley Railroad	*3' gauge*
MTDB	Metropolitan Transit Development Board - "San Diego Trolley"	*750V dc overhead*

MARK	COMPANY TITLE	REMARKS
MTM	Montana-Tonopah Mining Co.	
MTMW	Mt Tampalias & Muir Woods Railway	
N&C	Nevada & California Railway	*3' gauge, later SP*
NCB	Nevada Copper Belt Railroad	
NCNG	Nevada County Narrow Gauge Railroad	*3' gauge*
NCO	Nevada-California-Oregon Railroad	*3' gauge, later SP*
NCRR	North Coast Railroad	
NCRY	Nevada Central Railway	*3' gauge*
NIS	Nevada Industrial Switch	
NLC	Navarro Lumber Co.	
NN	Nevada Northern Railway	
NPC	North Pacific Coast Railroad	*3' gauge, later NWP*
NRC	National Redwood Company Railroad	
NRR	Nevada Railroad	
NSL	Nevada Short Line Railway	*3' gauge*
NVRR	Napa Valley Railroad - "Napa Valley Wine Train"	
NVS	Nevada Southern Railway	*later CE*
NWP	Northwestern Pacific Railroad	*SP subsidiary, later EUKA & CFNR*
OCE	Oregon California & Eastern Railway	
OSL	Oregon Short Line	*UP subsidiary*
OSR	Ocean Shore Railroad	
OTR	Oakland Terminal Railway	*ATSF-UP joint*
P&B	Pioche & Bullionville Railroad	*3' gauge*
P&W	Patterson & Western Railroad	*3' gauge*
PCB	Pacific Coast Borax Co.	*3' gauge*
PCM	Prince Consolidated Mining Co.	
PCR	Pacific Coast Railway	*3' gauge*
PE	Pacific Electric Railway	*SP subsidiary*
PLA	Pacific Locomotive Assoc. - "Niles Canyon Rly"	
PLC	Pickering Lumber Co.	
PLW	Pacific Lumber & Wood Co.	
PLX	Pacific Lumber Co.	
PP	Pioche Pacific Transportation Co.	*3' gauge*
PPC	Pacific Portland Cement Co.	*later USGX*
PSR	Petaluma & Santa Rosa Railroad	*SP subsidiary*
PRT	Parr Terminal	
PVC	Pajaro Valley Consolidated Railroad	*3' gauge*
QMC	Quartette Mining Co.	*3' gauge*
QRR	Quincy Railroad	
RAND	Randsburg Railway	*later ATSF*
RBR	Richmond Belt Railroad	*ATSF-SP joint*
RC&BT	Roaring Camp & Big Trees Narrow Gauge Railroad	*3' gauge*
RH	Ruby Hill Railroad	*3' gauge*
RL	Redwood Lumber Co.	
RRRR	Red Rock Railroad	
SBC	Ferrocarril Sonora-Baja California /Sonora-Baja California Railway	
SC	Santa Cruz Railroad	*3' gauge*
SCAX	Southern California Regional Rail Authority -"Metrolink"	
SCBG	Santa Cruz Big Trees & Pacific Railway	
SCI	Six Companies Inc.	
SCLC	Santa Cruz Lumber Co.	
SCRTD	Southern California Rapid Transit District	*750V dc overhead*
SDAE	San Diego & Arizona Eastern Railway	*SP subsidiary later SDIV*
SDIV	San Diego & Imperial Valley Railroad	
SDNR	San Diego Northern Railroad	*non-operational*
SERA	Sierra Railroad	*common carrier*
SERY	Sierra Railway	*tourist operation*
SFBR	San Francisco Belt Railroad	

MARK	COMPANY TITLE	REMARKS
SFOSJ	San Francisco Oakland & San Jose Railway -"Key System"	
SGL	Sanger Lumber Co.	
SJE	San Joaquin & Eastern Railroad	
SJSN	San Joaquin & Sierra Nevada Railroad	*3' gauge later SP*
SL	Shaver Lake Railroad	
SMV	Santa Maria Valley Railroad	
SN	Sacramento Northern Railway	*WP subsidiary later UP*
SNWL	Sierra Nevada Wood & Lumber Co.	*3' gauge*
SP	Southern Pacific Transportation Co.	
SPBR	Stockton Public Belt Railroad	*ATSF-SP-UP operated*
SPC	South Pacific Coast Railroad	*3' gauge later SP*
SPL	Sugar Pine Lumber	
SRT	Sacramento Regional Transit - "RT Metro"	*750V dc overhead*
SSR	Sacramento Southern Railroad	*CSRM tourist operation*
STE	Stockton Terminal & Eastern Railroad	
SUN	Sunset Railway	*ATSF-SP joint*
SV	Sonoma Valley Railroad	*3' gauge later NWP*
SVL	San Vincent Lumber Co.	
SVM	Sierra Valley & Mohawk Railroad	*3' gauge*
SYPB	Sacramento-Yolo Port District Belt Railroad	*SP-UP operated*
SWPC	Southwestern Portland Cement Co.	
T&G	Tonopah & Goldfield Railroad	
T&T	Tonopah & Tidewater Railroad	
TBDC	Tonopah Belmont Development Corp.	
TEC	Tecopa Railroad	
TLC	Truckee Lumber Co.	
TMC	Tonopah Mining Co.	
TON	Tonopah Railroad	*3' gauge later T&G*
TRC	Trona Railway	
TS	Tidewater Southern Railway	*WP subsidiary later UP*
TTRY	Tijuana & Tecate Railway	*SP subsidiary later SDIV*
TVRR	Tulare Valley Railroad	*SJVR affiliate*
TW	Turlock Western Railroad	
UP	Union Pacific Railroad	
USA	United States Army	
USAF	United States Air Force	
USCG	United States Coast Guard	
USG	United States Government	
USGX	United States Gypsum Corp.	*3' and standard gauge*
USMC	United States Marine Corps.	
USN	United States Navy	
USSX	United States Steel Corp.	
V&T	Virginia & Truckee Railroad	
VCY	Ventura County Railroad	
VE	Visalia Electric Railroad	*SP subsidiary*
VLC	Verdi Lumber Co.	
WMC	Waterloo Mining Co.	*3' gauge*
WSL	West Side Lumber Co.	*3' gauge*
WP	Western Pacific Railroad	*later UP*
YLCO	Yosemite Lumber Co.	
YMSP	Yosemite Mountain-Sugar Pine Railroad	*3' gauge*
YPM	Yellow Pine Mining Co.	*3' gauge*
YSLR	Yolo Short Line Railroad	
YSPL	Yosemite Sugar Pine Lumber Co.	
YV	Yosemite Valley Railway	
YW	Yreka Western Railroad	

INDEX

Each page of this volume is divided into a 6 x 4 grid of squares lettered from West to East and numbered from North to South. This index places all locations into one of these squares.

The entry for each location comprises Place name, State Code and map reference. The map reference for any location in the index is made up of a combination of a page number and grid square (e.g. 29B4 places a location on page 29, column 2, row 4).

All names shown on the maps appear in the index with the following exceptions; milepost locations (MP), numbered control points (CP), numbered tunnels and workshops and engine facilities where they are located adjacent to the town/city/station/yard of the same name.

In crowded urban areas some locations sharing the same name are differentiated by the initials of either the current or former owner.

Entries whose names begin with a number will be found at the beginning of the index. In the case of names such as St Andrews, these will be found under 'St' rather than the full spelling of 'Saint'.

Conventional two letter codes are used to identify the various States and Canadian Provinces with 'MX' indicating Mexico.

Richard J Cossey - Worthing

Graham J S Pike - Horsham

Name	State	Page	Grid
Bakersfield	CA	36	A2
Bakersfield Corrals	CA	36	A2
Balboa	CA	43	A5
Balboa Avenue	CA	50	A1
Balboa Park	CA	21	A3
Balch	CA	39	A4
Baldwin Avenue	CA	51	D3
Baldwin Park	CA	43	A2
Baldwin Park	CA	52	B4
Ballico	CA	25	D4
Ballou	CA	53	C4
Baltic	NV	67	F1
Baltimore Park	CA	20	B3
Bandini	CA	51	C5
Bango	NV	66	D3
Banning	CA	44	B3
Bannock	CA	40	B4
Banta	CA	25	A3
Barber	CA	11	E1
Barclay	NV	73	C4
Bard	NV	72	B2
Barlow	CA	15	D6
Barlow	CA	16	A3
Barnwell	CA	39	D3
Baroda	CA	34	C5
Barranca	CA	52	C3
Barrett	CA	26	A3
Barrio Logan	CA	49	B3
Barstow	CA	37	D4
Barstow	CA	38	A4
Barth	NV	61	A1
Barth	NV	61	C3
Bartle	CA	7	E1
Bartlett	CA	31	D3
Bartolo	CA	43	A3
Bartolo	CA	51	D5
Bartonette	CA	32	B5
Basalt	NV	68	B3
Bascule Bridge [Stockton]	CA	24	B2
Basin	CA	38	D4
Bass	CA	43	D1
Bass	CA	44	A1
Bassett	CA	43	A3
Bassett	CA	52	A4
Basta	CA	55	D2
Basta	CA	56	A2
Bastanchury	CA	56	A2
Bataques	MX	48	D4
Batavia	CA	16	E3
Battle Mountain	NV	60	F3
Battle Mountain	NV	61	A3
Battles	CA	34	C4
Baumberg	CA	23	A1
Baxter	CA	13	C3
Bay Bridge	CA	21	B1
Bay Fair	CA	21	F3
Bay Meadows	CA	22	B2
Bay Street	CA	21	A1
Bayley	CA	9	D1
Bayshore	CA	21	B3
Bayshore Yard	CA	21	A3
Bayside	CA	14	B1
Bayside Junction	CA	14	B1
Beale Air Force Base	CA	13	A3
Bealville	CA	36	A5
Bealville	CA	36	B3
Bear Creek	CA	17	B4
Bear Creek	CA	25	B1
Bear Harbor	CA	14	B5
Bear Valley	CA	13	E1
Beard Industrial District	CA	25	C3
Beardsley	CA	17	F4
Beardsley	CA	26	B1
Beatrice	CA	14	A2
Beatrice	CA	16	F2
Beatrice	CA	24	A1
Beatty	NV	69	C4
Beatty Junction	NV	69	C4
Beaumont	CA	44	A3
Beckwourth	CA	12	E4
Beer Flat	CA	7	F2
Belden	CA	12	B3
Bell	CA	42	F3
Bell	CA	51	A5
Bell Mountain	CA	37	D6
Bell Springs	CA	14	D5
Bella Vista	CA	7	D4
Belle Haven	CA	22	D3
Belleview	OR	6	C1
Belleview	CA	26	C6
Belleville	NV	68	C2
Bellevue	CA	16	B3
Bellevue	CA	25	D4
Bellevue	CA	26	A4
Bellflower	CA	55	B2
Bellota	CA	17	C4
Bellota	CA	25	C1
Belmont	CA	22	C3
Belmont	NV	68	E1
Belmont Avenue	CA	30	B2
Belmont Pier	CA	55	A4
Beltaine	CA	16	B3
Ben Lomond	CA	18	B6
Bena	CA	36	B2
Benali	CA	24	C1
Bench	CA	43	C2
Bench	CA	57	D2
Benicia	CA	16	D4
Benicia	CA	18	B1
Benicia	CA	19	B2
Benicia Junction	CA	16	D4
Benicia Junction	CA	19	B2
Benito	CA	29	B1
Benkert	CA	50	C4
Benton	CA	27	D2
Benton	CA	68	B4
Beowawe	NV	61	B3
Berenda	CA	26	B6
Berg	CA	11	F3
Bergamot	CA	50	A4
Berkeley (ATSF)	CA	20	F4
Berkeley (SP)	CA	20	E4
Berkeley Downtown	CA	20	F4
Berkeley North	CA	20	F4
Bernal	CA	21	A2
Berry	CA	7	F3
Berry Creek	CA	13	A1
Berryessa	CA	22	B5
Berryessa	CA	23	D5
Berteleda	CA	6	A2
Bertram	CA	45	B6
Bethany	CA	25	A2
Bethel	CA	51	D6
Bethel	CA	55	C1
Bethune	CA	57	D2
Betteravia	CA	34	C4
Betteravia Junction	CA	34	C4
Beverley Glen Boulevard	CA	50	B4
Beverley Hills	CA	50	B4
Beyer Boulevard	CA	49	C6
Biddy McCarthy Mine	CA	41	D2
Bidwell	CA	11	F1
Bidwell	CA	13	A1
Bieber	CA	9	B2
Bieber Line Junction	OR	6	F1
Big Bunch	CA	30	B2
Big Canon	CA	7	D1
Big Creek	CA	27	A5
Bigelow	CA	7	E1
Bigelow	CA	32	B2
Biggs	CA	11	F2
Bijou	CA	13	F4
Bijou	CA	67	A2
Binney Junction	CA	11	F3
Binney Junction	CA	13	A3
Biola	CA	29	D1
Biola Junction	CA	29	D1
Biola Junction	CA	32	A4
Birch	CA	26	D6
Bishop	CA	27	D4
Bishop	CA	32	B1
Bissel	CA	37	A4
Bivalve	CA	16	A4
Bixby Heights	CA	54	D3
Bixby Heights	CA	55	A3
Bixler	CA	18	D2
Black Butte	CA	6	C4
Black Butte	CA	7	D1
Black Point	CA	16	B4
Black Point	CA	18	A1
Blackburn	CA	39	D4
Blackburn	CA	40	A4
Blackburns	NV	62	E1
Blacklands	CA	17	B4
Blacklands	CA	25	B1
Blair	UT	64	F3
Blair	NV	68	D4
Blair Junction	NV	68	D3
Blairsden	CA	12	D4
Blakes Landing	CA	16	A4
Blanco	CA	30	B5
Blanding Avenue	CA	21	D2
Blavo	CA	11	F1
Blinnville	CA	54	D4
Blinzig	CA	13	A1
Bliss	CA	50	D2
Bliss	CA	51	A2
Bloomer	CA	11	F1
Bloomer	CA	13	A1
Bloomington	CA	57	C3
Bloss	CA	26	C3
Blossom Hill	CA	18	D5
Blue Anchor	CA	11	F4
Blue Canon	CA	13	D3
Blue Cut	CA	43	C2
Blue Diamond Mill	NV	72	A1
Blue Hills	CA	18	C5
Blue Lake	CA	14	B1
Bluestone Copper	NV	67	D2
Blunt	CA	10	D2
Blythe	CA	46	C5
Boaz	NV	64	B1
Boca	CA	13	F2
Boca	CA	66	A4
Bodega Road	CA	16	A3
Bodie	CA	27	B1
Bogue	CA	11	F3
Bolam	CA	6	D4
Bolinas Avenue	CA	20	B2
Bolsa	CA	25	A6
Bolsa	CA	28	B1
Bolsa Chica	CA	55	C6
Bombay	CA	16	F1
Bombay	CA	17	A1
Bonnie Claire	NV	69	B3
Borax	CA	38	B4
Borax	NV	39	D1
Borax	NV	72	B3
Borden	CA	26	B6
Borden	CA	29	D1
Boron	CA	37	B4
Borosolvay	CA	41	A4
Bothin Tunnel	CA	20	A2
Boulder Canyon Gravel Pit	AZ	71	D4
Boulder Canyon Gravel Pit	AZ	72	D1
Boulder City	NV	72	C2
Boulder Creek	CA	18	B5
Boulder Junction	NV	72	B1
Bowens Landing	CA	15	A5
Bowerbank	CA	35	C2
Bowles	CA	30	A2
Bowman	CA	13	C4
Box Springs	CA	43	D3
Box Springs	NV	61	C4
Box Springs	NV	62	E1
Boyd	NV	73	B4
Boyer	CA	11	E4
Boyes	CA	16	C3
Brack's Landing	CA	16	F4
Brack's Landing	CA	17	A4
Brack's Landing	CA	25	A1
Bracken	NV	71	B4
Bracken	NV	72	B1
Bradford	CA	41	E1
Bradford	CA	70	A4
Bradley	CA	29	A6
Brant	CA	39	C3
Brawley	CA	48	B2
Bray	CA	6	E3
Brazos	CA	16	C4
Brea Chem	CA	43	A3
Brea Chem	CA	56	B1
Bree	CA	56	B1
Brela	CA	17	C2
Brentwood	CA	18	D2
Brentwood Park	CA	50	A4
Briceburg	CA	26	C3
Bridge Yard [Oakland]	CA	21	C1
Bridgedale	CA	54	B2
Bridges	NV	62	A2
Briggs	CA	42	C1
Brighton	CA	17	A2
Brighton	CA	24	C2
Brighton	CA	50	C2
Brightside	CA	23	D1
Brisbane	CA	21	B3
Bristol	CA	56	B6
Broadmoor	CA	50	A1
Broadway	CA	22	A1
Broadway	CA	51	A4
Broadwell	CA	38	D4
Brock	CA	13	A4
Brock Creek	CA	14	C4
Broderick	CA	24	B2
Bromela	CA	34	C4
Bronco	CA	25	C4
Bronte	NV	59	B2
Brookdale	CA	18	B5
Brookhurst	CA	55	D3
Brooks	CA	16	D1
Brown	CA	31	D6
Brown	NV	73	D3
Brown's	NV	66	F1
Brown's Junction	NV	66	C3
Browning	CA	56	C5
Bryant	NV	59	B4
Bryman	CA	37	C5
Bryn Mawr	CA	57	E3
Buaro	CA	56	A5
Buchanan	CA	58	D3
Buchli	CA	16	C4
Buckhorn	CA	42	D1
Bucks Bar	CA	17	D2
Bucksport	CA	14	A1
Buena	CA	47	A1
Buena Park	CA	55	D2
Buena Vista	CA	16	C3
Buena Vista	CA	28	B2
Buenos Ayres	CA	50	B4
Bull Ring [Los Angeles]	CA	51	A4
Bullard	CA	17	C2
Bullfrog	NV	69	C4
Bullfrog Junction	NV	68	F1
Bullion	NV	61	C3
Bullionville	NV	73	C3
Bundy	CA	50	B5
Bundy Drive	CA	50	A4
Burbank	CA	42	F2
Burbank	CA	50	D2
Burbank Junction	CA	42	F2
Burbank Junction	CA	50	C2
Burbeck	CA	15	B2
Burdell	CA	16	B4
Burdell	CA	18	A1
Burke	CA	51	C6
Burleigh	CA	54	B2
Burlingame	CA	22	B1
Burness	CA	32	D5
Burney	CA	7	F3
Burnham	CA	25	B2
Burr	CA	33	B4
Burrell	CA	29	D3
Busch	CA	16	D4
Butler	CA	52	A3
Butler Road	CA	21	B4
Butte Creek	CA	11	E1
Butte Street Yard [Los Angeles]	CA	51	A5
Butterfield	CA	24	D2
Buttonwillow	CA	35	C2
Byron	CA	18	D2

C

Name	State	Page	Grid
C&H Sugar Refinery	CA	19	A2
Cabazon	CA	44	B3
Cabernet	CA	35	D1
Cable	CA	36	C3
Cabrilla	CA	50	A1
Cactave	CA	57	B2
Cactus	CA	48	E2
Cadenasso	CA	16	D1
Cadiz	CA	39	C6
Cadwell	CA	16	B3
Cahill	CA	22	A6
Cahill	CA	23	D6
Cahuenga Pass	CA	50	C3
Cairns	CA	33	B1
Cajon	CA	43	A1
Cajon	CA	43	C1
Cal-Ed Spur [Hivolt]	CA	43	C1
Calada	CA	39	D1
Calada	CA	72	B4
Calcite	CA	30	D4
Calcite	CA	33	D5
Caldor	CA	17	E2
Calexico	CA	48	B3
Calgro	CA	30	C3
Calico	CA	35	D1
Calico	CA	38	B4
Caliente	CA	36	A5
Caliente	CA	36	B3
Caliente	NV	73	B3
California Avenue	CA	23	A4
California Glass	CA	21	E3
California Park	CA	20	B2
California RR Museum	CA	24	B2
Calipatria	CA	48	B1
Calistoga	CA	16	B2
Calla	CA	25	B3
Callender	CA	34	C4
Calneva	CA	12	F3
Calneva	CA	59	A4
Calpack	CA	26	A5
Calpine	CA	13	E1
Calpine Junction	CA	12	E4
Calvada	CA	13	F2
Calvada	CA	66	A4
Calwa	CA	30	A2
Calwa	CA	32	B6
Calwa Crossing	CA	32	B6
Camarillo	CA	42	C2
Cambridge	CA	43	B2
Cambridge	CA	50	A4
Cambridge	CA	53	B3
Cameo	CA	30	A2
Cameo	CA	32	C5
Cameron	CA	36	D3
Camino	CA	17	D1
Camp 1	CA	26	C3
Camp 2	CA	27	A5
Camp 8	CA	26	B1
Camp 9	CA	14	B3
Camp 9	CA	26	D3
Camp 10	CA	26	C3
Camp 16	CA	26	C3
Camp 17	CA	26	C3
Camp 20	CA	15	A2
Camp 21	CA	26	C2
Camp 45	CA	26	C2
Camp Connell	CA	17	E3
Camp Four	CA	15	A2
Camp Meeker	CA	15	D6
Camp Meeker	CA	16	A2
Camp Noyo	CA	15	A2
Camp Pixley	CA	13	F1
Camp Pixley	CA	66	A3
Camp Richardson	CA	13	F4
Camp Richardson	CA	17	F1
Camp Richardson	CA	67	A3
Camp Rogers	CA	12	B3
Camp Taylor	CA	16	B4
Camp Three	CA	15	A2
Camp Two [MCR]	CA	7	F1
Camp Two [MCR]	CA	9	A1
Camp Two Ten Mile	CA	15	A1
Campbell	CA	18	C5
Campbell	CA	22	A6
Campbell	NV	67	D1
Camphora	CA	28	C3
Campo	CA	47	D4
Canal	CA	24	C5
Canal	CA	25	B2
Canby	CA	8	C4
Candelaria	NV	68	C3
Cannon	CA	16	D3
Canoga Park	CA	42	E2
Canon	NV	69	D5
Canon	NV	70	A2
Cantara Loops	CA	7	D1
Cantil	CA	37	A2
Cantu	CA	48	E3
Canyon	CA	43	A1
Canyon	NV	62	A2
Canyon Creek	CA	14	B1
Canyon Creek	CA	14	D2
Canyon Tank	CA	25	D3
Canyon Tank	CA	26	A3
Capay	CA	16	D1
Cape Horn	CA	13	C3
Cape of Good Hope	CA	51	C1
Capella	CA	15	C3
Capitan	CA	35	A6
Capitol	CA	24	B2

D

T

NOTES

NOTES